intermedia

Retail

&distribution

Roger Lewis and Roger Trevitt

Hodder & Stoughton

A MEMBER OF THE HODDER HEADLINE GROUP

ACKNOWLEDGEMENTS

The authors and publishers would like to thank the following for permission to use material in this book:

Seacon Holdings plc for Figure 1.1; Young & Co's Brewery for Figure 1.3; William Reed Publishing Ltd for the material from *The Grocer* (the articles on pages 5 and 112) and *Convenience Store* magazine (Figures 7.3, 8.3, 10.8 and 11.4); Knowles Transport Ltd for Figure 1.6; the Office for National Statistics for material from *Labour Market Trends* (Figures 1.7, 1.8 and 1.9); HMSO for material from the *Annual Abstract of Statistics* (Tables 2.1 and 2.2 and Figures 1.10, 1.11, 1.12, 1.14, 1.15 and 7.17), *Retailing Business Monitor* (Tables 1.1 and 1.2), *Social Trends 1995* (Table 3.2), *Regional Trends* (Table 6.1), the Central Statistical Office (Figure 7.1) and the Department of Transport (Tables 2.4 and 2.5 and Figures 3.3 and 3.4); Business Monitor for material from *Size Analysis of United Kingdom Businesses* (Table 1.3 and Figure 1.16); D Brown and Sons Limited and Gerald Gabb for Figure 2.2(a); Eurostar (UK) Limited for Figures 2.2(b) and 6.4; Tony Sawyer, Managing Director of Instone for the case study on page 34; Pat Shirreff-Thomas at Cory Environmental Limited for Figure 2.3; Glyn Williams, Production Controller at Williams Press for the case study on page 45; Ken Bond for the case study on page 46; RSA for Figure 3.1; HarperCollins for Figures 3.2 and 3.5; Eurostat for Figures 3.3, 3.4 and 3.5; Office for Official Publications of the European Communities for Figures 3.6 and 3.7; Solo Syndication for the articles from the *Mail on Sunday* on page 68; NFC plc for Figure 3.9; *The Times* for the articles on pages 70 and 90; the AA for Figure 3.13 and the article on page 75; the RAC for the article on pages 78–9; EuroTunnel for Figure 3.17; News Shopper for the article on pages 96–7; Thurrock Lakeside for Table 4.1 and Figures 7.8, 7.19, 8.14 and 12.8; the *Guardian* for the articles on pages 98–9, 238, 259 and 310–11; Cite Europe for Figure 4.2; Cite Europe and The Glades Shopping Centre for Table 4.2; Steve King at CTL Bromley College for the activity on page 105; Nurdin & Peacock plc for Figures 4.4 and 5.1; Ryder and Gunns for Figure 4.5; the Post Office for the leaflet on page 122; Safeway plc for Figures 5.2 and 7.13; the Consumers Association for the *Which?* magazine cover on page 135; Tesco plc for Figures 5.3, 7.10, 7.11, 7.12, 7.21, 8.15, 9.2 and 12.10; Kentish Times Newspapers for the material from the *Bromley Times Leader* (extract on page 138); London Transport for Figure 5.4; Centre Court Shopping Centre for the case study on page 154; Euromonitor for Table 6.3; *The European* for Table 6.4; Consumerlink and Tefal UK Ltd for Figure 6.3; Portsmouth & Sutherland Newspapers for Figure 7.2; J Sainsbury for Figures 7.5 and 8.7 and the case studies on pages 224; 271-2 and 313-4; Henley School of Management for Figure 7.6; Pentos plc for Figure 7.13; Camelot for Figure 7.14; Wickes Building Supplies Ltd for Figure 7.15; Burton Retail Ltd for the article on page 208 and Figure 10.7; W H Smith, Kingfisher Group plc and Tesco plc for Figure 8.1; Mars UK Ltd for Figure 8.12; *Retail Newsagent* for Figure 8.13 and Table 10.3; Shell plc for the material on page 238; Audi UK Ltd for Figure 9.4; Peacocks Stores Limited for Figure 9.4; Kingfisher Group plc for Figures 7.16 and 9.9; Ford Motor Company for Figure 9.10; Dixons Ltd for Figure 9.12; Samsung for Figure 9.14; Traveller's Fare Limited for Figure 10.6; Emap Business Communications for the material from BRAD (the case study on page 277); Food Brokers Ltd for Figure 10.9; *Asian Trader* magazine for the material on page 282 and the article on page 310; Thomson Directories and British Telecommunications plc for Figure 11.3; Blockbuster Video for the material on page 320; and the John Lewis Partnership for Figure 12.7.

The two Rogers would also like to thank Justine Davis, Julian Thomas, Catherine Fear, Edward Millar and Tracey Maitland of Hodder & Stoughton for all their hard work and encouragement and, in particular, their families for their support in this project.

A catalogue record for this title is available from the British Library

ISBN 0 340 65472 4

First published 1996

Impression number	10	9	8	7	6	5	4	3	2	1
Year		1999	1998	1997	1996					

Typeset by Wearset, Boldon, Tyne and Wear.
Printed in Great Britain for Hodder & Stoughton Educational, a division of Hodder Headline Plc, 338 Euston Road, London NW1 3BH by Bath Press

CONTENTS

UNIT 3 RETAIL AND SALES

UNIT 4 ADMINISTRATION AND FINANCE

Using this book to build your portfolio

The chapters in this book follow the structure of the four mandatory units of the Intermediate GNVQ in Retail and Distributive Services. They also form a resource for the GNVQ additional unit 'Retailing' and provide background material for retail-based NVQs.

Whatever your course you will need to build a portfolio of evidence in order to claim that you are competent. This book will help you to do this:

- each chapter has short activities for you to attempt as you progress. Use these to help you check your understanding. They will also provide evidence for your portfolio
- the evidence indicators at the end of each chapter take the form of larger projects. These will provide your main portfolio evidence. You will see that this evidence can take many forms: reports, maps photographs, interviews, taped presentations and so on

YOUR COURSE CHECKLIST

There is a lot to know about NVQ and GNVQ courses and the responsibility for claiming that you are competent falls upon you, the student. Make sure that you have a copy of your course specification and that you understand what is involved. We suggest that you ask, and answer, the following questions at least:

- which mandatory and optional units will I study?
- which elements appear in each unit?
- how can I provide evidence for each element?
- what counts as evidence?

And for GNVQ courses only:

- What do the three key skills (application of number, communication and information technology) involve?
- how can I claim these key skills? (where possible it is best to claim key skills through mandatory and optional unit evidence)
- merit and distinction grades are achieved through the **four** grading themes (planning, information-seeking and handling and evaluation and quality of outcomes). How can I achieve these grades?
- my final grade depends upon one third of the portfolio – what does this mean?
- which units have an external test?
- which sources of information will I use and where can I get this information?

BEFORE YOU START

Set up a lever arch file for your portfolio evidence. Only work which is assessed as competent should be filed here. You will need a separate section for each unit with its own tracking sheet on which your assessor will sign off elements as they are achieved. The sheet will also show exactly where the evidence for each element is filed. The verifier will use these records when checking that your portfolio is complete.

Set up a separate series of working folders, ideally one for each unit. These are for your own notes, practice activities, research work, mock tests and so on. You may also file your evidence indicators here whilst you are working on them.

Make sure that you are properly equipped: not only with pens, pencils and paper but also with graph paper, a protractor, and a calculator. Buy at least two floppy discs and use one to store back-up copies of your work.

AND FINALLY   Remember that retailing is a particularly accessible area to investigate. Take notice of what you see around you, keep up with local and national developments through the media and get to know what your local library has to offer. You will need to work hard, but you will find it both interesting and rewarding. As long as you are organised and determined you will succeed.

Good luck

Roger Lewis and Roger Trevitt

Distribution, transport and storage

C H A P T E R   **1**

Investigating the role and importance of distribution

> In this chapter, we will:
>
> - describe distribution operations: transporting, warehousing, wholesaling and retailing
> - describe the role and contribution of the distribution sector
> - describe the structure of the supply chain
>
> We will cover Element 1.1, Performance Criteria 1, 2, 3, 4, 5.

INTRODUCTION – YOUR DAILY NEWSPAPER

Did you have a newspaper delivered this morning, or did you buy one in your local newsagent? Have you ever wondered how it is made or how it gets to you?

Here are some of the processes it goes through to reach you:

1. Renewable trees are grown in a forest in Scandinavia.
2. The trees are pulped and manufactured into paper.
3. The paper is delivered to newspaper publishers.
4. Newspapers are sent by road or rail to a local distributor.
5. The papers are delivered to each shop where they are bought by consumers.
6. The papers are also delivered to households either on foot or on a bicycle.

Figure 1.1 shows two stages in this sequence.

Figure 1.1 Two stages in the production of a newspaper: (i) 32 tonnes of woodpulp on the hook - direct from ship to store; (ii) the distribution of newsprint from the terminal

All of the above processes can be classified under three headings as shown in Figure 1.2.

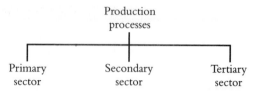

Figure 1.2 All production processes fall into three sectors

1 **Primary sector.** This consists of agriculture, forestry, fishing and mining. These are called **extractive industries** because natural resources are taken from the land or sea to produce goods. Coal-miners, farmers and foresters all work in the primary sector producing **primary goods**.
2 **Secondary sector.** This consists of manufacturing and construction industries. Workers who make cars, assemble TVs or manufacture cans of baked beans work in manufacturing, while bricklayers and plasterers work in the construction industry.
3 **Tertiary sector.** Workers in this sector provide **services**. Retailing, transport, wholesaling and warehousing are all services, as are teaching, insurance and banking.

1 Which of the three sectors do you think each of these jobs belong to: shop assistant, stores person, forestry worker, quarry worker, steel worker, wholesaler, librarian, oil-rig worker, travel agent, lorry driver?
2 Use your local Yellow Pages or Thomson Directory (these are directories of businesses in your area, including their telephone numbers and addresses) to identify five local businesses in each of the primary, secondary and tertiary sectors. If you are not able to find local business from every sector, what does it tell you about the types of business in your local area?

WHAT IS DISTRIBUTION?

In the dictionary, **distribution** is defined as 'the process of delivering, storing and selling goods so that they can be used by customers'.

1 *Delivering*: what types of transport have you seen today? Perhaps you saw cars, buses, cabs, bicycles, motorcycles, lorries, vans, trains, aeroplanes or boats? Which of these types of transport are mainly used for *carrying and delivering* goods (called **freight transport**)?
2 *Storing*: have you ever wondered where the goods you buy come from and how they get to the shops? What did you have for lunch? Did you eat in the canteen or did you go out? Did you have fresh

food, or was it frozen and then cooked? How is frozen food sent from the manufacturer, where is it *stored*?

3 *Selling*: have you been shopping? Did you buy anything in your local **retail outlet**? (**Retailing** is about *selling* goods – see Chapters 7–9.)

Distribution is about:

- getting goods from the manufacturer or producer to the consumer (who is someone who buys goods for their own or their family's use)
- getting goods from the manufacturer to the customer (this can be another business such as a wholesaler or retailer who will resell the goods on to someone else)
- meeting customers' and consumers' needs by providing goods in perfect condition and in sufficient quantities at the time when they are needed and at the place where they are needed. For example, if you need three loaves of bread at 7 pm on Saturday because guests have turned up unexpectedly to watch the National Lottery on TV, you should be able to buy them at that time

Distribution is a service, and is therefore part of the tertiary sector.

OPERATIONS IN THE DISTRIBUTION SECTOR

There are four operations in the distribution sector:

1 transporting
2 warehousing
3 wholesaling
4 retailing

and the whole chain of the distribution process runs as follows: from the manufacturer – via transport – to the warehouse/wholesaler, then – via transport – to the retailer, and finally – again via transport – to the consumer.

Let us now consider each of the above four operations.

Transporting

Transport is involved at every stage of the distribution process: raw materials are *transported* to the manufacturer, manufactured goods are *transported* to the wholesaler or retailer, and the retailer may *transport* goods to the consumer. The function of transport within the distribution sector is thus to carry, move or deliver goods to the places where they are needed at each stage in the chain of supply. In the UK, the main types of freight transport – see Chapter 2 for a more detailed discussion – are:

- *Rail*: freight trains;
- *Road*: lorries, vans, trucks and trailers, tankers;
- *Air*: freight aircraft;
- *Water*: canal barges, ships and ferries.

Goods can also be transported by:

- *people*: for example, in mountain areas where it is difficult to build roads, people have to *carry* everything they need
- *animals*: in some countries, donkeys and camels are used to carry goods. In the UK, horses are used to pull carts, and in some towns 'rag and bone' men can still be seen collecting unwanted metal items. In South London, Young & Co's brewery still sometimes uses horses to pull the *dray* (a brewer's cart) loaded with beer – see Figure 1.3. At one time, all beer was delivered this way. One of the authors remembers milk being delivered by horse and cart and being served straight from a large metal milk *churn* (can). Today, doorstep deliveries of milk are made using battery-operated milk floats. (Why do you think horses are no longer used? How many houses do you think a milk float can deliver to compared with a horse and cart?)

Figure 1.3 Horses pulling a dray (brewer's cart)

- *pipelines*: these are used to carry oil, natural gas or water. The longest oil pipeline in the world is over 1,700 miles long

Some goods have to travel many thousands of miles before they reach the final consumer. For example, it is estimated that breakfast cereal in the USA travels over 12,000 miles.

1 For your breakfast, you may have Danish bacon, an egg laid on a farm near Lincoln and a cup of Indian tea (with milk but no sugar). Estimate how far each item has travelled to reach your breakfast table. What is the total distance? (You will need to use a world atlas to work out the figures.) What effect do you think that distance has on the *price* of these goods?
2 Find the names of five road–haulage operators and five van and lorry hire businesses in your area. Why did you choose these businesses? Which of the two groups has the most number of businesses? Can you say why? (Hint: use the Yellow Pages or its equivalent.)

The warehouse

A **warehouse** is a building where goods are *stored* before they are distributed or resold to business customers. The term **storage warehouse** is sometimes used to describe premises where goods are stored for long periods. A **distribution warehouse** is a building where goods are collected and orders are assembled and then redistributed. Many of these warehouses store goods for less than a day. **Cash-and-carry warehouses**, such as Makro or Bestway (which has over 200 own-label products), buy goods in bulk from the manufacturer or producer. They 'break bulk' (see page 9 below) and sell goods to the retailer in boxes or cases. They hold or carry very large stocks of goods.

Retailers use warehouses in the same way that consumers use shops. Whenever the stock in the retail outlet is low, the retailer can obtain extra supplies from the warehouse. The retailer pays cash for the goods which they have to transport themselves. Retailers will break bulk (e.g. a case of baked beans) and sell individual tins to consumers (in French, 'retailer' means 'to cut again'). By using warehouses, retailers do not have to hold so much stock.

Warehouses are frequently used by small independent convenience stores and tobacconists because these shops do not have a regular order and can buy only what they need. Large chain stores and supermarkets do not use cash-and-carry warehouses because they have their own warehouses and distribution systems.

Designed for continuous growth

In its 25-year contract with Waitrose, Hays Distribution says that paramount to both parties are continuous improvements in costs and service.

Hays provides a distribution service for Waitrose's northern region, which is handled from a purpose-built 315,000-square-feet centre, dedicated to the retailer, at Hays' 26 acre site in Milton Keynes. From here, Hays delivers to all stores north of the Thames and the M4, while Waitrose serves stores south of this line from its own centre in Bracknell.

'Early in the planning stages for the Brinklow centre,' says Hays retail director Harry Cole, 'it was decided that, with over 550 lorry movements every day, optimum efficiency would be achieved if the arrivals and despatch vehicles were kept separate, even having their own entrances and exits. So the site is divided into two sections.'

There are 40 bays along one side, which accept incoming goods, while 40 on the other side load vehicles bound for stores. Traffic controllers oversee arrivals and despatch, ensuring goods go to the correct bays.

The multi-temperature fleet can be compartmentalised to carry a mix of products, and there are rigorous standards in place to ensure goods are transported at the correct temperatures.

(Source: The Grocer, 3 February 1996)

Case study: The mail order business

Every business wants to cut its distribution cost. Grattan, the mail order catalogue company, could send its goods direct to each customer. However, this would be very expensive. Instead, it therefore uses *agents* to minimise its costs – see Figure 1.4.

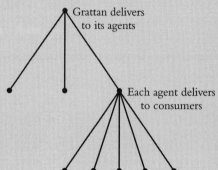

Figure 1.4 How Grattan uses agents to minimise its delivery costs

Case study: Warehouses at McDonald's, Kwik Save and Asda

1 In the UK, during any one week at McDonald's (the fast-food retailer), 90 vehicles will make over 2,000 deliveries and travel over 112,000 miles. Each vehicle can carry frozen, chilled and fresh goods at the same time. The vehicles will carry over 800 tonnes of french fries, 6.5 million buns and 100,000 gallons of milk to over 600 places. Nearly 6,000 suppliers are used. All the goods are channelled through warehouses at Heywood in Lancashire and Hemel Hempstead in Hertfordshire.

2 Kwik Save:
   ● have introduced a computerised warehouse management system
   ● have switched to a centralised warehouse system for the distribution of short-life chilled products. Previously, suppliers sent all these products directly to individual shops
   ● are building a new 250,000-square-feet specially designed distribution depot at Wellingborough in Northamptonshire

3 Asda are opening a new specialised temperature-controlled warehouse at Didcot to increase the amount of frozen and chilled foods that it can store before these are sent to the shops.

activity

Activities 2, 3 and 4 below should be done in a group, and notes should be produced as evidence of your activity.

1 Measure the size of the room you are now in. How many times would the room fit into the Kwik Save warehouse mentioned in the case study above? (Hint 1: length multiplied by width equals area; e.g. 4 metres × 3 metres = 12 square metres. Hint 2: the area of the warehouse divided by the area of your room equals the number of times your room could fit into the warehouse.)

2 Why do you think McDonald's has *two* warehouses, and that its suppliers do not deal *directly* with each restaurant?

3 Why do you think Kwik Save has a centralised warehouse system?

4 Discuss why Asda is increasing the amount of storage for frozen and chilled food.

Case study: Information processing in warehouses at J Sainsbury

J Sainsbury is a large UK chain comprising 370 supermarkets. These are located mainly in the North-West, West Midlands, South-East and London.

Computers are now widely used in all of Sainsbury's large warehouses. The next time you go shopping in a large Sainsbury's supermarket, look at your till receipt. Does it look something like the left-hand column below?

J S Cornflakes	0.89	(This is an **own-label** product which has been specially manufactured for J Sainsbury (JS) Plc. Nestlé, which makes Nescafé, does not make own-label coffee, despite the 'look alike' packaging and names. Nestlé has 'Gold Blend' and J Sainsbury has 'Gold Choice'. Heinz has only recently entered the own-label market because more people were buying own-label baked beans and Heinz were losing out. (In January 1996 there was a major price war on baked beans eaten in the UK. What price are they now?))
J S Diet Yogs X8	2.09	(This again is an own-label pack of 8 yoghurts. (Who buys packs of 8 yoghurts?))
Biactol 150ML	2.99	(This is a branded product. Biactol is a brand name for an anti-bacterial face wash. It is a registered trade mark

of Procter & Gamble (which also makes toothpastes and washing powders – look for the name on the packets), and no-one else is allowed to use this name. The advertising for this product is aimed at teenagers for 'daily cleansing which helps prevent spots'. (Do *you* buy Biactol? And at £2.99? How long does it last? It is made in France. Does this affect the price?))

3 ITEMS PURCHASED

Balance Due	5.97	(This is the amount the customer has to pay.)
EFT	5.97	(EFT – Electronic Funds Transaction. The customer has paid using a card with the long number shown on the next line. This is swiped (passed through) on the scanner.)
1234 5678 1234 5678		
Change	0.00	

The information on the receipt is stored on computers in the shop and sent to the head office and distribution warehouse daily by computer link.

How does the system work?

- Electronic checkout points in each store are used to record daily and weekly patterns of sales. This data is then used to predict future sales. The data is sent to the distribution warehouse and is used to determine the next order
- An electronic document system has replaced the paper forms and documents which used to be sent with deliveries made by truck drivers. Now, instead of delivery notes (see page 293), details of the stock held in the shops can be checked by computer. This means that the transport, warehousing and retailing operations are now linked automatically
- The fork-lift trucks used in the warehouses each have an on-board computer, and are linked by radio
- Computer systems are now used for load planning and route planning
- Specially designed computer software allows managers to find out immediately how much has been sold, how much is left and how much to reorder from suppliers
- Computer software is also used to show details of any customer complaints so that these can be dealt with quickly and efficiently

How does all this affect customers?

- Fresher produce
- More goods are likely to be in stock at any time
- Better service

How does all this affect Sainsbury's?

- It enables better control of stocks of goods
- It helps the shops to run more efficiently
- Managers have up-to-date and accurate information
- Better use is made of warehouse facilities
- Better use is made of delivery vehicles
- Goods can be delivered more quickly

The wholesaler In the chain we are considering, the **wholesaler** acts as the intermediate link between the producer and the retailer. One wholesaler will provide goods to a large number of retailers, and because of this, only a small number of wholesalers are needed in any one area (see Figure 1.5).

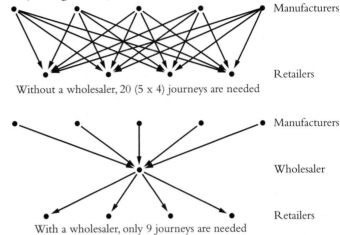

Without a wholesaler, 20 (5 x 4) journeys are needed

With a wholesaler, only 9 journeys are needed

Figure 1.5 How the presence of a wholesaler reduces the number of journeys required from manufacturer to retailer

WHAT DOES THE WHOLESALER DO?

The wholesaler:

- buys goods directly from the producer or manufacturer
- sells goods directly to the retailer, who is a business customer – this means that one distribution operator is selling to another distribution operator
- stores goods in places where retail customers want them. These are usually either in or close to large towns and cities
- buys large quantities in bulk from producers and sells smaller quantities to retailers. This very important function is called **breaking bulk**

Many retailers – for example, clothes shops and office-equipment suppliers – use wholesalers to obtain their supplies. A special group of wholesalers called **cash-and-carry** wholesalers provide many corner shops with almost all the goods they sell. There are only 15 of these listed in the Yellow Pages for London South-East, yet there are hundreds of shops listed as served by these special wholesalers. Similarly, there are 60 office-equipment retailers named, but only 2 related office-equipment wholesalers.

activity List the advantages, for both manufacturers and retailers, of using wholesalers.

1 Use the Yellow Pages for your area to find out:
   (a) the number of clothes shops – to get this information, you will have to include baby-goods shops, children's-wear shops, knitwear retailers, ladies-wear shops, lingerie retailers, maternity-wear shops, menswear shops, school outfitters, tailors (retail);
   (b) the number of clothing manufacturers and wholesalers.
   Once you have this information, locate the manufacturers and wholesalers on a map of the area covered by your Yellow Pages. Put your local clothing shops on the same map. What is the relationship between the wholesalers and the retailers?
2 What is the population of your local area? How many clothes shops are there per head of the population? For example, if the population is 20,000 and there are 20 clothes shops, this means that there is 1 clothes shop for every 1,000 people – i.e. 20,000 divided by 20. You could try this same exercise for other shops: for example, in Bromley there are 32,000 children aged 0 to 10 years and 22 children's-wear shops to cater for them – or 1 shop for every 1,455 children.

activity

Figure 1.6 shows an advertisement from *The Grocer*

KNOWLES WAREHOUSING & DISTRIBUTION

- ◆ 1 million square feet
- ◆ Ambient warehousing
- ◆ Racked storage
- ◆ Computer stock control
- ◆ H.M. Customs approved
- ◆ Break bulk
- ◆ Repacking facilities
- ◆ Modern fleet of vehicles
- ◆ Delivery service nationwide
- ◆ Major multiples serviced daily
- ◆ Good access for east coast ports

Figure 1.6 An advertisement for Knowles Transport Ltd

Write short notes explaining each of the points included in the advertisement.

Retailing　　The **retailer** is the last link in the chain which takes goods from the producer/manufacturer to the final consumer. **Shops** are retail outlets. These are places where goods are sold individually or in small quantities to consumers. You are a **consumer** when you go into a shop and purchase or buy something for your own use. Retailers sell to the general public. They do not usually sell to other businesses.

There are many different types of retail outlet, such as:

- **independent retailers**: these are not part of a larger organisation – e.g. a corner shop which is owned and operated by one person
- **chain stores**: these are a group of stores which trade under the same name and sell broadly similar goods – e.g. clothing, electrical goods or furniture
- **department stores**, which generally belong to a large group and sell a whole range of goods – e.g. clothing, electrical goods and furniture
- **voluntary trading 'symbol groups'**: Spar is the largest such retailing organisation in Europe with 250,000 outlets. Its headquarters are in the Netherlands. Mace is another such group.

We shall look at these outlets in detail in Chapter 7.

WHAT ARE THE FUNCTIONS OF THE RETAILER?

- To provide goods individually or in small quantities – e.g. one pot of jam
- To have goods in stock that people *want* to buy
- To buy goods in bulk or in large quantities from wholesalers or manufacturers and then 'break bulk' (see page 9 above). These goods often arrive at the store in cardboard boxes which have to be opened for the goods to be displayed on the shelves.
- To provide help and advice to the customer. For example, when you go into the local chemists, you expect them to be able to advise you on which medicine to take for a 'chesty cough'. This is a very important and responsible function, and is the major reason why chemists do not want supermarkets to sell a wider range of medicines
- To keep goods fresh and clean ready for reselling to the consumer
- To provide a personal service. Even in large supermarkets which are mainly self-service, there will often be a bakery or a fish or meat section which provides a personal service. (Clothing and footwear shops in particular are keen to retain personal service. Why do you think this is so?)
- To provide goods locally. Goods which we buy on a daily or weekly basis need to be available locally. These are provided by the shops which are within walking distance of people's homes, i.e.

newsagents/tobacconists, grocers, off-licences, video hire shops and hairdressers. These shops sell goods which satisfy personal needs. Such goods are called **consumer goods**.

1 **Convenience goods.** These are low-value goods which people buy frequently (daily or weekly), such as bread, milk and groceries. Little time is spent thinking about what to buy, and few comparisons are made between these goods.
2 **Shopping goods.** These are higher-priced goods which are bought less frequently, e.g. electrical goods such as toasters and irons. People spend considerable time here in comparing quality, style, price etc.
3 **Speciality goods.** These are goods with very special or unique features – e.g. a brand name or logo. One example is a Rolex watch. They tend to be very expensive goods which people buy for themselves.

1 Name five goods in each category. Give reasons for your choices.
2 Name three stores for each category. Again give reasons for your choice. Which of these stores provides a personal service?
3 What type of shops do you have in your local shopping parade? Can you say why these shops are present?

THE CONTRIBUTION OF THE DISTRIBUTION SECTOR TO THE ECONOMY
Contribution to the local economy

A good way of looking at the impact or effect of distribution operations on the local economy is to examine the benefits (advantages) and costs (disadvantages) of any particular relevant development, such as a superstore opening on the edge of a town or a shop closing on the local parade of shops.

Do you have a part-time job? Do you have a friend with a part-time job? Where do they work? It is more than likely that you or they will work either in retailing or in catering. For the majority of 16 and 17 year olds, retailing is a major source of employment. However, it is also a major source of employment for people of other ages in the local area.

Where do you spend the money you earn? Do you go to local shops? (Shopping is now considered a major social pastime by a large number of people.) Do you go to clubs or discos? Do you have a car? Whenever anyone works and earns and spends money, more jobs are created and the area prospers and improves. This process is sometimes called the **multiplier effect**. However, when businesses close, people have less money to spend, shops may close, there are fewer jobs and the area can become run-down.

activity

Carry out a small survey within your group to find out why people go to the shops. Is it because you can meet friends and go 'window shopping'?

Case study: the costs and benefits of opening a new out-of-town superstore

1 Costs (or disadvantages):
- More roads and other facilities may be needed
- There will be more congestion on the roads
- Conflict may arise between the shoppers and the local residents, e.g. over parking
- Local specialist shops may be forced to close because of the increased competition
- The new development may not fit into the surroundings
- There may be increased noise and pollution levels

2 Benefits (or advantages):
- More jobs for local residents will be created – e.g. a modern superstore can employ about 650 people and therefore people will have more money to spend
- Leisure and entertainment facilities could improve
- People will have more opportunities to meet each other because people enjoy shopping
- There will be less congestion in the centre of towns
- More restaurants and cafes may be attracted to the area

1 List the advantages and disadvantages of a new DIY superstore being opened (i) on the edge of a town, (ii) in the middle of a town.
2 List the advantages and disadvantages of existing shops closing in the middle of a town.
3 Using the publications *Regional Trends* and *Labour Market Trends* (published by HMSO) and your local Job Centre and TEC (Training and Enterprise Council), find out how many people work in the distribution sector in your local area or region. Show this information on a graph. How do you think this sector of employment helps the local area?

Contribution to the national economy

COMPARISONS OF DISTRIBUTION OPERATIONS BY THE NUMBER OF EMPLOYEES AND THE TYPES OF EMPLOYEE

Who works in distribution? Figure 1.7 shows the number of full-time and part-time male and female employees in transport in September 1994 and September 1995. The figures show that:

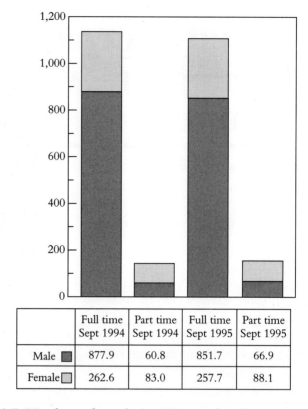

	Full time Sept 1994	Part time Sept 1994	Full time Sept 1995	Part time Sept 1995
Male	877.9	60.8	851.7	66.9
Female	262.6	83.0	257.7	88.1

Figure 1.7 Numbers of people (in 000s) employed in the transport sector in September 1994 and September 1995

1 the majority of employees are male;
2 the majority of employees are full-time;
3 there has been a reduction in full-time employees and a rise in part-time employees (see page 207).

'In 000s' means that, for example, there were 877,900 full-time males employed in transport in September 1994.

Look at Figure 1.8 which shows information on people employed in the wholesale trade, and Figure 1.9 which shows the same for the retail trade.

1 What comments can you make about the numbers of male and female full-time and part-time employees?
2 What are the differences between the transport, wholesale and retail figures? Can you suggest reasons?

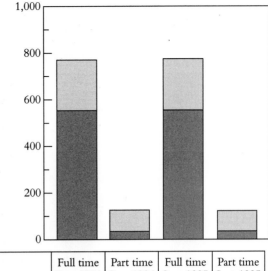

	Full time Sept 1994	Part time Sept 1994	Full time Sept 1995	Part time Sept 1995
Male	559.7	30.7	563.3	29.7
Female	207.3	92.5	210.3	86.8

Figure 1.8 The number of people (in 000s) employed in the wholesale trade in September 1994 and September 1995

	Full time Sept 1994	Part time Sept 1994	Full time Sept 1995	Part time Sept 1995
Male	529.6	214.8	519.6	226.6
Female	474.3	933.3	455.8	933.1

Figure 1.9 The number of people (in 000s) employed in the retail trade in September 1994 and September 1995

activity

You have been asked to produce a short article for your local newspaper on 'People employed in distribution'. Here are three more charts – see Figures 1.10, 1.11 and 1.12 – which will help you. Whenever possible, use your numeracy skills to calculate the percentage involved.

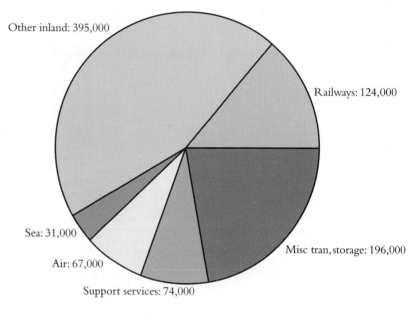

Misc tran = miscellaneous transport

Figure 1.10 People employed in transport, 1993

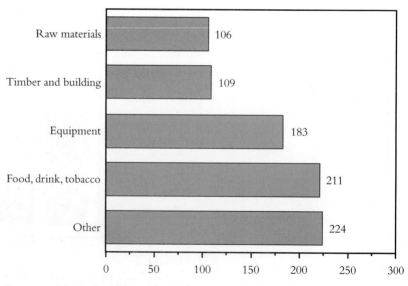

Raw materials = agriculture, textiles, fuel

Figure 1.11 People employed in wholesale distribution, 1993, in 000s

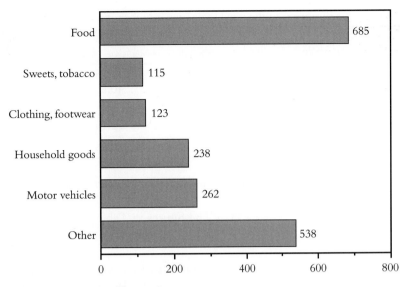

Motor vehicles includes filling stations
Sweets = confectioners
Source: Annual Abstract of Statistics

Figure 1.12 People employed in retail distribution, 1993, in 000s

A COMPARISON OF THE NUMBER OF BUSINESSES, THE NUMBER OF OUTLETS AND THE SIZE OF BUSINESSES IN THE RETAIL TRADE

Table 1.1 shows:

- Column 1: businesses categorised by the number of persons employed
- Column 2: the total number of retail businesses in the UK – i.e. 219,131. The vast majority of these (92%) employ fewer than ten persons. There are only 49 businesses which employ more than 5,000 people. These are the large supermarket chains and well-known high-street multiple retailers and department stores
- Column 3: the total number of outlets. An **outlet** is an individual shop or store. There are more outlets than businesses because a single business can have more than one outlet. The majority of businesses, however, only have one outlet – these are the small independent retailers. The largest 49 businesses, on the other hand, have over 25,000 outlets
- Column 4: the total number of persons employed in the retail trade – i.e. 2,325,000
- Column 5: the total turnover of retail businesses. **Turnover** is the value of the amount of sales made during one year. The largest 49 businesses have sales of over £72 billion

Table 1.1 Businesses in the retail trade: size, number and turnover figures, 1992

BUSINESSES HAVING:	NUMBER OF BUSINESSES	NUMBER OF OUTLETS	PERSONS EMPLOYED, IN 000s	TOTAL TURNOVER IN £ MILLION
under 10 persons	202,226	220,354	602	29,646
10–199 persons	16,403	40,884	348	17,840
200–999 persons	341	12,701	136	8,065
1,000–4,999 persons	112	19,611	239	15,848
over 5,000 persons	49	25,201	1,000	72,736
Total	219,131	318,751	2,325	144,135

Source: *Retailing Business Monitor*
Note: There are also some useful figures in *Annual Abstract of Statistics*, published annually by HMSO.

The figures in Table 1.2, with the same column headings as for Table 1.1, are for particular sections of the retail trade.

Table 1.2 Businesses in the retail trade: size, number and turnover figures, 1992, for particular sections of the trade

Food retailers	60,119	78,606	854	54,888
Drinks, tobacco and confectionery	46,671	57,999	254	14,051
Clothing, footwear and leather goods	24,923	51,319	264	12,687

Show the information using graphs or diagrams (use percentages when you can). What comments can you make?

Contribution to the international economy

We are all affected in some way by the international flow of goods into (i.e. **imports**) and out of (i.e. **exports**) the UK. Look at the labels on your clothes: where were they made? Look at the electrical goods in your home: where do they come from? What have you eaten today? Did you have an orange from Spain, grapefruit from Israel or tomatoes from the Canary Islands? Without imports, many of the things we now routinely enjoy would not be available. It is the distribution sector which gets these goods to the consumer. The simple supply chain in Figure 1.13 shows how tomatoes from the Canary Islands could reach your local supermarket:

- Stage 1: the tomatoes are grown under glass on Tenerife and Gran Canaria (you would see them growing alongside the road when you travel from the airport to your hotel)
- Stage 2: the tomatoes are picked and packed into cardboard boxes by the grower for export to the UK
- Stage 3: the tomatoes are unloaded and sent either to the distribution warehouse of a large supermarket or to the wholesaler
- Stage 4: the tomatoes are sold in supermarkets, greengrocers etc.

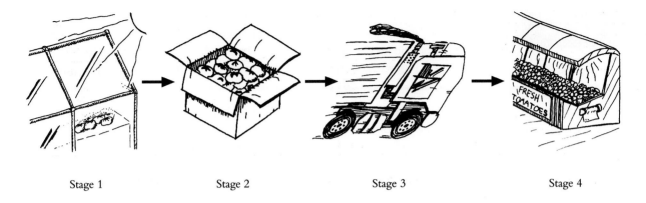

Stage 1   Stage 2   Stage 3   Stage 4

Figure 1.13 A supply chain for tomatoes: from greenhouse to supermarket

All of these stages of the international supply chain create jobs and wealth for the people involved – e.g. the growers and pickers of tomatoes, truck drivers, sea or air transporters, warehouse persons, wholesalers and retailers.

Look at Figure 1.14 which shows the types of products which the UK imports and exports. The UK imports more food than it exports, but it exports more 'drink' than it imports (mainly whisky). UK sea ports handle the majority of imports and exports (international trade). Look at Figure 3.3 on page 58 and you will see that large towns such as Southampton have grown up around these ports.

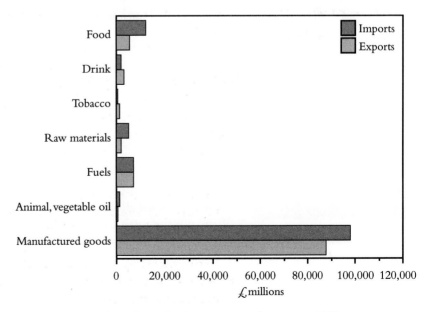

Figure 1.14 The value of UK imports and exports, 1992

1 Why do you think towns have developed at sea ports? What storage, loading and unloading facilities are needed?
2 Update the figures from the *Annual Abstract of Statistics* (HMSO) in Figure 1.14 and redraw the graph. What changes have taken place?

Look at Figure 1.15 which shows where the exports go to and where the imports come from (destination and source). For example, the UK imports more from the European Union (EU) than it exports. The majority of UK trade is with the EU. This means that the majority of ships entering or leaving UK trade with the EU. This is one of the reasons why Felixstowe has grown in the last 12 years.

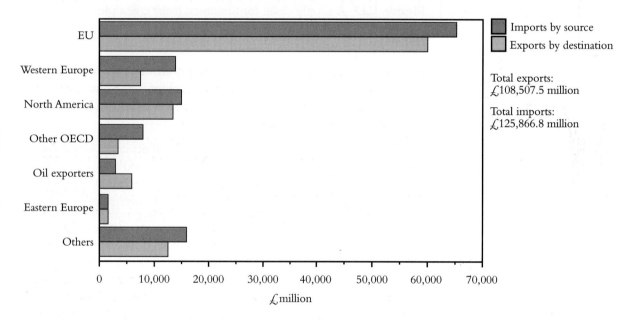

Other OECD means Japan, Australia and New Zealand
Eastern Europe includes the old USSR
EU = European Union

Figure 1.15 The value of UK imports and exports, 1992: source of imports and destination of exports

Describe the information shown in Figure 1.15. Update the figures from the *Annual Abstract of Statistics*. What changes have taken place? Write out the totals for imports and exports in words.

TYPES OF DISTRIBUTION BUSINESS

Table 1.3 Percentages of each type of business, 1994

	ALL BUSINESSES	PARTNERSHIPS	SOLE TRADERS	COMPANIES
Transport	4.3	2.9	5.3	4.4
Wholesale	8.2	5.1	6.1	13.7
Retail	14.2	21.2	16.1	6.9
Finance	11.0	8.4	11.3	12.5
Catering	7.3	11.2	6.6	3.2
Business services	8.8	4.2	6.7	15.5
Other services	9.2	6.6	9.7	9.1
Agriculture	10.0	19.4	11.0	1.8
Production	10.1	6.8	6.1	18.1
Construction	12.2	9.2	15.6	11.2
Motor trades	4.6	4.9	5.4	3.7

Source: *Size Analysis of United Kingdom Businesses, Business Monitor*, 1994.

Here are some of the key features from Table 1.3:

- Column 1: this lists the different sectors of industry
- Column 2: this shows the number of transport, retail businesses etc. as a percentage of all businesses. For example, 14.2% of all businesses are in retailing (this means that of every business you see, roughly 1 in 7 is likely to be in retailing). This is the largest number in any group. More businesses are in retailing than in any other category. Can you say why?
- Column 3: this shows, for example, that 21.2% of all partnerships are in retailing, and that only 2.9% are in transport. **Partnerships** are a very important form of business structure for retailers. Most partnerships are small, consisting only of family and friends of the founder of the business. John Lewis, on the other hand, is a large retailing partnership. It has a large store in Oxford Street in Central London, and sells its goods using the slogan 'Never knowingly undersold'. It also has a chain of food retailers under the 'Waitrose' name
- Column 4: 16.1% of all sole traders are in retailing. This is the largest figure for any sector. Only 5.4% of motor traders are sole traders. Most retailers are either sole traders or partnerships. Look back at Table 1.1, which shows that 92% of all retailers employ less than 10 people. This is because most retailers are small sole traders or partnerships
- Column 5: 6.9% of all companies are in retailing, but 13.7% are in wholesaling; this is the third largest group. Only 1.8% are in agriculture

activity

Draw charts which show this information. (Hint: we have found the best method is to draw individual pie charts for 'All businesses', 'Partnerships' etc. We have already done 'Sole traders' for you as an example – see Figure 1.16. Describe the main features of your charts.

(Note: a sole trader is a business owned by one person – e.g. most corner shops; a partnership is a business owned by two or more persons.)

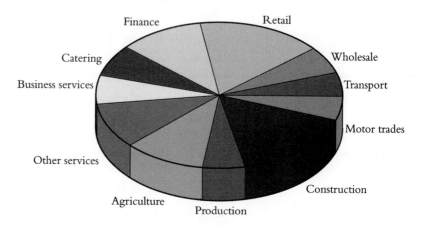

Figure 1.16 Pie chart for the percentage of sole traders in industry

THE STRUCTURE OF THE SUPPLY CHAIN

The interdependence of the supply chain

The **supply chain** is the route that goods take from the producer to the consumer. Traditionally, the supply chain is shown as involving four stages:

Producer → Wholesaler → Retailer → Consumer

So far in this chapter, we have looked at the role of wholesalers and retailers only. We now need to examine how *all* the various stages in the supply chain are linked or depend on each other. In the specification of the Intermediate GNVQ, this is called the **interdependence of the supply chain**. Look again at the above supply chain. Although the consumer is at the end of the chain, without consumers there would be no need for the first three stages. Whenever consumers buy particular goods in particular retail outlets, they are showing that they prefer one product or brand to another and one shop to another. Their decisions will trigger a chain reaction throughout the supply chain: the information that consumers are buying more or less of a particular product will be fed back to wholesalers and producers.

Here is an example of how this could work:

1 Consumers buy less butter → Food stores sell less butter → Stocks of butter remain unsold on the shelves → Fewer deliveries of butter are made.
2 Food stores order less butter from the wholesalers → Stocks of butter pile up at the wholesaler → Wholesalers order less butter from the manufacturer → Less refrigerated transport and warehousing is required.

3 Manufacturers make less butter → Farmers sell less milk → Fewer cows are needed for milk production.

Each part of the chain thus reacts to the original decision by consumers to buy less butter.

activity

Write notes which show what happens along the supply chain when:

1 people buy less butter;
2 people buy more or fewer Japanese cars;
3 people buy more or less wooden furniture made from valuable hardwoods – such as mahogany – from the tropical rainforests of Africa or South America.

INTERDEPENDENCE WITHIN THE SAME BUSINESS

Sometimes, all the functions involved in all the stages in the supply chain are carried out by one and the same organisation, and when this happens the business is said to be **vertically integrated**. J Sainsbury, Marks & Spencer, Asda and Iceland, for example, all operate their own retailing outlets, transport own-label goods in their own vehicles, and store and distribute goods from their own warehouses. They also have very close links with their suppliers. These companies do not generally own manufacturing facilities because they consider that their main or 'core' business is in retailing and distribution. However, they may make special arrangements with manufacturers to produce goods specially under their own label.

Case study: own-label goods

Own-label goods – see also page 7 above – are goods made exclusively by a manufacturer for a specific retailer. The retailer then sells the goods under its own label; for example, Marks & Spencer uses St Michael. Many famous food manufacturers make own-label goods in addition to their own brand-name products. Nestlé claims 'We do not make coffee for anyone else.' This means that they do not make own-label products. Why do you think they should want to stress this point in their advertising? H J Heinz ('Beanz meanz Heinz') has only recently started making own-label baked beans because the company was losing sales to the own-label brands sold very cheaply by the major food retailers such as Tesco and Kwik Save. (It is alleged that the own-label biscuits made by a leading biscuit manufacturer are all identical! Have you eaten any? If so, do they taste the same?) British retailers sell more own-label products than do retailers anywhere else because they make more profit on such goods.

The next time you buy an own-label product, look for the words 'Produced and packed specially for . . .' on the packaging.

Carry out a survey in your group to find out what proportion of the goods bought by members of the group or their families are own-label. Use notes and diagrams to show your results. What conclusions can you reach?

Features of vertically integrated distribution operations

1 The operator will have their own transport, and so will not have to rely on other companies to carry or deliver their goods.
2 The operator will be able to make better use of their transport by delivering to a series of outlets, so that the vehicle will be able to travel full instead of half-empty.
3 Better contact with and access to customers means that operators can react swiftly to any changes in customer demand.
4 There is more control over storage and distribution costs.
5 Less storage space is required because the operator can now make the best use of space. For example, they can have goods delivered only when they are needed. This is called **Just-in-Time** (JIT) delivery, meaning just in time for when they are needed.
6 Transport costs will be lower because routes can be planned more efficiently.
7 Fewer distribution outlets and warehouses are needed, again saving on costs.
8 Because vertically integrated companies are generally very large, they will have much greater control and power over their suppliers to get better prices. They can also buy and sell in bulk.
9 Better control of administration costs because with electronic systems such as EPOS (see page 204), orders can be passed directly from retail outlets to warehouses and even on to manufacturers.

Working as a group, give as many examples as you can of retail outlets which have their supplies delivered using their own transport.

INTERDEPENDENCE OF THE SUPPLY CHAIN BETWEEN BUSINESSES

Although there has been an increasing trend for distribution operator to take over or buy other distribution operators at different stages of the supply chain (vertical integration), there are still many examples where manufacturers, wholesalers and retailers have to deal with many separate independent businesses. Here are some examples:

● Independent wholesalers and cash-and-carry warehouses have to deal with a large range of retailers (see Figure 1.17)

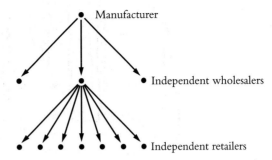

Figure 1.17 Independent wholesalers deal with many different retailers

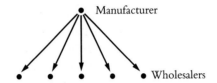

Figure 1.18 Manufacturers deal with many different wholesalers

- Manufacturers have to deal with many wholesalers so that their goods can be distributed (see Figure 1.18)
- Transport businesses have to obtain loads from a wide variety of businesses in order to survive and make profits
- Local corner shops or convenience stores have to deal with wholesalers

There are two disadvantages to this arrangement:

1 Administration costs are increased because operators will have to order from many other businesses and sell to many businesses. People will have to spend time making phone calls, writing and checking orders, following up queries etc.
2 Transport costs are increased because routes and deliveries will continually vary, which can lead to higher prices.

Self-test questions:
Chapter 1

1 Name the four operations which make up the distribution sector.
2 Name three roles of the distribution sector.
3 Complete this statement:
   A key role of the distribution sector is to get goods to the customer in the right _____, in the right _____, at the right _____.
4 Define primary sector, secondary sector and tertiary sector. Give examples of the goods or services produced by each sector.
5 Name two types of warehouse and describe their purpose.

6 Describe the functions of a wholesaler.
7 Describe the functions of a retailer.
8 Briefly describe how distribution contributes to the local, national and international economy.
9 Name four possible stages in the supply chain.
10 List the advantages of a vertically integrated supply chain.

Distribution operations

Using the activities in this chapter and your own investigation, produce a written and/or oral report which includes photographs, charts and diagrams. The report should:

1 Describe the main components of distribution: transporting, warehousing, wholesaling and retailing.
2 Describe the distribution operations in your local area, such as size and number of outlets by carrying out a survey. You will also find the business pages of telephone directories useful.
3 Describe the role of distribution in the economy.
4 Describe with examples, photographs, charts and diagrams the contribution that distribution makes to the local, national and international economy (note that not all the contribution is beneficial, e.g. some forms of transport can cause pollution, new buildings can damage the environment).
5 Describe with examples some typical supply chains, e.g. locally produced foodstuff. Use photographs or drawings to illustrate each part of the chain, including any transport.
6 In no more than 250 words, summarise the main conclusions for possible inclusion in the local paper.

Instructions for all evidence indicators

In order to get a distinction you must use the grading criteria by:

- producing a plan showing what evidence you will need and how and when you are going to get it
- including a list of all the sources you have used. Say, with reasons, which you found the most or least helpful
- stating what changes would you make if you had the opportunity to produce the assignment again; this will enable you to evaluate your work and avoid making the same mistakes again

Investigating types of transport for retail goods

In this chapter we will:

- compare road, rail, air and water transport
- describe the influence of journey features on the choice of transport
- identify features needed for different types of goods
- select which transport is best for carrying particular products

We will cover Element 1.2, Performance Criteria 1, 2, 3, 4, 5.

Transport is needed to carry people and freight. We will be looking at freight transport only (see Figure 2.1).

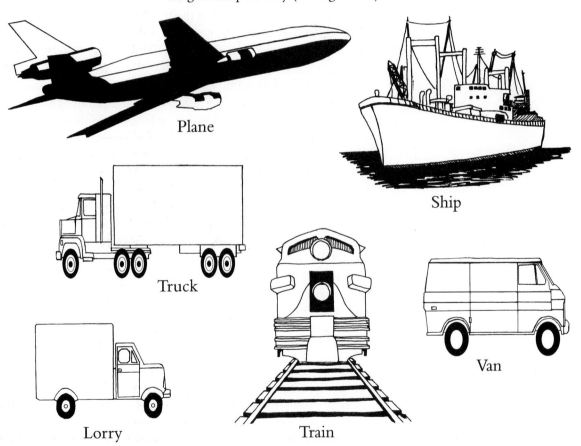

Plane

Ship

Truck

Train

Van

Lorry

Figure 2.1 The main types of freight transport

Hundreds of years ago, very little transport was needed because most villages were self-sufficient: they grew their own food and kept their own animals which were used for milk, meat and finally clothing. Any special items (i.e. the 'speciality goods' of today) were brought in by traders on horse and cart. Today in the UK society is more complex and we cannot live like this: the majority of people have to buy what they need from someone else. In order to satisfy the consumer's needs, goods have to be made, transported, stored and sold. An efficient transport system is vital if society is to continue to grow and prosper. Every business will have to take decisions about what transport to use for particular journeys or for carrying particular products. Transport is needed whenever goods move along the supply chain. It is the link that holds the supply chain together.

ROAD TRANSPORT

Road transport is the most popular form of transport world-wide. In Greece and Ireland, almost 100% of all freight is moved by road. The UK, Spain and Portugal move approximately 90% by road, whilst the Netherlands and Germany make the least use of road transport at about 40%; these last two countries make much more use of canals and inland waterways (for example, along the River Rhine).

You are to carry out a traffic survey. You will need to plan this survey very carefully (check with your tutor). The group should divide into teams of not less than six people: no-one should do this survey on their own. You will need to count the traffic that passes along a particular road in both directions during one hour. You will need to choose the roads very carefully. You must be able to count safely. You could choose, for example, a busy high street, a main road out of town, a road in a residential area or a minor road (see page 30). In order to make a fair estimate, you might have to do this over several days and at different times – we leave you to decide. (Check the GNVQ grading criteria in the Introduction – how do you get a distinction?) Your task is to find out the volume of traffic of each type that passes the chosen spot. You need to include bicycles, motorcycles, cars, vans, lorries and trucks, and specialist vehicles – e.g. milk floats.

When you have carried out your survey, compare your results with the survey carried out by the Department of Transport and published in *Social Trends* (see page 56).

1 Graph the results. What conclusions can you reach?
2 Present a written and oral report, showing your results and conclusions, to the rest of the group.

Advantages of road transport

- Goods can be picked up and delivered door-to-door
- Goods can be delivered almost everywhere in the UK by road. This cannot be done by rail which can only travel along a fixed track
- For short journeys, it can be much quicker and cheaper than other types of transport, provided there are no traffic jams. Almost 80% of all freight journeys made by road cover less than 60 miles, compared

with an average of 220 miles for inland waterways. (How many businesses in your area offer free delivery within 10 miles? Why do you think they do this?)

- Because there are many different types of van, lorry and trailer, different types of load can be carried. For example, milk is carried in specialised tankers, chilled and frozen foods are carried in refrigerated lorries, wide loads are carried on low loaders, and up to eight cars are carried on transporters
- For small loads, road transport can be cheaper because the road haulage businesses do not have to pay to maintain stations, tracks and signalling
- Unlike railways, road transport does not have to operate to a fixed timetable, so that goods can be picked and delivered to meet customers' needs
- Because it is quick and convenient, road transport is very good for carrying perishable items such as fruit, flowers and vegetables. These must be delivered at the time the customer needs them: if they are late, the customer may go to a competitor

Disadvantages of road transport

- Because of the limits on the size of vehicles, road transport is not very good for moving large quantities of heavy bulky goods such as the stone used for making roads, iron ore and steel coils (one of these can weigh up to 25 tonnes)
- **Heavy goods vehicles** (HGV) can cause pollution by creating noise, fumes and vibration, which is why many towns now have bypasses. Over 90% of road freight is now carried by HGV
- Roads can be closed, e.g. during bad weather: when there are high winds, high-sided vehicles cannot cross the Severn Bridges; and snow causes major problems in Scotland. Road works and burst water mains seem to occur regularly in most towns. Many local TV and radio stations and newspapers provide a road traffic service using the AA (Automobile Association) or RAC (Royal Automobile Club). Capital Radio in London has a helicopter called the 'flying eye' which reports regularly on traffic in the 'grid locked city'
- There are major restrictions on when and where goods can be delivered. (Look at the 'No Waiting' signs in your local high street)
- Traffic can be very slow. It is estimated that the average speed in London is 8 miles per hour (the average taxi does 60 miles in an eight-hour shift!)

activity

1 What road-information services are provided in your area?
2 The figures in Table 2.1 show how the importance of different methods of freight transport has changed since 1960. (All the figures (shown as a percentage) have been rounded to the nearest whole number, which is why some rows do not add up to 100%.) Draw a

graph of the figures. What can you say about the trends? Update the figures. (Use the *Annual Abstract of Statistics* (HMSO).) Have the trends continued?

Table 2.1   The relative importance (in percentages) of different methods of freight transport

YEAR	ROAD	RAIL	WATER	PIPELINE
1960	80	17	4	0
1965	83	12	3	1
1970	84	11	3	2
1975	85	10	3	3
1980	79	9	8	5
1985	80	7	8	5
1986	80	8	8	4
1987	81	7	7	4
1988	81	7	7	5
1989	82	7	7	4
1990	81	7	7	6
1991				
1992				
1993				
1994				
1995				

Table 2.2 gives figures for the road network in the UK. They show the number of kilometres of each type of road between 1983 and 1990.

1 Show this information on a year-by-year basis.
2 Describe any trends you can see. Why do you think these changes have happened? For example, have any new housing estates been built in your area? These could affect the figures for C roads and unclassified roads (see page 28).
3 Use the *Annual Abstract of Statistics* to update the figures. Have the trends continued?

Table 2.2   The extent (in kilometres) of different types of road in the UK, at 1 April in each year

	1983	1984	1985	1986	1987	1988	1989	1990
Motorway	2,741	2,786	2,813	2,920	2,975	2,992	2,995	3,070
Trunk	12,231	12,271	12,201	12,439	12,419	12,480	12,623	12,597
Principal	34,819	34,753	34,800	34,868	34,987	34,939	35,039	35,149
Other	295,985	297,779	298,885	299,849	302,314	303,904	305,946	307,142
Total	345,776	347,589	348,699	350,076	352,695	354,315	356,602	357,958

Source: Department of Transport
Note: 'Other' includes B roads, C roads and Unclassified roads

RAIL TRANSPORT

(a)

(b)

Figure 2.2 Railways old and new: (a) the Mumbles Railway; (b) Eurostar

The first regular rail passenger service in the world was the Mumbles Railway (see Figure 2.2(a)) which ran from Swansea to Mumbles on the Gower Peninsula in South Wales. It was opened in 1807, and shortly afterwards began carrying freight. In the past, railways were a very important form of transport for carrying goods of all kinds. Today, however, railways only carry about 5% of all freight. This is mainly heavy bulky goods such as coal, coke, iron ore, steel, gypsum and construction products. Very few retail products are carried by rail.

Advantages of rail transport

- It is ideal for carrying heavy bulky goods over long distances
- Goods can be carried in containers which are much safer and quicker to move
- One train can carry as much as a fleet of lorries
- Trains cause less pollution and are very safe and 'environment friendly'
- Goods can be carried in specialist wagons which are quick and easy to load and unload
- It is good for large businesses with bulky goods

Disadvantages of rail transport

- Goods cannot be delivered directly from supplier to customer – i.e. from door to door – without being loaded and unloaded
- It is not very useful for carrying goods over short distances
- Trains have to be run to fixed times because they are difficult to slot into complex timetables. This means they are less flexible than roads
- Freight trains usually have to give way to passenger trains
- It can be expensive particularly for short journeys
- It is not very good for small businesses except for the Red Star parcel service

Before 1994 railways in the UK operated as a state-run national system. At present (1996) the railways are being privatised. This means that they are being sold to the private sector so that they will no longer be owned by the state. Parts of the system are being sold separately so that, for example, train services in South Wales will be owned and operated by a different company from that operating services in the South-West of England. The three freight operations Loadhaul, Mainline Freight and Transrail were sold to an American freight company Wisconsin Central on 24 February 1996.

Brainstorm with the rest of the group how you think these developments could affect the delivery of freight.

AIR TRANSPORT

With the improvements in aircraft in recent years, moving freight by air transport is now the fastest-growing sector of the market. It is the fastest way of sending goods to places in Australia, Asia, Africa, North America and South America. Although any goods can be sent by air, dangerous and hazardous goods such as explosives are very strictly controlled by the International Civil Aviation Organisation, ICAO, which lays down rules and regulations which every sender and carrier of goods must follow.

How freight is carried

1 On passenger flights, freight is carried in the hold or 'belly' of the aircraft, which is below the passenger cabin floor. When you travel on an aircraft, this is where your baggage goes – you can sometimes hear it move when the plane takes off or lands. The Jumbo 747 for

example has a capacity of up to 20 tonnes, although many aircraft carry much less than this.

2 Some airlines operate aircraft which carry only freight, and these run scheduled (or fixed, timetabled) or charter services. Federal Express, for example, one of the biggest freight airlines in the world, promises 'next day by 10.30 am delivery throughout North America' for packages and documents, with a further 'fast and reliable' service to the Far East, Australasia etc.

Because of the increase in trade between the UK and the Far East, there has been an increase in demand for non-stop services such as London (Heathrow) to Singapore. This means that aircraft have to carry more fuel, and so are able to carry less freight. (What do you think happens to the price of carrying freight as a result?)

Fashion clothing, fresh vegetables, fruit and flowers are goods most often carried by air. For example, roses are air-freighted daily from Israel to France, and tomatoes are sent from the Canary Islands to the UK.

Factors affecting the price of air freight

- *Weight*: this is the most important factor. Heavier goods cost more to send than lighter goods. (Check this out by looking at the prices of airmail letters in your post office.)
- *The type of product*: boxed or crated products tend to cost less than goods which require more handling or packing
- *Distance*: higher prices are usually charged for longer distances
- *Fuel prices*: a rise or fall in fuel prices can affect freight prices. (Have you paid a 'fuel surcharge' (i.e. extra) on a continental holiday?)

Advantages of air transport

- It can be used to deliver urgent or emergency items across the world – e.g. medical supplies or documents
- It is the fastest form of transport
- It is ideal for light-weight perishable products, or for very expensive products where the extra cost of air transport is only a very small part of the final price so that the extra expense is worthwhile
- In some parts of the world which are very remote or inaccessible, such as Alaska or parts of Australia, it is the only form of transport which can be used
- It is very reliable

Disadvantages of air transport

- It is not suitable for bulky low-value products or heavy goods unless they are needed urgently
- Aircraft cause noise and pollute the atmosphere. (To reduce the nuisance caused by noise, several approaches have been taken, for example: aircraft are now built with quieter engines; aircraft have to take off very steeply to reduce the effects of noise; people living near

airports have had double glazing put in; only a small number of aircraft are allowed to land or take off between 11 pm and 6 am
- Aircraft can only operate between places which have runways
- Aircraft use a lot of fuel, which is a valuable natural resource and cannot be replaced
- Aircraft travel can be very expensive over short distances

1 Which form of transport is the cheapest over long distances?
2 Which form of transport is the cheapest over short distances?
3 Which forms of transport are most suitable for carrying bulky low-value products or heavy goods?

Case study: Instone Aviation

Instone Aviation, founded in 1919, is one of the original pioneers of air travel, flying from Croydon Airport (south of London) to Paris. It operates 24 hours a day, seven days a week: 'this is what our customers demand, we meet those demands.' It provides quality-assured professional air services for scheduled, charter, medical or even disaster and war-evacuation flights (e.g. during the Gulf War). It specialises in providing services to the marine and offshore oil industries, and has developed a wide range of new services to meet their ever-changing demands.

One of its functions is aircraft chartering: it will obtain the most suitable aircraft at the most competitive price to fly 'anything, anywhere, anytime'.

(with thanks to Tony Sawyer, Instone's Managing Director, for his help on this section)

1 Why do you think that Instone:
- has developed new services
- pays so much attention to customer needs
- is open 24 hours a day, seven days a week?
2 What factors should a business consider before deciding to charter an aircraft?

SEA TRANSPORT

The UK is a collection of islands. Its population cannot grow or make all that it needs to survive, so it has to bring in or import goods from other countries. However, there are certain products which the UK makes better than other countries. These goods are bought by other countries – i.e. sent overseas or exported.

This activity reviews your knowledge of the section on imports and exports in Chapter 1.

1 What are the main exports and imports?
2 Where do the imports come from?
3 Where do the exports go?
4 What do the figures on the sources of imports and destination of exports tell you about where the main sea routes are likely to be?

The main types of ship

CONTAINER SHIPS

These are ships which carry all their cargo in specially constructed standard-size containers (or 'boxes') which can be loaded from one type of transport to another – such as from rail to ship or ship to road. During the last 30 years, **container ships** have completely changed the face of sea transport: today, most goods are carried in containers. Most containers are either 20 feet or 40 feet long, 2.3 metres wide and 2.3 metres high. They open at one end only so that goods can be loaded and unloaded with a fork-lift truck. For large items of machinery, containers with a removable roof are available. Refrigerated containers are used to carry perishable, chilled or frozen goods, such as meat and butter from New Zealand and tomatoes from the Canary Islands. The average weight of a **full container load (FCL)** is about 17,000 kilogrammes. When a business has **less than a container load (LCL)** to send overseas, its packages will be combined with others (**consolidated**) to make a full load – e.g. hand-made woollen clothes, shortbread and orange marmalade sent together from Scotland to Japan. Exports of whisky are big enough to make up many FCLs.

1 Work out the volume of each of the containers mentioned above. You will need to multiply length × width × height. But you will also have to change either metres into feet or feet into metres so that you can work in the same units.
2 How many containers would be needed to ship 555,000 kilogrammes of goods?

ROLL-ON ROLL-OFF (RO-RO) SERVICES

You may well have travelled on a **Ro-Ro ship** between the UK and one of the English Channel ferry ports. Ro-Ro ships were originally designed to open at both the front and the back (fore and aft) so that any wheeled vehicles such as cars, buses, lorries, trailers, tractors and bulldozers could drive on at one end and drive off at the other end without turning around. (Since the sinking of the *Estonia* in the Baltic Sea, shipping authorities are now considering redesigning Ro-Ro ships so that they open at one end only. What effect will this have on lorry and car drivers? How might it affect the turnround time (the time taken for a ship to unload passengers and freight at the end of a trip and reload for the next trip) of the ferry companies? What would the operators of the Channel Tunnel say?) Ro-Ro ships are used to:

- carry people and freight from the UK to Europe – the Sally Line ship the *Sally Star*, for example, which crosses between Ramsgate and Dunkerque, can carry 1,800 passengers and 280 cars
- deliver new cars from Japan to the UK and the Middle East. If you have a car made in the Far East, it probably came to the UK on a Ro-Ro service and was driven off the ship straight onto a car transporter
- deliver goods from Europe to North Africa

In the last 10 years, Ro-Ro services have became very popular because ships can arrive at the port and leave or turn round very quickly. This saves time and money for both the shipping companies and the owners of the goods because loading and unloading is carried out very quickly: ships only make money when they are at sea.

TRADITIONAL CARGO SHIPS

Tramp ships
Tramp ships are cargo ships which operate when or where they are needed. They do not sail according to fixed timetables or on fixed routes, but instead they go wherever there is cargo. These ships are mainly used when:

- no container service is available – e.g. in small ports or where port facilities have not been built
- the goods do not fit into containers
- there is not enough to be carried in containers

Specialist ships
Specialist ships include:

- **bulk carriers**: these are used to transport one particular product such as coal, timber or cereals. For example, iron ore – which is used for making steel – is loaded directly into the hold of the ship at Narvik in Norway and unloaded at the deep-water harbour at Port Talbot in South Wales. Refrigerated ships are used for transporting frozen foods such as meat from Australia
- **tankers**: these are used for carrying crude oil, liquids and gases. The largest of these is over 1,500 feet long and weighs 564,759 tonnes (compare this with a car ferry at 15,000 tonnes)
- **coastal vessels**: these are usually smaller ships which stay close to the coastline, although you may sometimes see them crossing the

English Channel. They are used to carry heavy or bulky cargo
- **ocean-going ships**: these are larger ships which can carry cargo or passengers

Advantages of sea transport

- Large bulky and heavy goods can be carried
- It is ideal for goods which do not deteriorate – i.e. non-perishable goods
- It is ideal for delivering non-urgent items

Disadvantages of sea transport

- Many small ports cannot handle container ships because they do not have the facilities required
- Goods may need to be loaded and unloaded many times unless they are in containers
- It is very slow compared to other forms of transport. In addition, ships can run aground, spill their cargo and cause pollution – e.g. in February 1996 the *Sea Empress* went aground at Milford Haven, spilling 65,000 tonnes of crude oil

INLAND WATERWAYS

Inland waterways include canals and navigable rivers – e.g. the Manchester Ship Canal and the River Severn. Petroleum and oil products make up nearly 40% of the total carried by this form of transport, whilst wood and timber, construction materials and coal are also important. In the UK, there has been a rise in the use of inland waterways for leisure and boating activities, and only a very small fraction of transport here is used for carrying freight. This is not the case in Germany, Belgium and the Netherlands, where inland waterways are regularly used for carrying large amounts of freight. For example, in Belgium nearly 60% of all freight is carried by **barges** (these are the boats that are used).

Figure 2.3 A Cory Environmental tug transporting city waste down the River Thames to one of Cory's disposal sites

Case study: waterways and waste disposal

On 10 July 1995, the London *Evening Standard* reported that Westminster City Council, instead of sending nearly 150,000 tonnes of waste and rubbish down the River Thames in barges to be dumped out in the Thames estuary, would in future be sending it in lorries for burning at a new waste-disposal plant: 'Barges brought raw material for Londoners to work on coal to the power stations, flour to the bakeries, timber for building yards . . . industry has already abandoned inner London now the barges are going. This ignores a great asset – the working river.' A week later, it reported that the Corporation of London (the group that runs the City of London 'square mile' financial area which includes the Bank of England) would be continuing to send its rubbish in barges.

1 Construct a chart listing the advantages and disadvantages of using inland waterways.
2 Why do you think lorries are going to be used instead of barges? What effect will this have on the streets of London?
3 Which of the two decisions mentioned in the above case study would you support? Give your reasons.

FACTORS GOVERNING THE CHOICE OF FREIGHT TRANSPORT

Every business which sells a product, whether it is in manufacturing, wholesaling or retailing, will need to be able to distribute it profitably. This means getting the goods to the right places (e.g. shops, homes, wholesalers or other businesses) at the right time in the right quantity and in good condition so that the customers can buy them easily. A key decision that every business will have to make is: what type of transport should we use to move or distribute the goods? The business will have to compare the advantages and disadvantages of each type of transport. Here are some examples which you know: a local pizza company will use motorcycles; milk is delivered door-to-door using small battery-powered milk floats; a building supplier will deliver paving stones and gravel using a lorry. (Can you say why each of these methods of road transport was chosen? And can you name some other examples?)

The following are the points a business will have to consider when deciding what method of transport to use:

Speed

Water → Road → Rail → Air
Slowest ——————→ Fastest

Water is the slowest form of transport, and air transport is the quickest. Ask yourself these questions:

- Do all goods have to be delivered quickly?
  Answer: no, although there are some goods – such as medical supplies which are needed in an emergency, or spare parts which are essential to a production process, or perishable goods such as flowers, fruit and vegetables – where speed is vital
- Do all goods have to be delivered on time?
  Answer: yes. A company will not stay in business if it cannot deliver goods on time. This is a main feature of the advertising of many companies – e.g. Office Business World states 'Next day delivery anywhere in Britain guaranteed.' In most cases, it is more important for goods to be delivered on time than delivered quickly. For example, if supplies are needed weekly, then plans can be made to make sure that this happens using the best method of transport. This could be by road, rail, air and – for many islands – by sea. Perishable goods need to be delivered both quickly and on time

Whether a business buys or sells goods, it will need to compare the advantages and disadvantages of obtaining goods more quickly against the extra costs that could have to be paid. Generally, with quicker or faster delivery, transport costs will be higher.

Cost

The cost of transporting goods is made up of several different parts:

- *Packing*: this is the cost of the material used to protect goods whilst they are being transported. Generally, goods which are sent by sea need more secure and expensive packing than goods which are sent by road or air. Containers have helped to reduce the cost of packing (see page 35)

- *Handling*: this is the cost of loading and unloading. With some journeys, this can be very expensive, e.g. when goods change from one method of transport to another – such as road to air and then back to road
- *Freight charges*: this is the price charged by the company which carries the goods or freight. Sending goods by air is about 10 times more expensive than sending goods by sea
- *Insurance*: this is the amount of money which the sender has to pay to protect the goods against, for example, the risk of damage or theft. Generally, goods sent by sea cost more to insure than goods sent by air

See Table 2.3 for a summary.

Table 2.3   The comparative costs of sending goods by air or sea

COSTS	AIR	SEA
Packing	Average	Expensive
Handling	Average	Average
Freight carriage	Very high	Very low
Insurance	Average	Expensive

Case study: transport and insurance

In 1994, some 3,047 heavy goods vehicles were stolen, and 82% of these were never recovered. The total number of vehicles stolen in the UK in 1994 was 600,000, and nearly 250,000 of these were never seen again. The loss of a truck and its load can cost over £250,000.

(Reported in Trucking International, *July 1995)*

How do you think these statistics will affect **insurance premiums** (the money that has to be paid to get insurance cover)? How will it also affect the prices of goods?

 Find out the addresses and telephone numbers of the following delivery and collection service companies: Parceline, Parcel Force, TNT, Group 4, Securicor Omega. You will need these for a later activity. If you cannot find any of them, check out some local alternative companies offering the same service.

Availability and reliability

The availability of transport means the frequency of service or how often a particular service runs. Because of the intense competition between businesses in the transport industry, there are now frequent transport services available almost everywhere. For many large places, there will be a choice of methods of transport. For example, between London and Manchester, goods could be sent by road, rail or air. Frequent services are available to Europe, so that goods can be sent by Ro-Ro ferry or through the Channel Tunnel. Ships sail weekly from the UK to the Far East and North America (the *Lloyd's List* which is published daily gives details of shipping movements throughout the world). There are several flights each day to cities in North America. On the other hand, there are many places which are so remote and isolated that they are only accessible by road and do not have a regular transport service.

Whatever the speed, cost or frequency of a service, if it cannot be relied upon it is useless. You will probably have experienced the frustration of being told 'Yes, it will definitely be delivered on ————————', making special arrangements to stay in and then waiting for goods which never arrive! How often have you stood at the railway station and been told that the train you wanted has been delayed or cancelled? The railway businesses now have to publish and display charts showing the number of trains which have been cancelled (**reliability targets**) and the number of trains which arrive late at their destination (**punctuality targets**). Both these figures are shown as percentages – see Table 2.4. Check out what happens with privatisation.

Table 2.4 Railway performance indicators in the UK

	TRAINS ARRIVING WITHIN PUNCTUALITY TARGET (%)				TRAINS CANCELLED★ (%)			
	1986–87	1991–92	1992–93	1993–94	1986–87	1991–92	1992–93	1993–94
British Rail								
InterCity	85	84	85	89	0.8	2.3	1.7	1.7
Network SouthEast	91	91	91	92	1.6	1.2	1.5	1.1
Regional								
Express and long rural	} 91 {	92	91	92	} 0.5 {	1.3	1.1	2.7
Urban and short rural		89	91	91		1.6	1.6	1.9
London Underground	88	88	88	86	2.9	2.8	2.1	2.2
Docklands Light Railway	–	–	–	–	–	15.7	2.3	1.7

Source: Department of Transport
★ Percentage of scheduled services run for British Rail and scheduled kilometres operated for London Underground

Discuss whether the railway service has got better or worse. Do the figures shown in Table 2.4 reflect your own personal experiences?

Businesses which sell goods must deliver at the time they promise, particularly since many stores now operate Just-in-Time buying methods where everything that is needed for production or resale is delivered only at the time that it is needed so that it does not have to be stored on the buyer's premises. For some companies, this means that goods and materials are being delivered on a hourly basis. The buyer of the goods must plan ahead so that goods can be unloaded and used immediately, whilst the seller and carrier of the goods must be very efficient and make sure that the goods arrive on time for when they are needed.

1 Find out the cost of sending five copies of this book to a town in the UK which is approximately 200 miles away from your centre. You have promised that the parcel will definitely be with the buyer tomorrow morning.
2 Carry out the same exercise for Brussels, New York and Warsaw (the capital of Poland). You must find the cheapest and most reliable method. Do not forget to try the Post Office. Which service would you recommend, and why?

Loading and unloading

A major objective of every sender, buyer and carrier is to reduce the time taken loading and unloading or handling goods. On every journey, goods must be handled at least twice. Here are two examples showing when goods are handled (the loading and unloading are shown in brackets):

1 A manufacturer of clothes in Oldham (the clothes are wheeled onto trucks) sends dresses as 'hanging garments' by road to a retailer in Chatham (the clothes are wheeled off).
2 An electrical-goods retailer in the Galleria at Hatfield delivers a refrigerator (loaded using a trolley) onto a small van for a family in Wheathampstead. (Unloaded using a trolley) it is carried upstairs using two straps to take the weight.

A manufacturer sends goods by road to the docks. They are shipped to Rio de Janeiro (in Brazil), sent by rail to Brasília (about 1,200 kilometres north-west), and then carried by road to a customer located near the cathedral about 10 kilometres east of the station. How many times are the goods loaded and unloaded?

Every time goods are handled, this will add to the cost of the journey, add to the total time taken for the journey, and add to the price of the goods. Loading and unloading times – sometimes called **transfer times** – must always be taken into account when calculating the overall time for a journey.

Case study: manual handling

Figure 2.4 It is important to take care when carrying a heavy load

The majority of industrial accidents reported each year to the Health and Safety Executive (HSE) arise from manual handling – mainly back injuries. On average, each such injury results in 20 days off work.

Every employee has a duty to:

- follow appropriate systems of work laid down for their safety
- make proper use of the equipment provided
- cooperate with the employer on health and safety matters

The HSE's advice is:

- Can you make the load lighter or less bulky, easier to grasp, more stable, and less damaging to hold?
- Stop and think before you pick up a load

(Source: Manual Handling, *published by the Health and Safety Executive, September, 1994)*

 What effect do you think that industrial injuries could have on a distribution business?

Distance Distance is an important feature of any journey, and there is a very close relationship between the distance and the cost of a journey for different methods of transport – as Figure 2.5 shows.

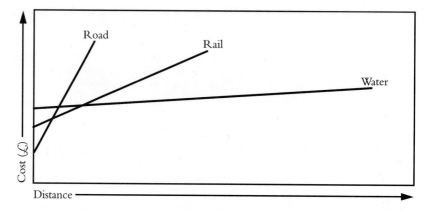

Figure 2.5 The cost of road, rail and water transport over short and long distances

What does Figure 2.5 tell us?

1 For short distances:
   ● road transport is very cheap;
   ● water transport is the most expensive;
   ● rail transport is relatively expensive.
2 For long distances:
   ● water transport is the cheapest;
   ● road transport is very expensive;
   ● rail transport is relatively expensive.

LOCAL JOURNEYS

Road is the most efficient form of transport for short journeys. Light vans and lorries are normally used to deliver goods within a 10-mile radius of a town. When small parcels and documents are needed urgently, motorcycle courier services are available. The effect of traffic delays on the time taken for a journey needs to be taken into account.

NATIONAL JOURNEYS

Although road transport is used to carry most freight, rail and air services are also available. Unless goods are in containers, it will be necessary to consider the location of the nearest station/airport both at the point of departure and at the destination. Road transport will be necessary for the collection and delivery of the goods. This will add to the time and cost.

For the vast majority of retail products, road is the preferred method of transport.

INTERNATIONAL JOURNEYS

Sea is the preferred method of transport for the majority of international freight journeys (excluding England, Wales and Scotland). (The majority of international long-distance *passenger* journeys, on the other hand, are made by air. Why do you think this is the case?)

Case study: Williams Press

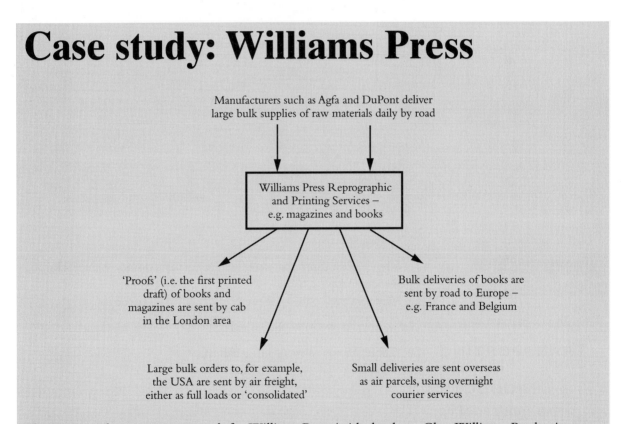

Figure 2.6 The transport network for Williams Press (with thanks to Glyn Williams, Production Controller at Williams Press)

1 What factors will Williams Press have to consider when choosing a method of transport for its products?
2 What do you think influenced its choice in the four cases shown in Figure 2.6?

Case study: Exotics, the tropical food importer

Lychees from Taiwan and Thailand are canned,
and the cans are put into cardboard cartons

↓

The cartons are shipped in containers to
the UK by sea at normal temperatures

↓ By road, still in containers

Importer breaks bulk into
shrink-wrap packs
of 12 or 6 cans

↓ By road

Wholesaler

Retailers

Figure 2.7 The transport arrangements for a tropical food importer (with thanks to Ken Bond)

1 Why do you think that wholesalers/retailers do not want packs of 24 cans of exotic fruit?
2 Why was each particular method of transport used?

TRANSPORTING RETAIL PRODUCTS

Goods transported by road

See Table 2.5 for relevant information.

Table 2.5   Products carried by road

PRODUCTS	CHARACTERISTICS	CATEGORY
Food, drink and tobacco: mainly manufactured from the secondary sector, but some primary goods also	High-value fast-selling consumer goods, short-to-medium shelf life	Perishable, non-perishable, dry, chilled, frozen, liquid
Fertilisers: mainly manufactured	High weight, high volume, medium value	Non-perishable, dry, liquid, hazardous
Wood and timber: wood is a primary product, timber is manufactured	Medium weight, high volume, medium value	Dry, generally non-perishable after preservation treatment
Crude minerals and ores: these are primary products which do not enter the retail sector	High weight, high volume, low-to-medium value	Non-perishable, dry
Coal and coke: coal is primary, coke is manufactured from coal. Very little now enters the retail market	High weight, high volume, low-to-medium value	Non-perishable, dry, can be hazardous under certain circumstances
Petrol: this is a manufactured product	High weight, high volume, high value	Liquid, very hazardous
Bulk chemicals: these include both primary and manufactured	High weight, high volume, high value	Perishable, non-perishable, chilled, dry, liquid (acids) very hazardous
Building materials: these include both primary (sand) and manufactured (cement)	High weight, high volume, low-to-medium value	mostly non-perishable, dry, can be hazardous
Machinery & metals: manufactured goods used in the secondary sector	High weight, high value	Dry, non-perishable

Source: Department of Transport
Note: Shows the most important products

Goods transported by rail

Today in the UK, rail transport is used mainly for transporting industrial goods:

- coal and coke: used for steel-making and generating electricity. This has decreased substantially since 1980
- metals including iron and steel: if you travel on the main railway line between Newport (Llanwern steelworks) and Port Talbot

(Margam steelworks) in South Wales, you will see steel coils being carried in open-top wagons

- construction materials: particularly bulk sand, roadstones, gravel and cement. These are mainly used in the construction industry
- oil and petrol: carried in specially designed wagons

Almost no retail products are carried by rail, with the exception of newspapers and some building materials. Contrast this with the situation in Switzerland or Peru in South America (the train goes over 15,000 feet high) where many high mountain villages are only accessible by rack or cog rail because it is impossible to build roads.

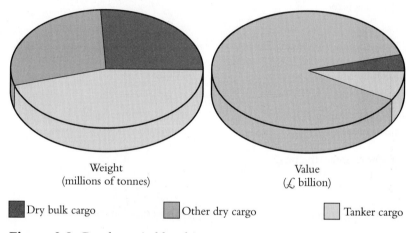

Weight	Value
(millions of tonnes)	(£ billion)

■ Dry bulk cargo   ▨ Other dry cargo   □ Tanker cargo

Figure 2.8 Goods carried by ship

Goods transported by ship

The pie charts in Figure 2.8 show:

1 that tanker cargo (mostly crude oil and petroleum) is most important in terms of weight;
2 that dry cargo (mostly manufactured goods) is most important in terms of value;
3 that although dry bulk cargo (e.g. cereals, coal, iron ore) is significant in terms of weight, it is not important in terms of value.

Figures 2.9 and 2.10 show the most popular choices of freight transport for different products.

1 What do the figures tell you about the choice of transport for each category of product? For example, what are the most and the least popular choices? Can you say why?
2 Can you say which goods are most often transported by road, rail, water or pipeline?

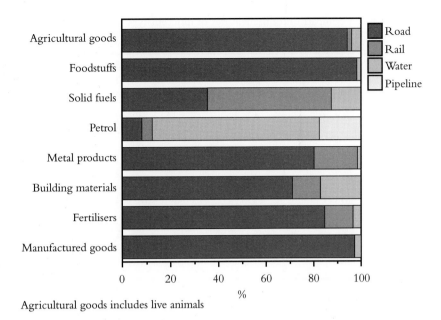

Agricultural goods includes live animals

Figure 2.9 The most popular choices of freight transport: bar chart

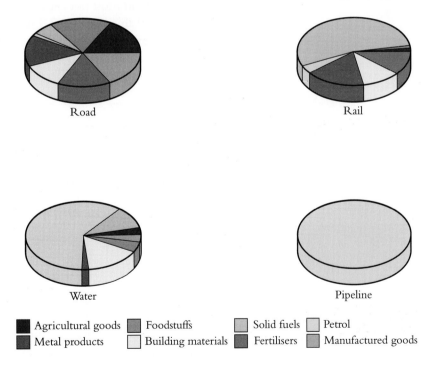

Figure 2.10 The most popular choices of freight transport: pie charts

Table 2.6   A comparison of the features of different types of freight transport

	SPEED	COST	FREQUENCY	AVAILABILITY	RELIABILITY	LOADING AND UNLOADING
Water	Very slow, but acceptable if pre-planned	Very cheap	Very few	Limited to navigable waterways	Satisfactory	Easy in containers, but can be difficult without good facilities
Rail	Medium	Medium	Few	Decreasing	Satisfactory	Lifting equipment is needed
Road	Fast	High	Very high	Available everywhere	Satisfactory	Straightforward with proper equipment
Air	Very fast	Very expensive	Medium	Limited	Very good	Easy in containers. Equipment is needed
Pipeline	Slow	Cheap	High	Very limited	Very good	Not needed. Pumping is required to keep the liquid moving

Produce a report or presentation showing the best method of transport for each of the products (numbers 1–13 on page 52). Give reasons for your choice. (You must put each product into its category and give its characteristics. Tables 2.7 and 2.8 will help you.) Because you may have to find out where various places are, you will probably need both a UK atlas and a world atlas.

Table 2.7   Distribution and categories of good

CATEGORIES OF GOODS	SIGNIFICANCE FOR DISTRIBUTION
Perishable Such as fresh food, fruit, vegetables, flowers and certain medicines	These are goods which deteriorate/rot quickly. They require e.g. • special storage such as chilled warehousing • special transport to avoid breakage, damage or rotting • a quick sale in the shop because they have a very short shelf-life
Non-perishable Such as tinned food, crockery (note that this is fragile because it can break easily), furniture, electrical goods	These are goods which do not rot quickly and have a long shelf-life. Generally, they do not need any special facilities for transport, storage, wholesaling or selling (fragile goods need to be protected from damage)
Chilled Foods such as pies, yoghurts, cheese, fresh meat and fish, delicatessen items; certain medicines	These are goods which need to be transported, stored and displayed in moderately cold conditions (chill cabinets)

Frozen

Such as meat, fish, convenience ready meals

These are goods which need to be transported, stored and displayed in extremely cold conditions (freezers)

Dry

Foods such as biscuits, rice, sugar, cereals; building materials e.g. cement

These goods must not be allowed to become damp or moist otherwise they will rot very quickly. The food must also be protected from insects and other creatures

Liquid

Hazardous liquids such as chemicals and acids; non-hazardous liquids such as milk, fruit juice

These are normally transported, stored and sold in sealed containers. Tankers are used for carrying bulk liquids, barrels are used for smaller quantities, and bottles and jars are used for the final sale

Hazardous

Such as household and garden goods, some toiletries, medicines

These are goods which can cause damage or harm under particular conditions, e.g. air freshener sprays are 'highly flammable and must be disposed of carefully'. There are strict regulations for controlling the transport and storage of hazardous goods

Table 2.8 Distribution and characteristics of goods

CHARACTERISTICS OF GOODS	SIGNIFICANCE FOR DISTRIBUTION
Weight Tinned goods, books and paper, building materials, tissues and cotton wool, chipboard furniture	Heavy items are best carried by sea, rail or road. High-value heavy items can be carried by air
Volume Toilet paper, cotton wool, wood and timber	Volume is the space taken up by the item. Small items can be carried by air. Large items can be carried by air (when the weight is low), road, rail or sea. Toilet paper is low-value/high-volume/low-weight and takes up a large amount of space on supermarket shelves
Value Jewellery, watches, cameras, computers	For long distances, high-value goods can be carried by air. Low-value goods would usually be carried by sea, rail or road. Good protection is needed against theft and damage during transport and storage
Fragile Pottery, crockery, electrical items	'If you break it, consider it sold!' said the sign in a pottery. Good protection and insurance is necessary for transporting, storing and selling the goods

Shelf-life

Foods, medicines, fashion clothing	Shelf-life is the length of time a product – usually food – will last before it deteriorates (see the sell-by and eat-by dates on sandwiches). Fast-selling items are usually placed at eye level on shelves. Shops will not stock goods which do not sell quickly because these can deteriorate

1 Sending tomatoes from the Canary Islands to the UK.
2 Sending frozen meat from New Zealand to the UK.
3 Sending flowers from the Netherlands to the UK.
4 Delivering electrical goods from a warehouse in Guildford to a shop in Swansea.
5 Delivering pizza within a 5-mile radius of a local shop.
6 Transporting a package of diamonds from London to New York.
7 Taking cabbages from a farm in Norfolk to the fruit and vegetable market in London.
8 Transporting very large and regular quantities of stone, for making roads, from a quarry near Hastings to a depot next to Chislehurst Station.
9 Transporting petrol from an oil refinery in Llandarcy (near Neath in South Wales) to the Bristol area.
10 Transporting crude oil from Saudi Arabia to the refinery at Milford Haven in South Wales.
11 Sending coal from Poland (Gdansk) to the UK.
12 Sending foodstuffs from your local town in the UK to Madrid in Spain.
13 Delivering beds made in Aspatria (Cumbria) to Walsall in the Midlands.

Self-test questions:
Chapter 2

1 List the advantages and disadvantages of road transport.
2 List the advantages and disadvantages of air transport.
3 List the advantages and disadvantages of rail transport.
4 List the advantages and disadvantages of water transport.
5 Which type of transport is fastest over short, medium and long distances?
6 Which type of transport is cheapest over short, medium and long distances?
7 Name three products most likely to be carried by ship. Give reasons for your choice.
8 Name three products most likely to be carried by rail. Give reasons for your choice.
9 How might weight, volume, value and shelf-life (all characteristics of goods) affect the type of transport chosen?

10 What type of transport is most likely to be used for carrying perishable, frozen, liquid and hazardous goods (categories of goods)?

evidence
indicators

Transporting retail goods

You should have now completed all the activities in this chapter, this means you have the evidence to show you are competent in this element, 'Investigating types of transport for retail goods'.

Gather the evidence together and sort it into the following headings:

* notes evaluating the features of different kinds of transport
* notes showing the effect of journey features on the choice of transport
* a report showing your choice of transport for carrying five different retail goods from different categories and with different characteristics

Label all your work, include a contents page and present it attractively.

Investigating transport networks

In this chapter we will:

- use maps to describe the UK and European transport network
- compare the volume of traffic carried by different types of transport
- describe methods of route planning, and calculate distances and journey times
- plan a transport route from the UK to a town in mainland Europe

We will cover Element 1.3, Performance Criteria 1, 2, 3, 4, 5, 6, 7.

THE MAJOR FEATURES OF THE LOCAL TRANSPORT SYSTEM

To be able to describe the major features of the local transport system, we need an Ordnance Survey (OS) map. Table 3.1 shows the most useful OS maps for planning routes.

Table 3.1 Ordnance Survey maps for route planning

ORDNANCE SURVEY MAP	SCALE	MAIN FEATURES	USE
Routemaster	1 cm = 2.5 km, or 1 cm = 250,000 cm	Shows major roads. Distances are shown between little marker flags. This technique is also used on Continental maps	Nine maps cover the UK. They are good for route planning. Little detail is given, so they are not useful for local deliveries
Landranger	1 cm = 0.5 km, or 1 cm = 50,000 cm	Because of the bigger scale, minor roads can also be shown	204 maps cover the UK. They are good for showing the details of a journey
Pathfinder	1 cm = 0.25 km, or 1 cm = 25,000 cm	Considerable detail is shown – e.g. footpaths	Used by walkers and ramblers. Not very useful for HGV drivers

Obtain a copy of the OS Landranger map for your area. Now look at the 'Key' which shows how features on the ground are represented by various symbols on the map. Can you find examples of the following on the map you are using?

- motorways with interchanges and junctions – shown in blue
- trunk roads: these are A or main roads – e.g. the A21(T) which runs between London and Hastings. They may have some long stretches of dual carriageway. They are suitable for heavy vehicles

- main roads or A roads: these are important roads which run between large towns
- secondary or B roads which link smaller towns. They may have some dual carriageways which allow slower vehicles to be passed
- narrow roads with places for passing
- minor roads with more or less than 4 metres of tarred surface. Heavy goods vehicles should avoid narrow or minor roads. (Measure out 4 metres. Could two vehicles pass each other in that width?)

Look at the symbols for gradients (hills) and vehicle ferries. Do you have examples of these in your area?

Canals

There are also three symbols for canals (can you find examples of these on your map?):

1 canal, lock (when the canal changes levels);
2 towpath (this is the path alongside the canal used for towing or pulling the boats);
3 canal dry.

Railways

There are four symbols here (can you also find examples of these on your map?):

1 track multiple (more than one line) or single;
2 track narrow gauge (less than the standard size – e.g. the Romney, Hythe and Dymchurch in south-east Kent);
3 freight lines only;
4 stations.

The group should form into two teams. Each team should prepare 10 questions using a local map of your area. Score 2 marks for each correct answer and 1 mark for a near miss – we leave you to judge this! Ask questions such as: where does the M(?) go to? How would you advise someone to go to town x? How would you advise someone to come from London? And from Newcastle? What is the canal here called? Where does the railway line go? Where is the nearest motorway junction? Where does the A(??) go? etc. The answers to the questions can be used to produce both a set of notes and a sketch map of the major features of the local transport system. (Figure 3.1 shows the main features of the system around Coventry.)

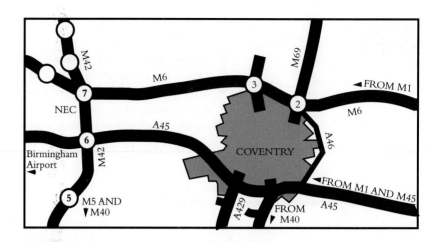

Figure 3.1 Major roads around Coventry

CONTINENTAL MAPS

The following are shown on the Michelin map of Belgium and Luxembourg (Map 409):

- motorways, with interchanges or junctions – which are the only places where you can join or leave a motorway – also shown
- dual carriageways, which are very similar to motorways and may have roads crossing them
- major trunk roads, with the number of lanes indicated
- secondary roads, with the number of lanes indicated
- distances between towns – shown with little marker flags
- roads classification numbers. For example, E roads are major international roads – such as the E 40 which runs through to Brussels and on to Cologne in Germany; A roads are the motorways; and N roads are other smaller, less important roads

MAJOR LINKS AND TRANSPORT SYSTEMS IN THE UK AND EUROPE

Table 3.2 shows the average daily flow of motor vehicles by class of road in the UK.

Table 3.2   The average daily flow of motor vehicles by class of road in the UK

| | 000s OF VEHICLES | | | |
	1981	1986	1991	1993
Motorways	30.6	38.3	53.9	55.2
Built–up roads:				
Trunk	13.6	16.5	18.5	18.5
Principal	12.3	12.8	15.2	14.8
Non–built–up roads:				
Trunk	9.0	11.5	15	15.1
Principal	4.5	5.5	6.8	6.9
All minor roads	1.0	1.1	1.3	1.3

The main conclusion is that traffic has increased on all roads, with the biggest increase – over 80% – in motorway traffic.

1 Draw line graphs of the data shown in Table 3.2. What other conclusions can you draw?
2 Compare the figures with those for the traffic survey you carried out earlier – see page 28.

The UK motorway, trunk road and ferry systems

The motorways are the major road routes. Figure 3.2 shows motorways and the principal trunk roads in the UK, as well as ferry routes from the UK.

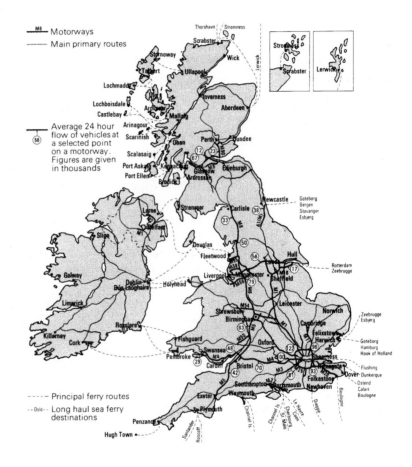

Figure 3.2 Motorways and principal trunk roads in the UK

1 Which motorway goes from:
   ● Birmingham to Bristol
   ● London to Cambridge
   ● Liverpool to Manchester
   ● Folkestone to London
   ● Glasgow to Perth?
   ● Carlisle to Dover
   ● Swansea to Birmingham

- Sheffield to Southampton
- Manchester to London
- Exeter to Shrewsbury?

3 Many capital cities now have motorways which go *around* them. The result is that heavy goods vehicles do not have to travel *through* the cities; and this means less pollution and fewer traffic jams. For example, Brussels has The Ring, and Paris has the Périférique.

A lorry is travelling on the M25 motorway around London (the London Orbital). Do some research to find out which exits it should take for Bristol, Gatwick, the Channel Tunnel, Oxford, Birmingham, Heathrow Airport (Terminal 4 and cargo), Southampton, Brighton and Lakeside.

UK ports and airports

1 Look at Figure 3.3 which shows the freight traffic at the main UK ports. Mark each port onto the map. What conclusions can you reach?

2 Look at Figure 3.4 which shows the freight traffic at the main UK airports. Mark each airport onto the map. How do the figures compare with those for European airports (see page 63)? What conclusions can you reach?

3 Compare the amount of freight which is moved through ports with the amount moved through airports. What conclusions can you reach?

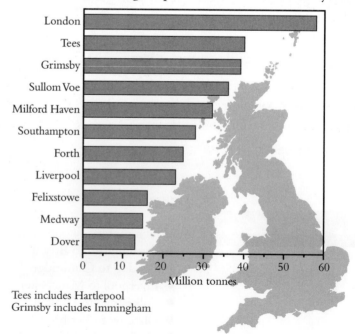

Tees includes Hartlepool
Grimsby includes Immingham

Figure 3.3 Freight traffic at the main UK ports

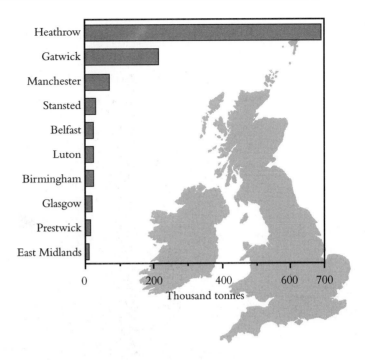

Figure 3.4 Freight traffic at the main UK airports

The UK railway system

Look at Figure 3.5 which shows the main railway lines in the UK.

1 Where is your nearest station which will accept freight?
2 Does your local station have a parcel service?
3 Why is the rail network different in England, Wales and Scotland?
4 Why are there more railway lines around the major towns?
5 How important is London in the railway system?

Transport networks in the European Union

Table 3.3 Road and rail networks in the European Union, 1992 (km)

	MOTORWAYS	OTHER ROADS★	NATIONAL RAIL NETWORKS
UK	3,259	383,287	16,881
Belgium	1,631	131,810	3,432
Denmark	653	70,389	2,344
France	7,408	908,243	33,555
Germany	11,013	628,792	40,816
Greece	280	40,550	2,484
Ireland	32	92,330	1,944
Italy	6,306	297,217	16,016
Luxembourg	95	5,108	275
The Netherlands	2,134	103,683	2,753
Portugal	519	65,576	3,054

Source: Eurostat
★ Different classifications of roads may affect totals

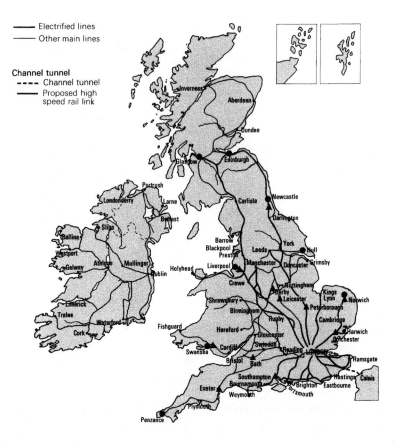

Figure 3.5 The main railway lines in the UK

Highlight the main features of Table 3.3. What conclusions can you reach? If you knew the size of each country, how would your conclusions change? (Remember how you get a distinction on this course – check the GNVQ grading criteria.)

EUROPEAN ROAD AND RAIL NETWORKS

Figure 3.6 shows the planned Transeuropean road network for the year 2002, whilst Figure 3.7 shows the planned high-speed rail network for the year 2010.

1 A distributor wants to go to Marseille in the South of France. What method of transport would you recommend?
2 Do you think that more roads or more railways should be built?

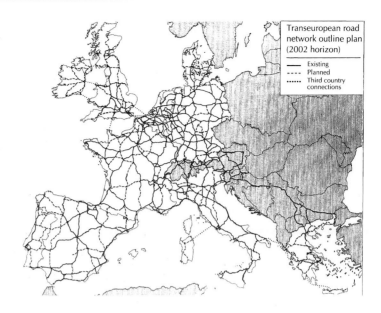

Figure 3.6 Outline plan for
the Transeuropean road
network for 2002

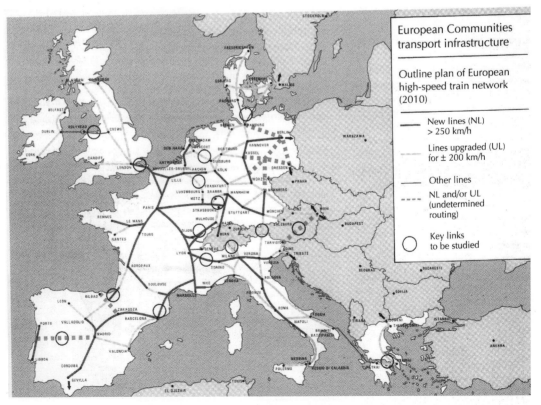

Figure 3.7 Outline plan for the European high-speed train network
for 2010

3 Do you think that there should be more high-speed rail lines in the UK? (The only one shown in Figure 3.7 is the link from St Pancras in London to the Channel Tunnel. The contract to build this was given to a group of private businesses (including Virgin) in February 1996.)

Here is some information which will help you to reach your decisions:

- In the countries of the European Union, goods and vehicles can move freely
- New production methods mean that supplies need to be delivered more frequently
- More people own and drive cars

THE VOLUME OF GOODS TRAFFIC CARRIED BY DIFFERENT TYPES OF TRANSPORT WITHIN EUROPE

Look at Table 3.4. As can be seen, road transport is used to carry the majority of freight. Inland waterways are significant in Belgium, France, West Germany and the Netherlands, whilst rail transport is important in the UK, France and West Germany.

1 Calculate the total inland freight for each country.
2 Calculate the total freight carried by road, rail and inland waterways.
3 Draw charts/diagrams to show the freight–transport proportions for each country.
4 What conclusions can you draw from the European totals calculated?
5 Calculate the figures as percentages. What percentage of Spanish freight is carried by rail? And by road? (You should be able to answer this question for all countries!)

Table 3.4   Inland freight transport within Europe in 1991, in million tonnes

COUNTRY	TOTAL	ROAD	RAIL	INLAND WATERWAY
UK		1,557.3	136.0	5.4
Belgium		355.2	60.4	91.4
Denmark		190.1	5.2	
France		1,444.6	130.0	61.1
West Germany		2,934.2	390.9	215.2
Greece		188.6	3.4	
Ireland		79.9	3.3	
Italy		923.2	60.9	
Luxembourg		24.3	12.8	1.9
Netherlands		457.8	17.6	242.5
Portugal		271.7	7.0	
Spain		700.2	24.4	
Total				

Source: Eurostat

The following figures show how goods are transported between the different Member States of the European Union: road 38%, sea 26%, inland waterway 18%, pipeline 9%, rail 7%, air 0.04%.

1 Draw a pie chart showing this information.
2 Use a map of Europe to plot the following sea routes: Dover–Calais, Harwich–Hook of Holland, Southampton–Cherbourg, Ramsgate–Ostend. What other ferry routes are there?

The figures in Table 3.5 show the amount of freight loaded and unloaded at major EU airports.

1 Put the airports on a map of Europe.
2 Draw a bar chart showing the figures. Compare the chart with that for the UK on page 59.

Table 3.5 Passenger and freight volumes at major EU airports

CITY	AIRPORT	PASSENGERS PER YEAR IN MILLIONS	FREIGHT LOADED AND UNLOADED, IN 000s TONNES
London	Heathrow	45	755
Frankfurt	Rhein Main	30	1,054
Paris	Charles de Gaulle	25	612
	Orly	25	275
London	Gatwick	20	190
Rome	Fiumicino	19	231
Amsterdam	Schipol	19	695
Madrid	Barajas	18	188
Copenhagen	Kastrup	12	146
Palma (Majorca)	San Juan	12	15
Manchester	Ringway	12	

Source: Eurostat

3 London (65 million – Heathrow and Gatwick) Paris (50 million) and Frankfurt (30 million) handle the most passengers. What conclusions can you reach? What do the figures tell you about the popularity of the places and the amount of traffic going to the airports?

Use a map of Europe to show the route between Manchester and Palma, Manchester and Copenhagen, Heathrow and Frankfurt, Heathrow and Madrid, Gatwick and Paris, Gatwick and Rome, and Amsterdam and Copenhagen.

METHODS OF ROUTE PLANNING

Manual or computer-based methods, or both, can be used for route planning.

Manual methods

CHOOSING AN ATLAS

Whether you are a driver or a dispatcher, it is essential to be able to find your way around the country. To do this successfully, you need to be able to use an atlas. There are several atlases available, although only a few of these are any good for truck drivers. Always make sure that you have the most up-to-date atlas.

Here are some useful hints when choosing an atlas:

- Scale: a large scale is good for detail but is less good for route-finding because the pages have to be turned more often
- Quality: is the print too small? Can it be read under yellow sodium street lights (green shows up much better than red here)? Is the paper strong enough (maps get very rough use in the cab of a truck)? Is the cover waterproof?
- Is it up-to-date? When was it last revised (new roads and service areas are built all the time – check inside the front cover)?
- Does it have detailed town and city plans on a larger scale? (These are important for getting through towns quickly)
- Does it have plans of docks and ports?

Here is a list of road atlases currently available for the UK:

- *AA Truckers Atlas of Britain* (scale: 3 miles = 1 inch). Currently, this is the only atlas which has been printed especially for truck drivers, and it includes the heights of low bridges in neat red triangles (how often have you seen pictures of lorries stuck under bridges?). It is essentially a road atlas, and does not show details such as 'viewpoints' which are shown on tourist maps (the authors were told 'truck drivers are not paid to admire the view'!).
- *AA Big Road Atlas Britain* (scale: 3 miles = 1 inch)
- *Collins Road Atlas Britain* (scale: 3.2 miles = 1 inch)
- *Geographers' A–Z Great Britain Road Atlas* (scale: 2.5 miles = 1 inch)
- *Michelin Motoring Atlas Great Britain & Ireland* (scale: 4.75 miles = 1 inch)
- *Ordnance Survey Motoring Atlas* (scale: 3 miles = 1 inch)
- *Philip's 1995 Road Atlas Britain* (scale: 3 miles = 1 inch)

You will need an equivalent road atlas for European countries to complete the assignment on planning a route to a town in mainland Europe (see page 80 later in this chapter).

USING AN ATLAS

At the back of every atlas there should be an index of places/streets etc.

For example, in the AA Atlas (scale: 4 miles = 1 inch) the entry for Lincoln reads: 'Lincoln Lincs. 32 SK 9771' (these figures are called **coordinates** or **reference points**):

- '32' is the page number
- 'SK' is the National Grid position used by the Ordnance Survey. This must be included so that it cannot be confused with anywhere else
- '97' is the **'easting'**: 9 can be found on the line on the bottom of the page, and 7 shows the number of imaginary lines of tenths of the square to count east of line 9
- '71' is the **'northing'**: 7 can be found on the left-hand side of the page, and 1 shows the number of imaginary lines of tenths of the square to count north of line 7
- Lincoln is situated where the two imaginary lines cross – see Figure 3.8.

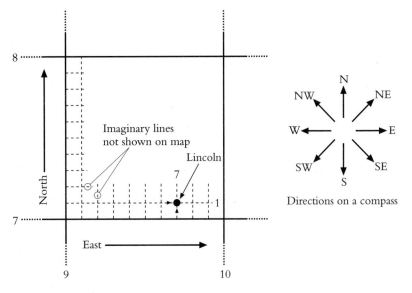

Figure 3.8 Using 'easting' and 'northing' to locate Lincoln on an atlas map

(Hint: eastings and northings can be remembered as (i) walking along the street and (ii) going up the block of flats.) A similar system for locating places is used on many atlases, maps and street plans.

HOW TO PLAN A JOURNEY

This method for planning applies to local, national and European journeys:

1 To get an overall view of the journey, use a route-planning map. This is a small-scale map which covers a very large area such as

Scotland, England and Wales and acts as the key map showing which further map to use for greater detail. It only shows motorways, primary routes, A roads and major centres of population (and therefore traffic jams). This map can also be used to locate the towns at the beginning and end of the journey.

2 Make a note of:
   - the road numbers
   - key towns along the route, to help with directions
   - junction numbers for joining and leaving motorways (motorway signs are always in blue)

3 Whenever possible, do not go through towns as this can cause severe delays. In addition, try to avoid rush hours such as the morning and afternoon when children are taken to and from school, and people are going to or coming home from work).

4 Try to go *against* the flow of traffic – i.e. *leave* a major city during the morning rush hour, go *into* a city in the evening. (Many HGVs travel at night. Why do you think they do this?)

5 Use a large-scale map or plan to work out the beginning and end of the journey, and to work out such things as where and when to join or leave the motorway network, or whether there is a one-way system or dual carriageway.

6 Check with the motoring organisations – e.g. AA Roadwatch – on road and weather conditions. Listen to road reports on local radio stations. You will find that by putting the station frequencies on a small card, you can tune in more easily – e.g. West Glamorgan 96.4 FM, Lincolnshire 94.9 FM etc.

7 Calculate the distance and time of the journey (see below). Be prepared to start/leave earlier or later than usual. For example, you do not want to be on the M6 around Birmingham between 4 and 5 pm!

8 Always allow extra time for delays, particularly when crossing the Channel (check weather conditions).

1 A distributor based in Shrewsbury has to make deliveries to: Church Stretton, Whitchurch, Market Drayton, Oswestry, Much Wenlock, Telford. Plan the route, giving the road numbers.

2 A distributor based in York has to make deliveries to: Malton, Fridaythorpe, Great Driffield, Staxton, Bainton. Plan the route, giving the road numbers and order of delivery. What type of vehicle would you recommend?

3 A distributor based in Oldham has to make deliveries to: Stockton, Bolton, Rochdale, Bury, Littleborough. Plan the route.

4 A distributor based at Newbury has to make deliveries to: south-west Swindon, Chippenham, Malmesbury, Chepstow. Plan the route.

Finding routes using a computer program

There are now several computer programs available which can plan cost-effective journeys for both the private car and heavy-goods-vehicle users – e.g. Truckstops (published by Kingswood) and AutoRoute Express (published by NextBase). Most of these work in the same way. Here is an example of how one of them works.

AA Milemaster 2, a DOS (disk-operating system) computer program which operates with a mouse, has the following features:

- It covers the UK, Europe and Ireland
- It calculates the quickest and shortest routes between places (right down to individual postcodes) so that deliveries and distribution can be made quickly and easily
- It can print out a full set of directions
- It produces mileage, cost and time charts
- An 'avoid' icon allows the user to keep away from motorways, toll roads (roads which you have to pay to use), cities, urban areas (towns) and high altitudes. This is important in planning a journey because towns and hills can slow down heavy goods vehicles, and any time wasted costs money
- Every transport company needs to be able to control its costs if it is going to make a profit. This program will calculate costs for each (per) mile and for each (per) driver hour, based on recommended speeds and roads. This is very important if the company has different types of vehicles and uses different routes
- It can give directions from one postcode to another

ADVANTAGES OF USING COMPUTER ROUTE-FINDING PROGRAMS

1 Better, shorter routes are generated which can take account of traffic jams.
2 Vehicles and drivers are used more effectively, so increasing productivity and cutting fuel costs.
3 Routes can be arranged quickly. This is important if goods have to be sent out immediately.
4 Administration time is saved.

Many large companies use some form of computerised route planning, including Nestlé, Sainsbury and Boots.

You will need a commercial route-finding computer software package for this activity. Repeat the activity on page 66 using the computer program. What are the differences in the suggested routes. Can you say why different routes were produced?

On-board electronic route-finding systems

In addition to the systems described in the two articles below, there are now several electronic aids which help with tracking both goods and vehicles on their way to the customer, e.g.:

- Cellular phones in truck cabs mean that drivers can be contacted anywhere in Europe and can inform the customer of any delays or route changes that may become necessary
- Satellite tracking systems mean that every vehicle can be tracked and located using a desktop computer based in the transport manager's office – see Figure 3.9

Look at the two articles below on the Blaupunkt and Phillips systems for navigation and route finding.

1 Who do you think is likely to use these systems?
2 What are the advantages and disadvantages of using these systems?

Electronic atlas can save time and fuel

The Philips Routefinder is an electronic road atlas that tells you how to get from A to B and also gives travel time, distance and mileage cost.

To operate it, simply key in the start point and the destination and within seconds Routefinder will calculate the quickest way to get there.

For those not keen on motorways, Routefinder can be programmed to bypass them. And when traffic jams are ahead, it can plan an alternative route.

From its AA-compiled database of more than 38,000 towns in England, Scotland and Wales, the Routefinder calculates the journey time and fuel consumption for each trip.

The LCD display can be backlit for night use.

By 1996, interchangeable ROM cards that can be inserted into Routefinder, loaded with data for other European countries, will be available.

(Source: Mail on Sunday, *15 October 1995)*

Figure 3.9 The computer tracking of loads in Europe, at NFC

Motorists need never be lost with CD-Rom maps

Getting lost in the car may become a problem of the past with the launch of a device that links the global positioning system (GPS) to CD-Rom maps to guide motorists to their destination.

The Blaupunkt system plots the car's position to within 100m by establishing where it is in relation to at least three of the 24 satellites that form the American Navstar system, better known as GPS. This is then narrowed down to within 5m by comparing this position with a CD-Rom map housed in a player in the boot and a compass under the parcel shelf. This is finally checked with direction detectors in the wheel hubs before the car's position is plotted on a small liquid crystal display (LCD) screen on the dashboard.

The driver can use the screen to visualise where he or she is in relation to surrounding roads and plot the most sensible route to any location.

This route flashes on screen. A blinking arrow represents the car. The system uses voice cues to warn when a left or right turn is needed, estimating in how many metres' time action needs to be taken. For complicated manoeuvres several instructions can be issued at the same time, such as 'Take the next left after 50 metres and then turn immediately right'.

Should you go wrong, it requests a U-turn, or, if ignored, will work out a new route.

(Source: The Sunday Times,
10 September 1995)

Calculating distances

MAPS AND SCALES

The **scale** on a map shows what the real distance on the ground is compared to the corresponding length shown on the map. Take an example where the scale is 1 cm = 1 km (cm = centimetre or 100th of a metre; km = kilometre or 1,000 metres):

0	1	2	3	4	5	6

This line is 6 cm long, so the actual distance on the ground is 6 km.

0	1	2	3	4	5	6	7 7.5

This line is 7.5 cm long, so the distance on the ground is 7.5 km.

When map makers want to cover a large area – such as a whole country – with one map, they use a smaller scale. For example, Michelin uses the scale 1 cm = 3.5 km for its map of Belgium (Map 409: Belgium and Luxembourg) and a scale of 1 cm = 10 km for its map covering Belgium, Luxembourg, the Netherlands, Austria and Germany (Map 987).

MEASURING DISTANCES

By measuring the relevant length on the map, it is thus possible to estimate the corresponding real distance on the ground. For example, on a map with a scale of 1 cm = 0.5 km, this means that for every 1 cm shown on the map you would have to travel 0.5 km along the road.

What is the real distance from Needles to Pinza?

Needles _____ Pinza

Length in cm = (measure the length of the line shown)
Therefore: line length in cm × 0.5 = the actual km distance to be travelled.

activity

1 Now it's your turn. What is the real distance on the ground for each of these?

_____ scale: 1 cm = 0.5 km
_____ scale: 1 cm = 2.5 km
_____ scale: 1 cm = 3.5 km
_____ scale:
1 cm = 10 km

2 See Figure 3.10. If a distributor located at D had to deliver to all the outlets (A, B etc.), what would be the total distance covered?

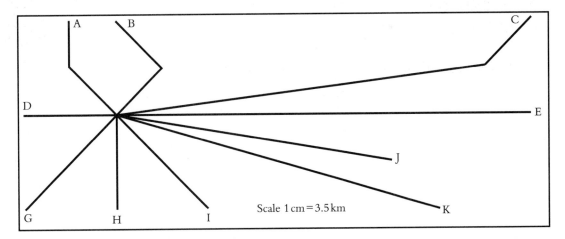

Figure 3.10 Distance calculation for straight routes

3 Not all roads, however, are as straight as the Romans built them. In the following example – see Figure 3.11 – you can use a strip of paper or piece of string to calculate the length of the roads as a straight line. Then, if the paper or string is placed against the scale, the distance along the ground – see Figure 3.12 – can be calculated. (Alternatively, use the width of your finger, which is roughly 2 cm).

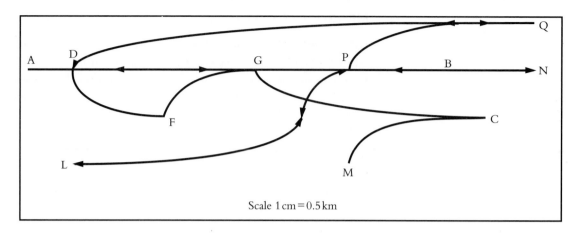

Figure 3.11 Distance calculation for curved routes

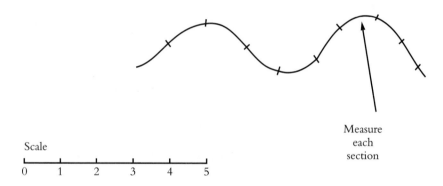

Figure 3.12 Measuring curved sections

Most camping or outdoor shops sell a **map measurer** for calculating distances (this looks like a pen with a small wheel on the tip).

4 A local delivery business makes the following journeys – see Figure 3.11 – during a day. What is the total distance covered?
   ● From A to N
   ● From A to D to F to G to C
   ● From A to M
   ● From A to F

Calculate the distances for each of the journeys in the activity on page 66. Do this both manually and using a computer program. Can you say why there are differences in your results?

DISTANCE CHARTS

A **distance chart** shows how far one place is from another using the best route that is available. It will use motorways wherever possible. For example, in Figure 3.13, the distance from Preston to Peterborough is shown in the square where the row from Preston meets the column from Peterborough. The distance in this case is 182 miles.

- Penzance to Plymouth is 77 miles
- Perth to Portsmouth is 504 miles
- Perth to Preston is 237 miles

Penzance					
614	Perth				
348	352	Peterborough			
77	545	279	Plymouth		
246	504	161	178	Portsmouth	
377	237	182	308	268	Preston

Source: AA based atlas

Figure 3.13 A distance chart

DISTANCE DATABASES

Distance databases use computer programs – such as those mentioned on page 67 – to calculate distances. Their main advantages over manual methods are:

- the speed at which information can be retrieved
- the large amount of data that can be stored. For example, the AA database contains over 38,000 entries – imagine this on a distance chart!
- the ease of access

Journey times   To be able to work out how long a particular journey will take, these are the factors we need to consider:

1 the average speed of the vehicle;
2 the time taken for loading and unloading and the number of deliveries;
3 the distance of the journey;
4 ferry or flight timetables;
5 constraints on drivers;
6 the volume of traffic;
7 the weight of loads.

AVERAGE SPEED

If you have been held up by a lorry going up a steep hill, you will know how slowly they go and how many gear changes they need to make (a truck with 16 gears is not unusual). Hills can severely slow down the speed of a vehicle, and this needs to be considered when working out how long a journey will take. The slopes or **gradients** of hills are shown on most road maps.

On Ordnance Survey maps, slopes are shown like this:

=================>===============   ================>>============

1 in 7 to 1 in 5   Over 1 in 5
or 14% to 20%   or over 20%

On Michelin maps, slopes are shown like this:

=================>===============   ================>>============

9% to 13%   over 13%

High percentage figures mean very steep hills. The arrows point *downhill*.

Motorways have very low gradients because these have been smoothed out by the construction of cuttings, viaducts and tunnels. This means that lorries can maintain *higher* average speeds. However, fuel consumption and fuel costs both increase with higher speeds (10 miles per gallon is considered excellent for a fully loaded truck!), so there is always a cost incentive for vehicles to travel more slowly. (Do people you drive with think about this?) Airlines consider this very important, and it now takes longer to fly to Paris than it did 10 years ago. On the other hand, with Ro-Ro ferries and trucks carrying perishable goods, speed is more important than the possible saving on fuel costs achieved by going more slowly.

The *type* of road used will also affect the average speed. For example, the legal maximum speed on UK motorways is 70 miles per hour (mph), although 56% of cars, 37% of motorcycles and 21% of buses and coaches do more than this. The legal limit on other roads is 60 mph, with 30 mph in built-up areas. Many towns are introducing traffic-calming measures, such as bumps in the road, to slow down the traffic. The highest speeds are thus achieved on motorways, with the slowest speeds in built-up areas.

Speed controls – sufficient safeguards?

Up to 200,000 vehicles travel daily on the south-west section of the M25. And at peak times the traffic is so heavy it eventually results in long queues of stationary traffic.

Since September, a pilot scheme has been in operation on this section. An automatically set speed limit is imposed at the busiest times: sensors detect traffic building up and set a speed limit of 50–60 mph, depending on conditions. This 'controlled' motorway will be closely monitored during the next year. 'The AA supports the concept of controlled motorways' says Paul Watters, head of roads and transportation policy. 'This system actually allows people to get along the congested parts more quickly – it smooths the traffic flow, making driving more comfortable, and it squeezes in more traffic.

(Source: AA Magazine)

1 With your group, discuss whether you think that excessive speed on motorways causes accidents? What happens in fog? In February 1996, there was a 100-vehicle pile-up on a Belgian motorway between Antwerp and Bruges, due to unexpected fog.
2 What effects do traffic-calming measures have on cars, delivery vehicles, emergency vehicles (ambulances, fire engines), pedestrians and surrounding streets?
3 At what average speed would a vehicle need to travel to cover a journey of 210 miles in under 8 hours, including a one-hour rest stop?

LOADING AND UNLOADING, AND THE NUMBER OF DELIVERIES

The time taken to load and unload a vehicle is very important when calculating the overall journey time. When companies such as Boots and Argos build new stores, a great deal of thought goes into the layout and design of the unloading and storage facilities.

Fork-lift trucks are now in common use for loading and unloading a wide range of goods which have been stacked on **pallets**. These are small wooden/plastic movable platforms which can be used to store or carry goods. They can hold about 1,000 kilogrammes. It takes about 6 to 8 minutes to unload a pallet using a fork-lift. Trucks which have to make several deliveries should be loaded on the basis of first in last out, last in first out.

activity

What is the average time taken to load and unload a vehicle with 16 pallets?

DISTANCE

Distance is obviously a vital factor to be considered when calculating journey times. However, it is equally important to examine various other factors concerning the journey. For example:

- a journey of 200 miles on a *motorway* would be much faster than the same journey on secondary roads. Whenever possible, HGVs use motorways
- Do **tolls** have to be paid? For example, a toll has to be paid to use the Dartford Tunnel (this goes under the River Thames and links the southern and northern sections of the M25). Long queues may also have to be taken into account. There is a toll of £11.10 for trucks crossing the Severn Bridges (M4) between England and Wales. This high price 'has pushed trucks off the motorway network and on to unsuitable single-carriageway A roads . . . an extra 200 trucks a day on the A48 and an extra 100 a day on the A40' reported *Trucking International*, July 1995. Motorway tolls are also payable in Austria, France, Italy, Spain and Switzerland

activity

1 Check out the A roads mentioned in the quotation above. Which towns are affected? How many extra miles have to be covered to get from Bristol to Newport?
2 Using the distance chart shown on page 73, calculate how long it would take a truck with an average speed of 27 mph to get from Penzance to Plymouth, Peterborough to Portsmouth (including a 45-minute stop), and Perth to Preston (with a 1-hour stop).

FERRY OR FLIGHT TIMETABLES

activity

Times on ferry and flight timetables are usually shown using the 24-hour clock. Look at the Sally Line ferry timetable for the sailings to and from Dunkerque.

RAMSGATE TO DUNKERQUE			DUNKERQUE TO RAMSGATE		
DEPART		ARRIVE	DEPART		ARRIVE
2.30 am	0230			0400	
	0840			0830	
11.30 am	1130		1.30 pm	1330	
4.00 pm	1600			1700	
	1930			2030	
	2300		11.59 pm	2359	

Note that the sailing time is 2 hours 30 minutes, and that Continental time is one hour ahead of the UK throughout the year, so that, for example, when it is 1 pm or 1300 in the UK, it is 2 pm or 1400 on the Continent.

1 Calculate all arrival times in local time – e.g. the 0230 arrives in Dunkerque at 0600: 2 hours 30 minutes for the journey plus the 1-hour time difference. In addition, fill in the missing 12-hour-clock times for departures.
2 Show all times calculated in terms of the 24-hour and the 12-hour clock.

CONSTRAINTS ON DRIVERS

The main constraint on drivers concerns the number of hours for which they are allowed to drive before taking compulsory rest periods. Everything which a driver does at work is now recorded using a **tachograph** – see Figure 3.14. This measures the speed and distance covered by a vehicle, and the written record which it produces is called a **tachogram**.

The rules and regulations about the number of hours which drivers are allowed to drive for are very strict and complicated. It is an offence if any of these rules are broken. The rules are intended to stop drivers from driving for too many hours without adequate rest periods. For example, drivers must take a 1–hour break after driving for $4\frac{1}{2}$ hours. (Do you think that this same rule should apply to car drivers?) You should use this rule when calculating journey times.

THE VOLUME OF TRAFFIC

The volume of traffic refers to the number of vehicles that use a particular route. Generally, when there is a large volume of traffic, journeys will take longer. The word 'traffic' can be used to describe *any* form of transport – e.g. air traffic, sea traffic and road traffic.

The volume of traffic depends on:

Steering wheel refers to driving time.

Crossed hammers refer to all other periods of work.

The rectangle with a diagonal line refers to other periods of availability, namely;
(a) waiting time, i.e. periods during which drivers need to remain at their posts only for the purpose of answering any calls to start or resume driving or to carry out other work; and
(b) time spent beside the driver or on a bunk while the vehicle is in motion.

The bed refers to breaks in work and daily rest periods.

Figure 3.14 Symbols used in tachograph records

- the popularity or importance of the route. For example, routes between large cities are always crowded and very busy – e.g. London/Birmingham, Liverpool/Manchester, Paris/Marseille, Cologne/Frankfurt, Antwerp/Rotterdam, or even London to Paris by air when planes are held in queues before they can land
- the time of day – e.g. travelling into a town or city in the morning at 7–9 am or leaving in the evenings between 4–6 pm. These are the rush hours or peak times when traffic jams occur. Local traffic jams can occur at the start and end of the school day. At 8 am, 60,000 cars are estimated to join the M25
- location: traffic is always busy within large towns – e.g. in London it can often take an hour to cover 15 miles

Drivers could be stuck in traffic jams all day

Maps published by the RAC (Royal Automobile Club) in *Funding and Managing the Future of Transport in the United Kingdom* show that motorists could be stuck in traffic jams all day by the year 2015 if the present growth in traffic continues.

The road stress maps shown on page 79 were originally produced by the Department of Transport. They show the Government's own forecasts of likely congestion levels on the motorway and trunk road network over the next 20 years. The RAC said they show 'chronic congestion and possible gridlock for large sections of the road network.'

The roads most affected will be the majority of the M25, the routes into and out of London including the M1, M2, M3, M4, M11 and M40 (where will you be able to go from London?) and motorway networks around Manchester,

Birmingham, Leeds and Sheffield.

The RAC says 'The maps present a picture which is totally unacceptable in terms of delay, inconvenience, restriction of freedom of movement and economic cost to the country. It is also wholly unacceptable in environmental terms, congestion being one of the worst culprits in causing pollution'. (Can you say why? Congestion occurs on motorways and trunk roads but it also occurs in most towns.) Congestion is already estimated to cost the economy £20 billion a year (e.g. the loss of production due to delays in deliveries of raw materials, and staff being late for work. Do you have to stay on at work if you are late?). The RAC forecasts that if congestion continues to increase then congestion costs 'will be approaching £40 billion a year by 2005'. Look at the maps which show the congestion.

1995 Road Network

2015 Road Network

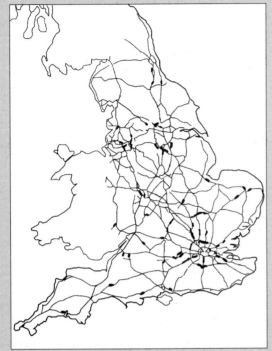
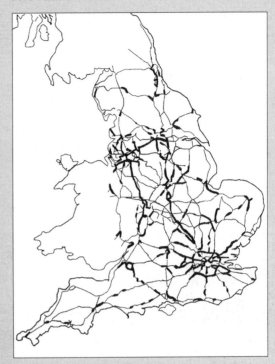

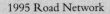 = stress of congestion

Figure 3.15 Traffic 'stress' maps for 1995 and 2015

- how do you think distribution businesses will be affected?
- how do you think that prices in the shops will be affected?
- how do you think that private motorists will be affected?
- what do you think will happen to traffic on other roads?
- what do you think will be the effect on other types of transport?
- suggest ways in which the UK can solve the possible problems, e.g. putting up the price of petrol or charging for using roads
- locate your area on the map. How will it be affected? Will you be driving a car?

(With thanks to Richard Woods at the RAC)

THE WEIGHT OF LOADS

This affects both the speed of the vehicle and the amount of fuel used. Loads must always be evenly distributed, and it is illegal if you *overload* any vehicle.

1 How do you think distributors will be affected by the predictions made in the article above?
2 Estimate the journey times for the four routes in the activity on page 66. You should make clear and detailed notes for each route, showing the effect of each factor – distance, speed, whether it is a built-up area or motorway, etc. What conclusions can you reach? Try to compare your manual calculations with the computer-generated versions. Draw sketch maps of the routes, or highlight them on a map.

Planning a transport route to a town in mainland Europe

The route we are planning here is from Bromley to Bruges in Belgium via Ramsgate/Dunkerque, and the goods to be carried are hand-knitted sweaters.

Here is a checklist which will help you to plan the route:

What time is the delivery expected in Bruges?	Between 1.30 pm and 2 pm.
Which route is best for our purposes?	Both ferry and train are possible.
Which port is best?	Either Dover or Ramsgate.
Can we go by Le Shuttle?	Yes.
What time is the ferry/train?	Ferry 8 am from Dover. Ferry 8.40 am from Ramsgate. Train (three shuttles per hour).
How long does the ferry journey take?	2 hours 30 minutes from Ramsgate by Sally Line, or 1 hour 15 minutes to 1 hour 30 minutes from Dover depending on the boat/ferry company (P & O/Stenna).
How long does the train journey take?	35 minutes to Coquelles just outside Calais.
What time do we have to have to leave Bromley?	We would need to be at the port 30 minutes before the boat is due to sail, therefore depart Bromley 6 am.
How long is the journey from Bromley to the port/train?	Allow 2 hours.
How long is the drive on the other side of the Channel?	Allow 1 hour 30 minutes or 2 hours 30 minutes, depending on the route.
When is the best time to travel?	Consider overnight, with a cabin on the ferry – e.g. Ramsgate to Ostend.

THE CHOSEN ROUTE AND ITINERARY FOR FEBRUARY 1996

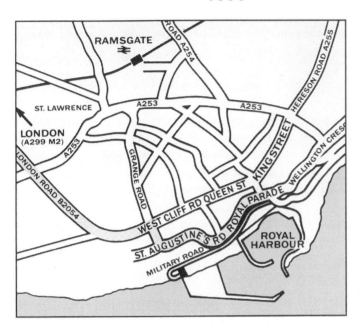

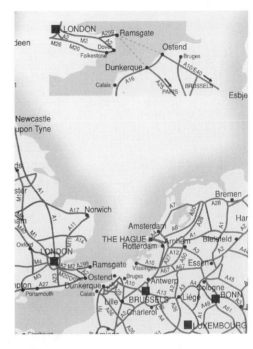

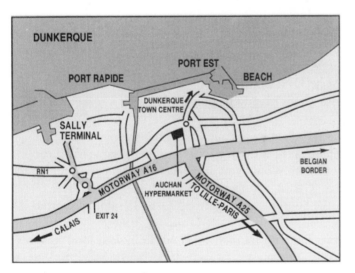

DISTANCES FROM DUNKERQUE		
	Miles	Km
Barcelona	867	1396
Bordeaux	551	887
Brussels	109	176
Geneva	523	842
Innsbruck	670	1079
Lille	53	86
Lyon	475	765
Milan	676	1088
Nice	769	1238
Paris	189	305

Figure 3.16 Maps showing the chosen route from Bromley to Bruges

- Leave Bromley by the A222 towards Sidcup (check that you have all necessary documents – valid passport, insurance, Customs Export Licence etc. – plus currency)
- Join the A20 in the direction of Swanley/Dartford Tunnel/Dover
- Join the M25 at Junction 3, and head north towards Dartford Tunnel

- Exit the M25 at Junction 2, and join the A2/M2 towards Rochester/Dover
- Exit the M2 at Junction 7 at the end of the motorway
- Take the A299 and then the A253 to Ramsgate (this can be a very slow road, particularly during the Summer. You should also therefore consider other routes)
- Check the map of Ramsgate – see Figure 3.16 – and follow the 'To Ferry' signs
- Arrive at the port at 8 am, check in and clear customs – this usually takes about 30 minutes if documents are all in order
- Take the 8.40 am ferry to Dunkerque, and have breakfast on the boat (as much as you can eat for £7.50!)
- Arrive at Dunkerque 12.10 pm (remember that you have added an hour)
- Clear the docks – you should be able to get straight off the ferry and drive away (see the map of Dunkerque in Figure 3.16) – and follow signs to Belgium
- Take the A16 motorway north, and continue following signs to Belgium
- Leave the motorway, following the old road around Veurne (take care: the road is not well signposted, and can be very slow)
- Join the E40 at Junction 1 towards Bruges/Brussels
- Exit the E40 at Junction 8 towards Bruges
- Enter Bruges along Boeverie Straat (a street), turn right (after a large open square) into Noordzand Straat, then turn right for Steen Straat (note: one-way system here)
- Arrive at *Quatre Vents* clothes shop in Bruges 1.40 pm. Limited parking means goods have to be unloaded quickly

1 Follow the route taken by the authors on the appropriate maps shown in Figure 3.16. Would you have taken the same route for this journey or not? Would you have taken a shorter sea route with a longer drive (Calais), a longer sea route with a shorter drive (Ostend), or Le Shuttle – see Figure 3.17 – at 35 minutes (but no breakfast!)?

2 Plan your own route for transferring goods from your local area to a town in Europe. You must:
- calculate distances and estimate journey times for each stage of the journey
- provide an itinerary and details of your chosen route, giving reasons why you rejected the alternative options
- describe how you planned the route, naming the sources you used (i.e. which maps or software)

**FOLKESTONE
EN 35 MN
A PARTIR DE
290 F A/R JOURNEE***

... Quel que soit l'état de la mer !

Avec Le Shuttle, qu'il vente, qu'il pleuve ou qu'il neige, vous arrivez à Folkestone en 35 mn. De plus, du 1er octobre 1995 au 7 janvier 1996, Le Shuttle vous fait une offre exceptionnelle : 290 F seulement l'aller-retour journée si vous prenez Le Shuttle du mardi au jeudi et 350 F A/R si vous voyagez du vendredi au lundi. Pour bénéficier de cette offre* partez avant 12 h et commandez votre billet au minimum 24 H à l'avance au 21 00 61 00 ou auprès de votre agence de voyages.

le Shuttle

La Navette d'Eurotunnel — EURO TUNNEL

* Par véhicule, quel que soit le nombre de passagers. Offre valable uniquement au départ de la France et non disponible au péage. Billet non remboursable ni modifiable.

Figure 3.17 An advertisement for Le Shuttle

Self-test questions:
Chapter 3

1 Name and give the main features of three particular Ordnance Survey (OS) maps.
2 Check out the main OS transport symbols for road, rail and canal features.
3 What are the destinations of the motorways out of London?
4 What are the advantages and disadvantages of using computer programs for route planning?
5 A map has a scale of 1:250,000. If the distance on the map between two places is 27 centimetres, what is the actual distance on the ground?
6 A map has a scale of 1:50,000. If the distance on the map between two places is 27 centimetres, what is the actual distance on the ground?
7 On a map, what would these letters and numbers indicate: TQ 86 15?
8 What factors are most likely to affect the time taken to complete a road journey?
9 If it is 227 miles between two towns. How long would it take an HGV with an average speed of 31 miles per hour, plus a stop of 38 minutes, to complete the journey between these two towns?
10 A lorry travels for 4 hours and 15 minutes at an average speed of 45 miles an hour. What distance has it covered?

evidence
indicators

The route to Europe

A local business intends to export goods to a town in mainland Europe. You have been asked to produce the route. You can choose any town, for example, the twin town to your home town.

Make any reasonable assumptions you think are necessary, such as, is an overnight stay required? You must state the category and characteristics of the goods that will be exported, as this will affect the choice of transport and choice of route.

1 Make notes on the major features of your local transport system, paying particular attention to the routes into and out of town, and noting any rush hours (these will affect the timing of any journey). Include sketch maps of the major features.
2 Make notes on the methods of route planning you have or could have used.
3 Make notes showing the volume of goods transported by the different types of transport in the UK and your chosen country. Include both figures and charts.
4 Find out what routes are available to your chosen town. Calculate the distances and the journey times for each route. List the advantages and disadvantages of each route and give reasons why you have chosen a particular route.

5 Find out what methods of transport are available. List the advantages and disadvantages of each and give reasons why you have chosen a particular method.

6 Describe the main links between the different types of transport (you will find the literature produced by motoring organisations, ferry companies and Le Shuttle helpful for this).

7 Draw sketch maps showing the route you have chosen, include photocopies of any maps you use and mark the route using coloured felt tips. Use photographs and pictures whenever you can.

8 Make a presentation to your group, using the overhead projector.

Investigating the supply chain for retail goods

In this chapter we will:

- describe supply chains
- explain the purpose of distribution outlets
- describe the location of distribution outlets
- identify factors which affect location
- explain the requirements for handling and storing different retail goods

We will cover Element 1.4, Performance Criteria 1, 2, 3, 4, 5.

SUPPLY CHAINS

The **supply chain** or **channel of distribution** is the route by which goods which are made by a producer or manufacturer reach the consumer or final user. Figure 4.1 shows the range of routes open to manufacturers to get their goods to consumers.

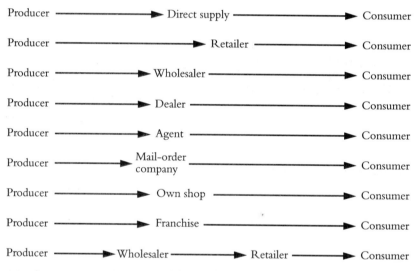

Figure 4.1 The range of routes from producer to consumer

Direct supply: from producer to consumer

The shortest route, i.e. from producer straight to consumer, is called **direct supply**, **direct selling** or **single-stage channel distribution**. The simplest form of this route is a bakery where bread and cakes are made on the premises and then sold directly to consumers. In addition, some farms and out-of-town garden centres advertise 'Pick your own fruit and vegetables' (PYO).

There are also an increasing number of manufacturers who are selling direct to the public, missing out the wholesaler and retailer. For example, most double-glazing companies which advertise in the local press claim their windows 'are made to measure with quality materials in our own factory.' Fitted kitchens and bathrooms are sold in the same way: 'Direct to you – we make them, we install them, you save £££s.' Clothing manufacturers advertising in the glossy Sunday magazines claim 'We cut out the middleman (the stage between the producer and the consumer). Deal with us direct and save yourself pounds.' Computer manufacturers also deal directly with the consumer: for example, Dell Direct will sell you 'A PC that's packed with features', together with a Hardware Technical Support Service. Amstrad Direct sells fax machines, personal computers (PCs), and electronic notepads and notebooks (with a 12-month guarantee to return the goods to the factory facility if anything goes wrong).

Many manufacturers now sell their goods direct to the public using a **mail–order catalogue**. This catalogue will have an order form at the back which the customer can use to buy the goods.

Almost all such services are provided direct to the consumer without an intermediary being involved. Teachers and opticians are two good examples of direct-supply services: you cannot get *someone else* to sit in a class or have their eyes tested on your behalf!

Independent Retail News reported in its December 1995 edition that Bass, the giant brewery, was about to stop its home-delivery scheme involving providing beer direct to the public following protests by Nurdin & Peacock the cash-and-carry wholesaler (the Happy Shopper brand) and off-licensees. Why do you think there were objections to this scheme?

Advantages of direct supply

- The manufacturer should be able to make larger profits (why do you think this is so?)
- Because the manufacturer is in direct contact with the consumer, they are able both to respond more quickly to changes in demand and to deal more quickly with complaints or problems
- The manufacturer is able to provide an after-sales service – as do Dell Direct and Amstrad, for example
- The consumer has plenty of time to look at the catalogue without the expense of going to the shops
- People living in remote or isolated areas find it easier to buy goods through direct supply
- The manufacturer can introduce new products without having to find a distributor for these products

DISADVANTAGES OF DIRECT SUPPLY

- Direct supply does not work with **seasonal** products because there is no regular demand here and the manufacturer may therefore have to close for part of the year
- It is not suitable for low-value items unless there are a large number of customers
- It is not possible to examine the product before it is purchased. This is why many items which are purchased through a mail-order catalogue have to be returned

In Chapter 1 we saw that the goods produced by the primary sector were called **primary goods**. These included milk, fish, timber, oil, fruit, vegetables etc. Manufactured products are made by the secondary sector, and include clothing, footwear, furniture etc.

1 Collect examples of products which are sold directly to the public, and in each case say why the direct-supply method has been used.
2 List the advantages and disadvantages of direct supply from the point of view of both the manufacturer and the consumer.

The two-stage supply chain, or short channel of distribution

Here are some examples of **short channels of distribution**:

1 Producer → Retailer → Consumer
   Supermarkets such as Tesco and large stores such as Boots deal directly with manufacturers. Many manufacturers of ceramics and china, such as Portmeirion, Poole and Wedgwood, deal direct with a wide range of small, medium and large retailers.
2 Producer → Wholesaler → Consumer
   Wholesalers such as Nurdin & Peacock and Bestway deal direct with manufacturers because this enables them to buy goods in bulk. This in turn makes it worthwhile for the manufacturer to deal direct.
3 Producer → Dealer → Consumer
   Examples here are dealers for Honda, Suzuki, Kawasaki, Ducati and Yamaha motorbikes. (Where are the dealers for these bikes in your area? How many are there? Is this enough?) The Ford Motor Company also sends cars direct to its dealers for sale to consumers. (How many Ford dealers are there?)
4 Producer → Agent → Consumer
   The most famous examples of this distribution channel are Avon Cosmetics, which concentrates on selling door-to-door, and Tupperware (look in the cupboard under the sink – you will probably find one plastic lid!) which has over 100,000 agents holding home and (also now) office parties world-wide. A Tupperware party selling a range of plastic containers is being held somewhere in the world every 15 seconds.

5 Producer → Mail-order company → Consumer
   Mail-order companies such as Grattan and Freemans (with a large
   distribution centre just outside Peterborough) sell a wide range of
   branded goods direct to the consumer. Great Universal Stores, with
   11 catalogues including Kays and Family Album, was the top retailer
   in Europe in 1992 (based on its before-tax profit margin).

6 Producer → Own shop → Consumer
   Some manufacturers also sell their goods through their own shops.
   This is a very popular method for shoe manufacturers such as
   Clark's. Even Cadbury's has its own shop at its factory in Bournville
   (Birmingham) – you can also visit the factory to see how chocolates
   are made. Another example is MFI (usually to be found on the edge
   of town) which is the UK's biggest retailer and manufacturer of
   bathroom and kitchen furniture. Although MFI also uses other
   manufacturers, since 1995 it has been making more of its products
   itself because this is more profitable.

7 Producer → Franchise → Consumer
   A good example of this kind of supply chain is The Body Shop
   which makes its products in Littlehampton and distributes these to
   its UK franchises using its own transport. The European franchises
   are supplied using a specialist haulage business.

WORKING WITH SUPPLIERS IN SHORT CHANNELS

Boots, J Sainsbury, Tesco and Marks & Spencer, for example, all work
with their own suppliers. Marks & Spencer works closely with
suppliers of ready-made meals to improve its existing products and
develop new ideas. Staff at M&S will taste each meal and make detailed
specifications for every aspect of the product such as the colour, taste,
texture and ingredients. J Sainsbury works with its suppliers of potted
plants, fruit and vegetables to make sure that these reach the shop in
good condition.

Many large retailers are now trying to reduce the number of
suppliers they use in an attempt to cut costs and improve profits. The
Tesco initiative described in the following extract is designed to cut the
number of vehicles Tesco uses to distribute goods by 25%:

Squaring an endless delivery cycle

Given so little latitude to raise prices without losing sales to competitors, Britain's supermarket groups are left with little option but to scrutinise every aspect of their cost bases to try to lift profits and margins.

About 18 months ago, in the search for cost savings, retailers started to focus on the seemingly simple process of moving products from the manufacturer to the retailer's distribution depots and then to the customer. They ruthlessly attacked the system of transporting products from depots to stores, injecting greater efficiency and reaping substantial cost savings.

According to Tesco, the same number of vehicle trips now deliver three times the volume of produce to their stores daily, and fuel consumption is down by almost a fifth. But the process of shifting goods from the manufacturer to the depots was left alone.

The reason was simple. The first stage of goods movement, called 'primary distribution', fell to the individual suppliers to organise. But attention has now begun to switch to primary distribution, with Tesco leading the way.

At first glance, primary distribution could be considered as interesting as watching bread defrost, but the implications of its management are far-reaching and often provoke outbursts of invective from the public.

A common feature of Britain's motorways is the seemingly endless stream of swaying lorries. Country lanes and villages are plagued by thundering trailers racing along in their quest to drop off that day's supplies of kippers and lettuces to supermarket groups' distribution depots scattered around the country.

The situation is made markedly worse by the knowledge that many lorries are trundling around either empty or only half full.

David Smith, Tesco's head of primary distribution, says: 'Each of our depots has an average of 200 lorries arriving each day, about 15 per cent of which are probably half empty when they set out from the supplier. Overall, about 30 per cent of all mileage travelled in this country is thought to be travelled empty.'

The inefficiencies in the system are mainly the fault of the system itself. The short lifespan of many items means that supermarkets demand fresh stock on a daily basis and manufacturers are almost constantly on the move in a never-ending delivery cycle. The result is that manufacturers supplying a limited line on a national basis often embark on their journeys with surplus space and then make the return journey emptyhanded.

In principle, the burden of the transport bill rests with the supplier, but, in reality, these costs are added to the price charged to the retailer for the products. It is this that has spurred Tesco into action.

The supermarket group is overhauling the outmoded system, in a move that is expected to save millions of pounds as well as to produce the welcome by-product of markedly cutting the number of lorries on Britain's roads, as well as pollution.

(Source: The Times, *5 February 1996)*

Once you have read the article, answer these questions:

1 Why is Tesco trying to introduce a new delivery system?
2 What is the possible effect on haulage companies?

Case study: Kennedy's

Kennedy's is a private limited company based in South-East London. It is a food manufacturer which makes a range of sausages, cooked meats and savoury and sweet pies. It has 10 retail outlets, which are all within 8 miles of the place where the sausages are made. Each customer is served personally by the staff who work behind the display counter.

The food is made fresh each day and delivered daily to each shop – there are no chilled or frozen foods. All the food delivered is sold each day. Vans are used to take the food to each shop every morning. The driver will also take the food into the shop. The shops are very popular and sell out each day.

1 Why do you think that Kennedy's does not use a wholesaler?
2 If Kennedy's wanted to expand, how do you think it could do it?
3 Would the current system still work if the sausages were made 100 miles away from the outlets?

ADVANTAGES OF SHORT CHANNELS

The manufacturer is able to:

- keep control of the sale of the product. This is particularly important with the sale of expensive goods such as cars and motorcycles. Many manufacturers have dealers/car showrooms which are only allowed to sell and service one make of car. Staff can be trained and will have much better knowledge of the product. The dealer will also be able to offer an after-sales service and give guarantees. (If you have a new car, it must be serviced by an authorised dealer. If it is serviced elsewhere, then the guarantee does not apply – one of the authors has personal experience of this!)
- monitor sales relatively quickly and easily
- provide the dealer with advertising and promotion material
- give discounts and incentives to dealers and retailers

DISADVANTAGES OF SHORT CHANNELS

- The large retailers will be in a better position to bargain with the manufacturer. Although this is an advantage for the retailer, it could be a disadvantage for the manufacturer
- Distribution costs can increase because the manufacturer may have to supply to a large number of retailers. This in turn could increase the price which the consumer has to pay

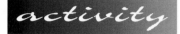

1 Using real examples, draw diagrams which describe two short channels of distribution.
2 List the advantages and disadvantages of two-stage supply chains from the point of view of both the manufacturer and the retailer. How is the consumer affected?

The three-stage supply chain or long channel of distribution

Here are two examples of this type of distribution:

1 Producer → Wholesaler → Retailer → Consumer
2 Producer → Agent or Distributor → Retailer → Consumer

These are the traditional methods of distribution for a wide range of products. Many small retailers will get their goods – such as cigarettes and sweets – from a wholesaler. Over 90% of independent corner shops and convenience stores selling groceries will obtain their goods from an independent wholesaler on 'cash and carry' terms (retailers pay cash for goods which they have to carry away themselves). Only 7% of retailers will have their stock delivered by a wholesaler. Retailers which belong to a symbol group such as Mace or Spar will get their goods from Mace or Spar wholesalers.

ADVANTAGES AND DISADVANTAGES OF LONG CHANNELS

- The retailer gets all the benefits of dealing with a wholesaler
- The consumer is able to buy goods individually or in small quantities
- However, the consumer usually has to pay higher prices. This is because small retailers cannot usually buy in bulk and therefore have to pay higher prices for their goods which are then passed on to the consumer. Whenever goods 'change hands' or move from one business to another – for example from a manufacturer to a wholesaler, from a wholesaler to a retailer, or from a retailer to a consumer – the prices will rise because each business in the chain is trying to make a profit. When there are many stages in the channel of distribution, the price paid by the consumer is therefore likely to be high.

1 Working in groups, carry out a small survey comparing the prices of goods in your local corner shop with those of the same goods in your local supermarket. For example, you could compare branded with own-label goods. Each group should look at different products – e.g. tinned vegetables, fresh vegetables, bread etc. What conclusions can you reach?

2 Find out about, and make notes and diagrams on, the supply chains for the following products: milk, petrol, chocolates.

THE PURPOSE OF DISTRIBUTION OUTLETS

1 Look at Chapter 1 again and write short notes explaining the purpose of retail, wholesale and warehouse outlets.

THE LOCATION OF DISTRIBUTION OUTLETS

In this section we will look at the location of retail, wholesale and warehouse outlets.

The location of retail outlets

Anyone who wishes to open a shop has to choose the location very carefully. (Where do you go shopping? Why do you go there? Is there a part of your high street which people rarely use? Are there some sites which always seem to fail?) A good location can make or break a business. Where are the shops located in your area? The simple answer should be: wherever there are people or wherever these shops are needed.

What affects location?

- The number of possible or potential customers. The terms **catchment area** or **trading area** are sometimes used to describe where a store's customers live. The **primary catchment area** will include most of the possible customers. This is usually the area closest to the store. For a convenience store or corner shop, this area can be as small as a few streets (it is estimated that most corner shops can survive with about 250 regular customers). The **secondary catchment area** will contain the rest of the possible customers. Very often, these two areas will overlap. (If you have a choice of two shops, which do you choose?)
- The number of customers who are pedestrians – i.e. people who *walk*. For many corner shops and community or neighbourhood stores, these are likely to make up the majority of possible customers
- The transport facilities that are available. For example, is there a bus or train station? Many places – e.g. Coventry – are now providing

'Park and Ride' services so that people do not have to drive their cars into the town centre

- The parking facilities that are available. Many shopkeepers are now complaining about the parking restrictions outside their stores – e.g. single/double yellow lines, no unloading at certain times, bus-only lanes, 'red routes' (no-stopping routes). At all new shopping centres, the number of car-parking spaces that can be built is an absolutely vital factor to take into account when choosing a site
- The number of possible sites which are available – e.g. which shops are vacant or unoccupied? The size of the site and its position will also be important. For example, corner sites have always been valuable because they can be seen from *two* roads
- The costs of running the business – e.g. the rent and business rates. These costs will change depending on where the shop is situated or located. Shops in better locations usually have higher costs to pay. Shops which are located in a shopping centre will have to pay the owners of the centre a management fee. This is a sum of money which pays for security, cleaning, maintenance of the centre and the premises, and the heating and lighting of the communal areas. It may also include storage in a secure area; this often involves a simple lock-up facility behind metal bars. The centre managers will carry out the advertising and marketing of the centre
- Competition. The number and type of other retailers in the area (sometimes called the **retail mix**) will greatly affect the success or failure of a business. Will a new retailer be able to attract customers from other shops selling similar goods? Two newsagents may find it difficult to compete if they are close together, whilst two or more clothes shops that are close together, on the other hand, could actually sell *more* because people believe that they have a better chance of finding something they like
- Access roads. It is important for both suppliers and customers that goods be easily unloaded and loaded

Write notes describing the location of three contrasting retail outlets in your local area.

THE VILLAGE STORE

Although 25% or nearly 13 million of the population of the UK lives in rural areas (i.e. villages in the countryside), almost 70% of parishes do not have a food shop and only 60% of parishes have a permanent shop. *Independent Retail News*, in its December 1995 edition, reported that the rural charity Voluntary Action Cumbria was trying to stop the decline of the traditional village shop by offering shopkeepers free carrier bags with the message 'more from your village store'.

1 Why do you think so many village stores have closed?
2 What effect do you think that closure will have on the village? Does it matter?
3 Read the article below:

Small shopkeepers hit back at Safeway

Many town centres are dying as more and more supermarkets are opened on the outskirts of towns.

Can small shopkeepers do anything?

In some places shopkeepers have been unwilling or unable to do anything. However the following example shows the positive approach taken by small shopkeepers at Leominster ('Lemster' to the locals) in Herefordshire.

Leominster is an attractive market town with a long history. Its old narrow high street runs from North to South and beautiful 'olde worlde' shops and houses line the street.

Safeway opens

A Safeway store was opened nearly four years ago on the outskirts of the town. Since then the small shops and businesses in the high street have found it increasingly difficult to survive. Butchers, greengrocers, grocers, cafés, a pub and a petrol station have all closed. The new Safeway store has meant that:

- people can buy everything at one store
- there is better car parking
- prices are lower because of special offers and discounts

Shopkeepers fight back

Shopkeepers have started a campaign to bring shoppers back to the high street. 'We need to fight the supermarkets at their own game and show people the benefits of high street shopping; we must tempt shoppers back. This is up to us not the local council,' said a local shopkeeper.

Loyalty cards and discounts

The high street shops are competing by:

- offering high street loyalty cards which can be used in many shops
- giving high street discounts
- using special offers, e.g. 'buy two pounds of tomatoes from the greengrocers at Broad Street and get 20% off a bottle of mayonnaise from the grocers in the high street'
- giving away carrier bags with the slogan 'Support your local high street'
- giving away free pens with purchases

(Adapted from an article in the Guardian)

What has happened in your own town? Do you think that what the local shopkeepers are doing is a good idea? Do you think that it will bring back trade? Do you agree that it is up to the customer to decide?

THE TOWN CENTRE

In most towns, the town centre or high street is the most important shopping centre. This is the street that is likely to have all the 'big shops'. These are the department stores such as Marks & Spencer, Debenhams, Littlewoods, BHS and C&A. New shopping centres try to get as many of these 'anchor stores' as possible. In a city such as Birmingham, the most important centre is the central business district.

1 Carry out a survey of your local high street. What retail outlets are there? Can you put these into groups – clothes shops, shoe shops etc.? Is there any other way of classifying them? What factors have affected the location of these retail outlets? Put these outlets on a map and show the car-parking facilities (are these free? How long can you stay? How many spaces are there? Is this enough?).
2 Read the following article:

Appeal to council over high street

Beckenham residents and shopkeepers are calling on Bromley Council for a lifeline to save the High Street trade from dying.

The Copers Cope Area Residents Association (CCARA) wants council action to boost trading. Officers were invited to yesterday's AGM to discuss the problem.

Chairman Colin Watts told the *News Shopper* before the meeting: 'We don't actually know what we want to achieve, we are just hoping that the council will have some ideas about what we can do.'

Mr Watts said Beckenham's main problems are:

- high rents forcing small businesses out
- too many charity shops undermining traditional stores
- high business rates
- severe lack of parking
- large supermarkets drawing shoppers away
- high crime rate

He admitted some difficulties couldn't change overnight: 'We have already spoken to them about parking, and we can see that there just isn't the physical space to have extra parking near the High Street.

'We are not expecting miracles, but we

want to know what the council is prepared to do about Beckenham's problems.'

Out of 179 premises in the High Street, just over half are traditional shops. The remaining trading outlets are made up from estate agents, banks and building societies, charity shops or just stand empty.

Peter Martin, planning policy manager at Bromley Council was due to attend the open meeting.

(*Source:* News Shopper, *7 February 1996*)

How does it compare with your local high street? Can you say why it is the same or different? Can you make any suggestions to improve the situation? (Note that the high street is about 2 miles from the centre of Bromley and the new Glades shopping centre.) Compare the article with the previous one on page 95. What are the similarities/differences? Which approach do you think is best?

OUT-OF-TOWN SHOPPING CENTRES

Since the 1980s, there has been a large growth in out-of-town shopping centres. Many of these are located on ring roads or bypasses around towns. The result of this development has been that many town centres have become deserted, with shops that are boarded up or that sell poor-quality goods. Many corner shops have closed. The poor and the elderly have been very badly affected by these developments, particularly since 25% of the population does not have cars. Some of these out-of-town centres can be very large. For example, the Metro Centre in Gateshead, Tyne and Wear (the brainchild of Sir John Hall, Chairman of Newcastle United) has over 340 retail outlets, a leisure centre, a bowling alley and a cinema.

Case study: Lakeside

Lakeside, off Exits 30 and 31 of the M25 (the motorway which rings London), attracts people from all over the South-East of England – it is a regional shopping centre. Lakeside's anchor outlets are House of Fraser, BHS, W H Smith, M&S, Bentalls, Woolworths, Argos, C&A, Boots and Debenhams. There is free parking for 12,000 cars and 250 coaches, and there is a 7-screen cinema. Table 4.1 gives a full breakdown of retail outlets at Lakeside.

Table 4.1 Breakdown of retail outlets at Lakeside shopping centre

STORES	NUMBERS	STORES	NUMBERS	STORES	NUMBERS
Department stores	14	Dry cleaners	1	Lingerie	2
Gift stores	27	Electrical	13	Men's fashion	20
Banks etc.	8	Fabrics	1	Musical	1
Books	7	Florists	3	Off-licence	1
Bookmakers	1	Food	7	Optician	5
Cards	4	Furniture	8	Outdoor	1
Chemists	4	Gas	1	Pets	1
Children's wear	5	Hair	5	Post Office	1
Cinema	5	Jewellery	12	Records	4
Computers	4	Ladies' fashion	33	Restaurants etc.	33
Confectionery	9	Leather	7	Services	2
Shoes	16	Teenage fashion	2	Travel agents	3
Sports	11	Toys	11	Unisex fashion	17

1 Draw charts to show the information in Table 4.1. What can you conclude? How does it compare with The Glades and Le Cité in France (see page 101)? (For example, is there the same percentage of ladies' clothes shops?)

2 What does the pattern of shops say about
(a) the pattern of spending, and
(b) lifestyles in the region?

Out-of-town superstores

The government has become increasingly worried by the growth of out-of-town shopping centres.

'Nation of redundant shopkeepers'

Britain will become a nation of redundant shopkeepers unless the growth in out-of-town shopping centres is halted, the chairman of the Commons environment select committee said yesterday.

The report by the committee says that during the 1980s development policies allowed too many superstores and other large retail developments to be built in places which were inappropriate on environmental, heritage and social grounds.

The committee chairman, Barry Field, said the policy 'has turned too many of our town centres into shopping deserts'. The committee felt it was time to require developers to prove that new stores would not harm town centres.

'All too often, we are inclined to deplore the death of once vibrant town and village centres, while enjoying for ourselves the convenience of out-of-town shopping. We all mourn the loss of "our" corner shop, but if we don't use it we lose it.'

The committee recommends significant changes to government planning guidance and says effective public transport must be developed.

Government guidance to local authorities has already changed this year, with superstores now unacceptable if they would cause 'demonstrable harm' to nearby town centres. But the committee said that this and subsequent guidance, combined with ministerial speeches, had left a sometimes contradictory picture.

The committee recommends that the guidance should be amended to say superstores are best built in or on the edges of town centres unless there are very strong reasons to the contrary. It suggests a new booklet should be issued setting out conditions for permission so that developers, local authorities and planning inspectors all work to the same rules. 'We recommend that no proposals for superstores or other large retail developments in or around market towns should be considered, unless they are accompanied by a comprehensive study of the possible retail effects over the whole of each proposal's catchment area.'

The committee points out that 24 per cent of the population do not have use of a car. Problems are caused for these people by 'planning creep,' where out-of-town centres offer more and more services such as chemists' shops and post offices. This threatens the continuation of such services in town centres, which are more easily reached by the poor and elderly who need them most.

The report details visits to various towns where new out-of-town shopping malls have sucked the life out of traditional town centres. It quotes evidence from companies such as Boots, which told the committee it opposed out of town shopping but was forced to follow the trend: 'It would be commercial suicide not to seek representation.'

Some 89 town managers have been appointed to help to revitalise local centres, but most do not have the resources or status to succeed. Restrictions on the compulsory purchase powers of local authorities make it difficult for the necessary public and private partnerships to be developed. The committee urges the Government to give local authorities more freedom and to find ways of financing town centre revitalisation.

(Source: The Guardian, *2 November 1994)*

NEW SHOPPING CENTRES IN THE CENTRE OF TOWNS

Many towns now have indoor or enclosed shopping centres in the centre of town, e.g. at Leamington Spa (behind the main street), Bromley (parallel to and behind the high street), Aberavon (where it has replaced the high street), Birmingham (next to a main railway station), Wimbledon (next to the railway station) and Wood Green ('Shopping City'). At The Glades in Bromley (Kent), there is a wide range of shops which are all indoors (so that people do not have to get wet or cold when they go out shopping), parking spaces for 1,500 cars, and several cafes and restaurants.

The first shopping centre in the world was completed in 1896 in the USA. The largest is currently in Edmonton in Alberta, Canada, with over 800 outlets, 11 anchor stores and parking for 20,000 cars.

NEIGHBOURHOOD SHOPPING

Neighbourhood shopping facilities are sometimes called **shopping parades**, and are normally found within walking distance of blocks of houses or flats. They consist mostly of convenience stores such as grocers, greengrocers – which sell fresh fruit and vegetables – newsagents and tobacconists, a Post Office and perhaps an off-licence. Before people had cars, the majority of families would have bought all their everyday goods in these stores, and before the development of supermarkets, people used to buy their goods daily. (Before people had fridges and freezers, people had to buy fresh food daily.) Today, however, people spend much less money in their neighbourhood stores because people with cars tend to travel to their local supermarket for 'one-stop shopping'.

Write notes describing the retail outlets on your local shopping parade. Who are the customers? Why are these shops there?

Case study: supermarket shopping in Europe

In Belgium, GB and Delhaze are two of the biggest food supermarket chains. You can find these two supermarkets on the edge of most large Belgian towns, e.g. Wavre and Bruges (try finding these on a map of Belgium).

In France, Intermarche and Leclerc are two of the largest independent retailers in Europe. If you have been on a day trip to France, you might have visited Continent in Cherbourg, Carrefour in Calais or Auchan in Dunkerque (check Figure 3.16 on page 81).

Aldi is the biggest food retailer in

Germany. It is also the second biggest food retailer in Europe. It is beginning to open stores in the UK. At the same time, UK food retailers are opening stores on mainland Europe – e.g. Marks & Spencer (which has stores in Paris – where white sliced bread is one of the biggest selling items – Madrid and Gibraltar where Christmas puddings sell well) and Tesco with stores in Northern France and Hungary.

Although there are now many large supermarkets in Europe, many Europeans still prefer to shop in specialist stores with a personal service. If you go to almost any French or Belgian town, you will see shops which only sell bread (boulangeries), cakes and pastries (pâtisseries) or meat (boucheries). Compare this with the position in the UK where many small stores have had to close because of the competition from supermarkets (see page 95).

activity

The figures in Table 4.2 show the distribution of retail outlets in Cité Europe and The Glades respectively.

● Cité Europe (see Figure 4.2) is at the mouth of the Channel Tunnel at Coquelles just outside Calais in Northern France. This shopping centre has been built where Le Shuttle trains stop when they come out of the tunnel. Le Shuttle trains carry cars and lorries from Folkestone to Calais. (Eurostar trains carry people from Waterloo Station in London to either Paris or Brussels.) Folkestone is advertised as being in White Cliffs Country just 35 minutes away

● In order to build The Glades in Bromley, Kent, several streets of old houses were pulled down

Table 4.2   Breakdown of retail outlets at La Cité and The Glades

STORES	LA CITÉ	THE GLADES
Hypermarket/department stores	1	4
Women's fashions	20	15
Men's fashions	11	13
Unisex fashions	2	11
Children's fashions	7	4
Sport	4	4
Shoes	10	6
Leather goods	1	1
Scarves	1	2
Jewellery	7	5
Cosmetics	2	3
Hairdressers	3	3
Health	1	
Opticians	3	2
Gifts/records/toys	13	20
Home decoration	4	3
Services	12	7
Restaurants/food	31	12

1 Draw a bar chart showing the number of shops in each category – women's fashion, children's fashion etc. – for Cité Europe and The Glades. Then say how Cité Europe and The Glades are the same or different. Give reasons for your answers.

2 Give reasons why Cité Europe was built at Coquelles.

3 What do the figures tell you about shopping habits and lifestyles in the UK and France?

4 If there is a new shopping centre near to you, suggest reasons for its location.

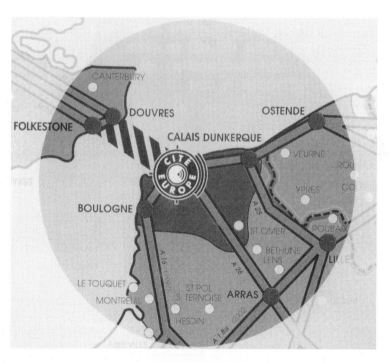

Figure 4.2 The location of Cité Europe

Outlets

Florist	Estate agent (2)
Supermarket (2)	Men's clothes shop
Newsagents (2)	Women's clothes shop (2)
Shoe shop	Electrical shop
Bank (2)	Fast-food restaurant
Post office	Toy shop
Cafe	

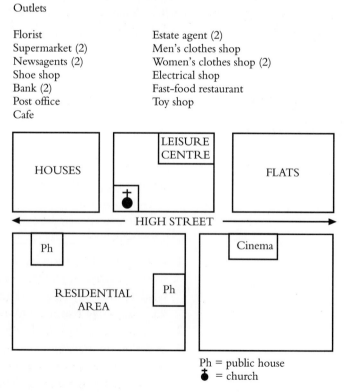

Figure 4.3 A street plan with outlets to be located

activity   Put the outlets onto the street plan, as shown in Figure 4.3. Give reasons for your suggestions for the locations.

Case study: voluntary groups of retailers

Table 4.3 shows the major voluntary 'symbol' groups of food retailers.

These independent grocers have come together in order to be able to compete more successfully against the large supermarket chains. They gain many benefits from being part of a large group. For example, they are able to buy in bulk from manufacturers and get better prices.

Table 4.3 The major voluntary 'symbol' groups of food retailers

GROUP	APPROXIMATE NUMBER OF CONVENIENCE STORES
Spar	2,400
Londis	1,500
Mace	1,200
NISA-Today's	1,000
VG	700
Costcutter	500

activity   Draw a pie chart showing the information in Table 4.3.

The location of wholesale outlets

Until about 30 years ago, many wholesalers were located in Central London. Goods were brought from all over the UK for resale; for example, fish would be brought from the North of England, sold by wholesalers to retailers at Billingsgate Market and then sent back to the North of England. The situation today, however, is different:

- Billingsgate Market is now closed
- Smithfield Market (meat wholesalers) has also now closed down One trader said 'Meat no longer comes here from overseas. The large supermarkets will buy the whole boat and deal with it themselves, or else they will agree to buy everything that a farmer will produce. We have nothing to do: the supermarkets have cut out the middleman, meat wholesalers are no longer needed.' The turkey that you eat at Christmas now goes straight from the farm to the supermarket

- Covent Garden was once a busy fruit-and-vegetables market in Central London. It closed down because the lorries needed to bring in the fruit and vegetables caused continuous traffic jams. The market has now moved to Nine Elms in South London where there is much better access for the large trucks that are now used. There are also better storage and parking facilities here. As one trader said, 'Although working conditions are better here, I miss the atmosphere.' The old site at Covent Garden is now a major tourist centre, as is the old fruit-and-vegetable market, Les Halles, in Central Paris

Case study: the family trip to the wholesale market

'Come on Steve, time to get up. Margaret, are you up?' Dad was always the early bird. Always worried about time, he would never be late for an appointment.

'But it is only half past three in the morning. Surely we have not got to get up this early every morning, have we?'

'Look, I have told you, if you want to go into the fruit and vegetable business, you have to be at market most mornings by four o' clock.' Dad reinforcing what he had been saying many times before.

The new Sherpa van they had purchased drove well. They hoped that it would be big enough for their new venture. It was a thirty hundredweight capacity van which meant that it would carry sixty sacks of potatoes or their equivalent. 'Don't get overloading it, because you will get done by the police', Dad always said.

For our first venture to a market, we thought we would go to Spitalfields, since Dad was well known there and hopefully we could get lots of tips and helpful information from the salespeople and porters on all the various stands around the market.

It was just approaching four o'clock in the morning when we arrived at Spitalfields Market. Steve was surprised at seeing so many people at this time in the morning. There was a hive of activity. Large trailers were being unloaded, and large articulated lorries were driving around trying to park to deliver goods from across the world. Porters were barrowing produce to various lorries and vans. It was just like the market mum worked on at Woolwich but much larger and items were sold in containers rather than loose by the weight. Different stalls or stands – as was the technical name for them – would specialise in different countries. One stand, for example, may be a Spanish importer and so would specialise in all produce from Spain. Therefore, it might have Spanish tomatoes, peppers, Spanish onions, lettuce (especially icebergs), oranges and grapes. Another stand may be part of an English farm and so may specialise in home-grown produce like potatoes, greens, cabbage, onions, leeks and carrots. There were probably 60 or so different stands located in and around the market. It was a good thing that Dad had some idea of who sold what.

The family enjoyed the market life once they got used to getting up early. The business got off to a very good start. The local customers enjoyed talking to mum and became regulars, and trade with the restaurants and hotels developed as Steve hoped it would. After a couple of years of successful trading, they started looking for another shop. This would provide another outlet and opportunities to buy larger quantities, which in turn would mean cheaper prices.

Whilst this business was expanding and developing, something else was developing in the background which was to have a devastating effect on the small retailer. Since 1980, when this business opened up, until it was sold in 1990, the growth of out-of-town shopping and the supermarket retailer began to take off to such an extent that within the space of these 10 years, 10 large supermarkets opened within a 10-mile radius, which took much of the trade away from the small retailer.

1 In the text, it was mentioned that prices in the wholesale markets were quoted by the box or container. See if you can find out five different sizes of container which fresh produce would be sold in. Make a table showing the different types of produce which would come in the different sizes of package. For example, tomatoes from the Canary Islands come in 6-kilogramme boxes, but English apples are often sold in 15-kilogramme boxes. See if you can calculate how much a retailer would make when he has sold the full container. Add another column, and try to find out the wholesale price also. A useful guide for prices is a trade magazine called *The Caterer*.

2 Why do you think supermarkets have become so popular in the UK?

3 Why do people choose to shop at the local supermarket rather than the local retailer?

4 How can the small retailer compete with the supermarket?

5 Why do small retailers use fruit and vegetable wholesale markets?

6 Why do you think the market opened so early?

(With thanks to Steve King CTL Bromley College)

Here is a list of factors which could affect the location of wholesale outlets:

● The cost of the land. This will include the amount of rent and business rates

● The amount of land available. This needs to be quite large

● Access roads. Good access is needed for both suppliers and customers: suppliers will need space and facilities for unloading – lorries will need to be able to turn around and reverse safely; and customers will need to be able to load their purchases

- Today, many wholesalers are locating in specially built premises on industrial or trading estates on the edge of towns – also called **industrial parks**, **business centres** or **trading centres**. This is shown by the location of electrical-supplies wholesalers in the South-East of the UK – e.g. BDC electrical distributors at Beddington Trading Park, Britannia Enterprises Ltd at Canal Road Industrial Park, and CEF Ltd at Faraday Industrial Estate

activity

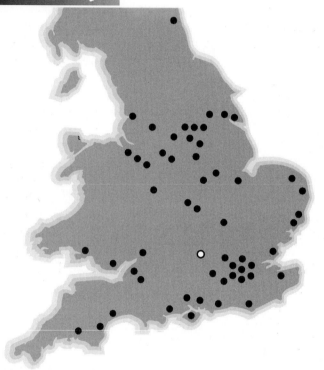

•	Ipswich	62,775
•	Keynsham	83,250
•	Kingswinford	79,000
•	Leeds	105,150
•	Leeds	67,225
•	Lowestoft	58,650
•	Luton	79,300
•	Manchester	121,600
•	Medway	86,100
•	Northampton	79.800
•	Norwich	60,500
•	Nottingham	76,300
•	Nuneaton	87,325
•	Paignton	72,950
•	Peterborough	83,375
•	Plymouth	75,125
•	Portsmouth	83,530
•	Reading	96,000
•	Rochdale	61,750
•	Sheffield	113,000
•	Sidcup	74,375
•	Southend	86,825
•	Staines	22,320
•	Stoke on Trent	91,000
•	Swansea	83,275
•	Watford	63,790
•	Wimbledon	96,350
•	Wolverhampton	90,300
•	York	74,600

Total Sales Area   5,564,450

Figure 4.4 The locations and size of Nurdin & Peacock wholesale outlets

Look at a map of population distribution in the UK (this shows where people live). What is the relationship between the location of Nurdin & Peacock's outlets (shown in the figure) and the size of towns?

The location of warehouse outlets

Many manufacturers and retailers will have to make decisions about warehousing facilities, such as: how many warehouses should we have? Where should they be located? What facilities should they have? Here is a list of factors which each business will have to consider before it can answer these questions:

- Access to all major transport routes such as the motorway and rail networks. Air and sea ports could be important to businesses which export goods overseas or import goods from overseas. Many wholesalers are also importers
- Good access to the customers. These customers can be either independent retailers or branches of a retail chain. Generally, it is much better if warehouses are located close to the customer, because this reduces collection costs
- The needs of the customers. How often do customers need deliveries? What quantities do they need? If deliveries are needed daily – e.g. fresh or perishable goods or goods which are constantly in demand – it will be necessary for the warehouse to be located close to the customer. However, if deliveries are needed less often, the warehouse can be located further away and can serve a much bigger area
- The number of customers
- The physical environment. This refers to the land on which the premises are built. Today, there are many groups of people who are concerned with protecting the environment
- Planning permission. Every new development must have permission from the local council before it can be built. Every developer must give plans of their proposed premises to the local council. These can be seen and inspected at the local council offices, and often they are published in the local newspaper. Local councillors, residents and businesses then have the opportunity to object to the proposed designs. The council has the right to change the design, or to say yes or no to the proposals.

  The council will ask: will the development:
  - cause traffic congestion? How will this be reduced? Will special access roads be built? Is there enough parking space for trucks and trailers?
  - fit in with the surrounding area? If not, how will it be changed? For example, will the height be reduced, and will the building materials be changed?
  - cause waste or pollution? How will these be reduced? For example, could noise be reduced with a screen of trees or specially constructed fencing?
  - reduce the amount of countryside? For example, could existing trees be kept, and could new ones be planted?

Case study: 'planning gain'

'Can we build a new supermarket on this bit of countryside if we give you a nice new community centre?'

In order to get planning permission, developers of out-of-town shopping centres offer inducements or sweeteners, says a report by the House of Commons Environment Committee called *Shopping Centres and Their Future*, published in 1995. The process is called 'planning gain', and examples include road improvements, community centres and landscaped open spaces. The Committee said that the process should not be encouraged. If a new development was no good, then no amount of planning gain would make it better.

1 Which would you prefer, the countryside or the new shopping centre?
2 Why do people fight to keep the countryside?
3 Give some examples of advantages and disadvantages of 'planning gain' (hint: see page 13).

REQUIREMENTS FOR MOVING DIFFERENT CATEGORIES OF GOOD ALONG THE SUPPLY CHAIN

Packaging

The purpose of packaging is:

- to protect goods when they are being moved – i.e. during **transit**
- to advertise and promote the product
- to provide customer information

The type of packaging that will be used will depend on:

- the type of transport: e.g. if fully loaded trucks or containers are used, then less packing is needed. (Can you say why?)
- the weather: e.g. can the goods be carried in open-top vehicles, or will they need covering? Containers can get very hot or very cold, depending on where they are sent, and suitable protection is therefore needed
- road conditions: e.g. are the roads likely to be bumpy or smooth?

- the type of goods: e.g. delicate or fragile items which are easily broken will need stronger packing during transit. Valuable items are also usually given better packaging protection. Dangerous goods in turn need to be specially packed, and may need to be labelled with 'HAZ CHEM.' ('Hazardous Chemicals') notices to tell people to take care. The fire service uses these notices when deciding how to deal with fires (many products give off dangerous fumes and vapours)

TYPES OF PACKING

- *Pallets*: these are simple wooden – and more recently plastic – frames on which goods are stacked. A whole pallet can be lifted with a fork-lift truck. The method is quick and efficient: boxes, cartons and sacks can be moved easily. Pallets are frequently used by supermarkets to transfer goods from the distribution warehouse to the delivery truck and then to the supermarket warehouse
- *Boxes*: although these are expensive to make because they are frequently made of wood, they are widely used in sea and road transport because they give good protection
- *Bags*: these can be made of sacking (a coarse cloth), plastic or paper, and can be used to carry, e.g., cement, sand, potatoes or garden fertiliser – the choice of material will depend on the type of product and the climate. (Can you say why? What would you use for frozen goods?)
- *Cartons*: usually made of cardboard, these are widely used for transporting goods over short distances. Most goods delivered to supermarkets come in cartons. Many of these are **recycled** (what does this mean?). On farms, the cardboard is delivered flat ready for making into cartons for transporting fruit and vegetables
- *Barrels and drums*: these are widely used for transporting liquids such as beer
- *Shrink wrapping*: this is a plastic sheet which is tightly stretched around cartons to give added protection and make them easier to transport. (If you have to unwrap them, take great care)

activity

Your friend wants to move to another area, and asks your advice about how they should pack the items in their kitchen. These items include a freezer and washing machine. Write notes explaining what they should do.

Specialist transport   We have already seen in Chapter 2 the types of transport which are available. In this section, we shall look at specialist road transport which is available. The choice of transport here will depend upon the category of goods which needs to be moved. For example, frozen goods and hazardous goods will need different types of road vehicle.

Here is a selection of the types of specialist road vehicles which can be used:

- *Curtain-sided vehicles*: these are large vehicles covered only with soft plastic sides, and used for low-value items. The 'curtains' can be easily moved to allow for loading and unloading
- *Boxes* (box vehicles): these have hard sides, and so are more secure. They can be used to carry, e.g., clothing, vehicle parts, sugar and all kinds of pallet loads
- *Tipper trucks*: these can be open or closed, and are used for transporting building materials such as sand and cement. The truck can be tilted so that the materials can be easily unloaded
- *Refrigerated vehicles*: these can be used for transporting chilled or frozen goods. New trucks have separate compartments for carrying frozen, chilled and fresh produce all at the same time
- *Tankers*: these can be used for carrying liquids such as petrol, milk and orange juice, and chemicals and dry goods such as flour. Inside these tankers there are separate compartments which can be used to carry different materials
- *Container trucks*: these are used for carrying containers either within the UK or overseas. Containers can be easily lifted from truck to ship using specialised cranes. Once containers have been closed and sealed, they cannot be opened until they reach their final destination. This means they are very secure
- *Trombone and low loader trailers*: these are used for heavy or long loads. The trombone is a low loader that can be extended to 60 feet
- *Hiab*: this is an open-top lorry with a crane attached for loading and unloading heavy equipment, machinery, timber and building materials

1 The above vehicles can all be hired or rented for any length of time. Check in the Yellow Pages under 'Van and lorry hire' to find out what is available in your area and how much it costs (Figure 4.5 gives two examples).
2 Which vehicles would you use for transporting the following: frozen ready meals, potatoes, garden turf, crazy-paving stone, a new refrigerator, sacks of flour, loaves of bread, Coca-Cola, milk, petrol, 40 feet of steel pipes, furniture, scaffolding, garden soil, glass? Give reasons for your answers.

Specialist storage   Efficient storage facilities are vital for any large distribution operation. We have already seen how warehouses and wholesalers operate (see Chapter 2). Here are some examples of the types of specialised storage facility that are available for a modern supermarket. The following facilities are for Waitrose – which is part of the John Lewis partnership – although they apply equally to any other group of supermarkets:

Figure 4.5 Two examples of Yellow Pages adverts for vehicle hire

- *Cold storage areas*: the air here is cooled to very low temperatures. These areas are equivalent to 'walk-in' deep freezers, and are used for all frozen meat, fish and vegetables, plus convenience ready-to-cook foods. Bread dough is also stored in this way, ready for defrosting and baking
- *Chilled storage areas*: the air here is cooled to slightly higher temperatures. These areas are used for yoghurts, milk, cheese, delicatessen, chilled cooked meats, some fresh produce and flowers (they can be kept fresh longer)
- *Dry non-perishable goods storage*: the majority of space in a warehouse is used for the storage of dry goods. The area is divided into separate sections – for tinned goods, household products etc. Cigarettes and tobacco are stored in a separate locked metal cage. Alcohol is stored in a separate locked room for security reasons

Case study: warehousing at Cadbury Schweppes

HANDLING LARGE SCALE SYSTEMS EFFICIENTLY

As retailers and manufacturers alike continue their efforts to drive down costs, warehousing has become the latest focus of attention.

Suppliers are not only starting to invest large sums in EDI (electronic data interchange) systems, but they are also starting to re-evaluate space utilisation and racking.

One of the latest state-of-the-art warehouses – with new racking and crane technology – is near Bournville, at Cadbury Schweppes' Minworth facility.

At the end of the 1980s there was a lot of growth at the seasonal end of Cadbury's business, namely Easter eggs and Selection Boxes. In fact, says distribution manager, Peter Norman, sales over the 10 week Easter period account for 10% of the company's total business.

The products are manufactured year round, and are then stored to meet the seasonal highs.

At that time, Cadbury had five main centres at Birmingham, Manchester, Liverpool, Crewe and Bristol and about seven smaller ones which, says Norman, were getting smaller and further away. 'We were looking at going into a thirteenth and with the stock in so many different locations, it was becoming difficult, and expensive, in terms of transport,' he says.

'There was no room for a warehouse at Bournville, so Minworth seemed ideal, not least because our major grocery customers are serviced by the motorway network. Here at Minworth we have access to the M1, the M5, the M6 and the M40.'

The decision was taken to centralise storage, for the reasons mentioned above as well as the fact that some existing facilities, such as the one in Liverpool, were old, and were raising quality issues. At £24 million Minworth is, points out Norman, the single biggest investment Cadbury has ever made.

The new facility had to cope with huge surges in demand, as well as being able to offer guaranteed chilled storage at constant temperature and humidity.

... 'It's one of the biggest chilled warehouses in Europe, and is equal in size to 5% of the UK's total cold storage capacity,' says Norman.

(Source: The Grocer, 3 February 1996)

Health and safety requirements Whenever goods are handled, lifted, moved or stored, great care must be taken to make sure that every aspect of health and safety law is obeyed. There are strict regulations about:

- the weight that can be carried by an individual (if you have to lift a heavy box or carton, always keep your back straight and bend from the knees). Always use whatever mechanical aids that are available, such as straps or stair lifts
- the amount that can be loaded onto trucks and railway wagons
- how goods should be stored. For example: dangerous goods need to be stored in a separate sealed area; many goods need to be kept cold; some cannot be shaken; some cannot be exposed to sunlight; chemicals can only be transported if the packing material can absorb any spillage (the author has found cat litter very useful for this purpose!). There are very strict hygiene regulations which apply to the storage and sale of food

Categories of retail product

Different categories of retail product – such as frozen goods or hazardous goods – need to be packed, transported and stored in different ways.

PERISHABLE GOODS

Perishable goods are goods which tend to rot quickly, especially during transit, and may therefore require chilled or frozen transit or storage. The temperature at which foodstuffs are kept is rigidly controlled: e.g. deep frozen, 0 °C for fresh fish and meat, 3 °C for apples, 10 °C for exotic fruits, 15 °C for bread and bananas, and room temperature for tinned foods – see Figure 4.6.

    Sell-by dates and **use-by dates** are now used to alert people to the length of time for which perishable goods can be stored or displayed. **Shelf-life** is the length of time a product will last before deteriorating. (How do you store fruit and vegetables in your home? Do you keep them in plastic bags? What happens if you do?)

NON-PERISHABLE GOODS

Non-perishable goods are goods which do not rot or deteriorate quickly, and so do not need to be stored in chilled or cold storage warehouses. However, they may need:

- clean, safe and secure conditions which prevent theft or loss
- good ventilation, to be kept away from sunlight (e.g. photographic materials), to be kept upright, to be kept dry etc.

Look at the four international symbols in Figure 4.7 which show how goods should be stored.

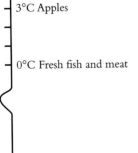

20°C Tinned foods

15°C Bread and bananas

10°C Exotic fruits

3°C Apples

0°C Fresh fish and meat

Figure 4.6 Transit/storage temperatures for foodstuffs as shown on a thermometer

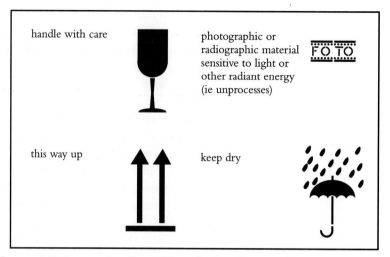

Figure 4.7 International markings for handling packages

There are many different types of non-perishables, such as:

- delicate or fragile goods: these can be easily broken during transit. Glass, crockery, electrical goods and computers, for example, all require very careful packing. Moveable parts need to be fixed to prevent damage or packed separately in the white rigid foam **polystyrene**
- clothing: frequently transported as 'hanging garments'. For example, coats and dresses are put on hangers on clothing rails which can then be wheeled directly onto aircraft or trucks and into the shops. Exel Logistics (part of NFC, one of the world's largest logistics and moving services companies) has developed an automated hanging-garment system for BHS. Garments are automatically wrapped with polythene and put onto trucks

FROZEN GOODS

Frozen goods are transported all over the world at temperatures of −18 °C, and need specialist packing – e.g. insulation against heat, specialist refrigerated transport (in countries where this is not available – such as the Ukraine – people eat fresh food), specialist refrigerated storage. (How do you carry frozen food from the supermarket?) Most meat, fish, fruit and vegetables can be frozen. Once frozen goods have defrosted, they must not (for health reasons) be refrozen. (New deliveries of frozen goods are always put underneath existing stock. Why do you think this is done?)

CHILLED GOODS

These include a wide range of convenience foods – meats, pies, flans etc. The main difference between chilled and frozen storage is the temperature at which the goods have to be kept. Chilled goods need to be kept in refrigerators, whilst frozen goods need freezers.

HAZARDOUS OR DANGEROUS GOODS

Great care needs to be taken when arranging the transport of hazardous or dangerous goods such as chemicals, acids or bottled gases such as oxygen or acetylene (when lit and used together, they can cut through thick metal). Some goods can become dangerous if they are packed in large quantities. For example, spirits such as brandy can ignite (catch alight) above certain temperatures, and aerosol sprays give off fumes and vapours. 'HAZ CHEM.' ('Hazardous Chemicals') notices are needed on all hazardous goods. Special regulations apply when such goods are moved by rail, road, air or sea.

1 Collect examples of the storage instructions on a range of foods and household products. (For example, on a can of fly and wasp killer it says 'Protect from sunlight.') What can you conclude about the storage instructions on different categories of retail products, e.g. frozen, perishable, etc.?
2 Give five examples of perishable, non-perishable, chilled, frozen, dry, liquid and hazardous retail products.
3 Now choose two products from each category and draw up a table like the one below, showing the requirements at each stage of the supply chain.

	PACKAGING REQUIREMENTS	TRANSPORT REQUIREMENTS	STORAGE REQUIREMENTS	HEALTH AND SAFETY REQUIREMENTS
Perishable Non-perishable Chilled Frozen Dry Liquid Hazardous				

Self-test questions:
Chapter 4

1 Identify the purpose of retail, wholesale and warehouse outlets.
2 Give examples of short and long supply chains.
3 List the advantages and disadvantages of direct supply.
4 What are the advantages and disadvantages of short channels of supply?
5 What are the main factors which affect the location of retail outlets?

6 What are the main factors which affect the location of wholesalers?

7 What are the main requirements for moving different categories of goods along the supply chain?

8 What are the main packaging requirements for different categories of foods?

9 What are the main storage requirements for different categories of goods?

10 What are the main health and safety requirements for different categories of goods?

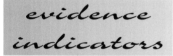

Supply chains

You work as an administrator in the Business Advice Unit of the local council. You are required to produce a report for your supervisor by four weeks today. The report should describe:

1 The purpose of the warehouses, wholesalers and retailers in the local area. You will find it helpful to use real named examples such as 'Kenny and Josie' the local newsagents/Post Office and general store use the wholesalers Makro.

2 The location of the warehouses, wholesalers and retailers in the local area. You should mark these on a map of the local area. You will find it helpful to use the local *Yellow Pages* published by British Telecommunications PLC and/or *The Thomson Local* published by Thomson Directories Limited.

3 The shops nearest to you in detail, this could be a local shopping parade or High Street. (Note; for example if you live in the centre of Birmingham you should still choose the shops nearest to you).

4 The factors which affect the location of the warehouses, wholesalers and retailers. You could ask the local shop owner and wholesaler. Check out the local details of the 1991 Census of Population. How does population affect location?

5 The supply chains for five products, (two of which must be primary and two of which must be manufactured). Use diagrams and notes, give real examples using named wholesalers and retailers in the local area. You should explain how the goods are handled and stored at each stage along the supply chain.

UNIT 1 DISTRIBUTION, TRANSPORT AND STORAGE END TEST

When two answers are required
   a = 1 and 2
   b = 2 and 3

c = 3 and 4

d = 1 and 4

1 A distribution operator which sells mainly to the general public is a
   a transporter
   b wholesaler
   c warehouse
   d retailer

2 A wholesaler is a business which
   a buys goods from and sells goods to retailers
   b buys goods in bulk and sells them in smaller quantities
   c buys goods from manufacturers to sell to other wholesalers
   d buys goods in small quantities and sells them in large quantities

3 The main purpose of a warehouse is to
   a sell goods to retailers and wholesalers
   b store goods for consumers
   c store goods for retailers and wholesalers
   d buy goods from retailers

4 Which two of these statements best describes the main role of the distribution sector?
   1 importing goods at the right time
   2 getting goods to consumers and customers
   3 meeting customer needs
   4 exporting goods at the right time

5 The main contribution of the distribution sector to the economy is to
   a improve the environment
   b renew town centres
   c provide employment
   d improve the high street

6 The main role of the distribution sector in the international economy is
   a to keep the sea routes clear
   b to make sure that trade is free
   c to carry imports and exports
   d to help overseas countries

7 The most likely structure of a supply chain is
   a retailer → manufacturer → consumer
   b manufacturer → consumer → retailer
   c wholesaler → manufacturer → retailer
   d manufacturer → wholesaler → retailer

8 Which of the following best describes sea transport?
   a it is very fast over long distances

b it is very cheap over long distances

c it is very expensive over long distances

d it is very convenient for carrying perishable goods

9 The best type of transport for short in-town journeys is most likely to be

a inland waterways

b railway wagons

c air transport

d road transport

10 A UK manufacturer distributes large volumes of lightweight goods to UK wholesalers. Which is the most flexible method of transporting these goods?

a rail

b road

c air

d canal

11 A European manufacturer distributes high value, lightweight, short shelf-life goods throughout Europe. Which forms of transport are most likely to be used?

a sea and canal

b canal and road

c sea and rail

d air and road

12 A retailer uses a lorry to distribute building materials to local residential customers. The main reason for doing this is because

a competitors use lorries

b customers prefer lorries

c lorries are flexible and convenient

d lorries are useful for carrying fragile goods

13 A home delivery pizza company uses motor cyclists to deliver the pizzas. The main reason for using this type of transport is because

a motor cyclists are more willing to take risks

b learner drivers can ride motor cycles

c 16-year-olds can ride motor cycles

d motor cycles are fast and convenient

14 A company delivers milk using an electric powered milk float. The main reason for using this type of transport is because

a it is fast and easy to unload

b it is quiet and reliable

c there are many milk floats available

d they can be used over long distances

15 Which road has the Ordnance Survey symbol for gradient 1 in 5 and steeper?

```
a  ══════════════════++══════════
b  ═══════════⟹═════════════════
c  ═══════════════════⟹⟹═══════
d  ════════════════//═══════════
```

16 What is the main requirement when building an airport?
   a there should be many aircraft
   b there should be a large amount of freight
   c there should be many retail outlets
   d there should be a large area of flat land

17 The *two* main requirements for a container port are
   1 a large local population
   2 facilities for loading and unloading
   3 availability of transport services
   4 a variety of local retail outlets

18 Two towns are shown 8.5 centimetres apart on a map with a scale of 1 centimetre = 3 kilometres. What is the distance on the ground?
   a 26.5 kilometres
   b 11.5 kilometres
   c 25.5 kilometres
   d 36 kilometres

19 How long would it take a lorry travelling at 48 miles per hour, with a 20 minute stop for loading, to complete a journey of 192 miles?
   a 4 hours 10 minutes
   b 3 hours 40 minutes
   c 4 hours 20 minutes
   d 4 hours 40 minutes

20 A truck travels 120 miles at 40 miles per hour, it takes 40 minutes for goods to be loaded on to an aeroplane which then travels 2,500 miles at 500 miles per hour. How long does the journey take?
   a 7 hours 10 minutes
   b 8 hours 10 minutes
   c 8 hours 40 minutes
   d 7 hours 40 minutes

21 Which route is most suitable for a Heavy Goods Vehicle (HGV) travelling regularly between two large towns?
   a country lanes
   b minor roads
   c unfenced trunk roads
   d motorways

22 Which two of these factors is most likely to affect the choice of route for a transport business which delivers goods to France?

1 the size of drivers
2 the distance of the journey
3 ferry and train timetables
4 the colour of the vehicles

23 Which supply chain best describes a 'Pick Your Own' fruit and vegetable farm?
   a producer → retailer
   b producer → wholesaler
   c producer → warehouse
   d producer → consumer

24 Which supply chain shows the situation 'We cut out the middleman'?
   a producer → wholesaler
   b producer → warehouse
   c producer → retailer
   d producer → consumer

25 The main purpose of a wholesaler is
   a to store goods for consumers
   b to sell goods to manufacturers
   c to sell goods to retailers
   d to store goods for manufacturers

26 Small convenience stores are most likely to be located
   a on out-of-town sites
   b on motorways
   c in town centres
   d on local shopping parades

27 Which *two* factors are most likely to affect the location of a small retail outlet?
   1 the availability of electrical power
   2 the number of competitors
   3 the number of possible customers
   4 the availability of workers

28 Which *two* factors are most likely to affect the location of a national wholesale distributor?
   1 the availability of transport services
   2 the parking and access facilities
   3 the amount of administration
   4 the size of the local population

29 Which of these would be required for handling dangerous liquids along the supply chain?
   a open top containers
   b wooden boxes
   c sealed barrels

d plastic bags

30 Which of the following would be the most suitable method of storing milk and cheese along the supply chain?
   a cold storage areas
   b chilled storage areas
   c locked metal cages
   d open air facilities

For the answers, see p. 344 at the end of the book.

Quality and service to the customer

C H A P T E R 5

Investigating customer services provided by distribution outlets

In this chapter, we will look at:

- customer services which are provided by different distribution outlets
- how to monitor customer satisfaction
- forms of customer protection
- how to tell customers about the protection which is available
- how to provide customer service and meet customer needs

We will cover Element 2.1, Performance Criteria 1, 2, 3, 4, and Element 2.2, Performance Criteria 1, 2, 3, 4, 5.

OUR CUSTOMER CHARTER

"We aim to serve you better"

OUR CUSTOMER CHARTER

"... problem solving, quickly ..."

Complaints and Enquiries

Unfortunately sometimes things do go wrong. So if you do have any problems or queries, we will do our best to sort them out in the shortest possible time. You can contact us in a number of ways:

- talk to the person behind the counter
- ask to see the office manager or subpostmaster
- ring out customer Helpline, 0345 223344, where the calls are charged at the local rate
- write to your regional office at the address at the back of this leaflet
- refer to our Code of Practice leaflet.

If you write to us, our Customer Service Team will acknowledge your letter on the day it is received and will send a reply no more than seven working days later. In other words, you can normally expect a reply within about ten days of writing.

A leaflet produced by the Post Office to explain customer services

Customer service concerns the way in which a business deals with its customers, and is a very important part of the marketing policy and image of a business. Lloyds Bank advertises using the slogan or phrase 'Legendary service'. A local hardware shop uses the phrase 'Browsers are welcome, buyers are adored' to sell its goods. Almost 70% of retail businesses advertising in our local paper highlight or emphasise the quality of their service in some way or another. As a representative of Travis Perkins (the builders and plumbers merchants) told the present authors, 'Customer service is long remembered, but price is quickly forgotten.' Most people remember and repeat the complaints they have made, such as about waiting a long time at the checkout to pay 'my money to you' or about staying in all day waiting for a delivery or repair person to come. But they also remember those occasions on which the complaints were dealt with quickly and effectively. It is easy for a business to lose customers, but it is very difficult and expensive (because of the advertising needed) to gain new customers or to entice former customers back again. This is why it is important for distribution outlets to maintain and develop a reputation for quality and service.

WHY DO DISTRIBUTION OPERATORS PROVIDE CUSTOMER SERVICES?

There are two main reasons why distribution operators provide customer services:

1 to attract new customers
2 to keep existing customers.

More customers should mean larger sales, larger profits and a bigger share of the market. Almost all distribution operators are in competition with one another. A shop which sells clothes will be competing with other clothes shops, but it will also be competing against mail-order companies such as Grattan or Freemans, and against manufacturers which also sell clothes. Furthermore, because people do not have enough money to buy all they want, the clothes shop will also be in competition with electrical or furniture shops etc. Although many businesses try to charge lower prices than their rivals (which is called **price competition**), they also compete by trying to offer better services or a wider range of services than their competitors (often called **non-price competition**). Providing customer services is a way of advertising or promoting the business so as to attract more customers.

1 Collect examples of advertisements in your local paper and your local Yellow Pages or Thomson Directory which use the word 'service' to sell their products.
2 What percentage of retail businesses use the word 'service' in their advertising? Are there differences between, for example, double-glazing companies and furniture and bedding stores?

TYPES OF CUSTOMER SERVICE

Providing information and help to customers

Information is needed before, during and after purchasing a product:

- Retailers require information from wholesalers and manufacturers
- Consumers require information from the seller of the goods

It can be very expensive for buyers to obtain information. For example, it could be necessary to visit a range of outlets, make phone calls, obtain literature or speak to sales representatives, all of which takes time and money. An effective seller or supplier will therefore need to have systems in place for providing accurate information quickly and easily, or else the potential customer could go elsewhere.

The information needed will vary with every purchase. Here are some points that might be considered by a buyer, whether a retailer or a consumer:

- the price
- the quantity which is needed, and the quantity in which the product is sold
- the colour, make or brand
- the quality of the item (remember that price and quality can be related)
- the location of the outlet, and the type of outlet
- the methods of payment that are available – e.g. cash, credit or debit card (see page 338)
- whether there is a delivery service, and whether this is free (for example, will the old model be taken away if you are replacing your refrigerator?)

Collect information on the group of products shown in the table. How long did this take you? How much did it cost to collect the information?

	ELECTRIC KETTLE	TRAINERS	CD PLAYER	PERSONAL STEREO	WHERE THE INFORMATION CAME FROM	EASE OR DIFFICULTY OF OBTAINING THE INFORMATION
Minimum–maximum price						
Quantity or size available						
Colours available						
Main brands						

	ELECTRIC KETTLE	TRAINERS	CD PLAYER	PERSONAL STEREO	WHERE THE INFORMATION CAME FROM	EASE OR DIFFICULTY OF OBTAINING THE INFORMATION
Name of outlet where sold						
Method of payment						
Delivery service						
Other factors						

Where do retailers and consumers get information from?

- Personal knowledge. With convenience goods such as bread and milk and detergents, people tend always to purchase the same brand. Manufacturers reinforce this tendency with continuous advertising
- Recommendations from friends and family. This is a form of word-of-mouth advertising. Many people ask their family and friends about their views on, for example, a particular brand or shop before they make a purchase. (Do you do this? And how much notice do you take of their replies?)
- Catalogues, trade magazines (see page 277), leaflets and the media (e.g. newspapers and radio provide information about sales and special promotions). The Consumers Association publishes a magazine called *Which* that compares products using a star system. Products with the most stars are the best buys
- Sales people. Consumers get their information either from staff at the store or from the manufacturer if goods are supplied directly – as, for example, with double glazing. Retailers will get information from **sales representatives** (**'reps'**) who visit the store
- Retailers and consumers will visit stores to compare, for example, prices and the range of goods available. This is sometimes called **comparison shopping** or 'shopping around'
- Customer surveys can provide valuable information for retailers

Figure 5.1 shows advice provided by wholesalers Nurdin & Peacock for independent retailers, whilst Figure 5.2 shows an example of a leaflet provided by the retailers Safeway for consumers.

Once the information has been collected about the range of products that are available, the alternative options will need to be compared. With expensive items, this can be quite a complex process as people 'shop around'. People spend less time, on the other hand, searching for information when buying everyday convenience items. The actual purchase decision will be based on a comparison of the advantages and disadvantages of each product. Many magazines now publish their own consumer surveys in which they test several brands

MERCHANDISING FOR CHRISTMAS

Nurdin & Peacock offers the following tips for a successful Christmas:
- Ensure your store is bright and well lit
- Put promotions on gondola ends or opposite the counters
- Let your customers know when you are open over Christmas
- Why not host a shop party with a Father Christmas and free wine and mince pies, or raise money for a local charity
- Use linked promotions to boost sales such as canned fruit and jellies, washing up liquid and rubber gloves. Back up promotions with in-store sampling
- Stock-up well but if you're worried about unsold product, buy stock with overwraps so that it can then be sold without its seasonal covering.

Figure 5.1 Nurdin & Peacock's Christmas advice for independent retailers

We're changing to Metric

As a result of European Legislation, the Government is introducing regulations in October 1995 which require, by law, that pre-packed foods such as meat and cheese show the metric weight (grams/kilograms) rather than the imperial weight (ounces/pounds).

We hope this leaflet will answer some of the questions you may have and help you to fully understand the changes. The Ready Reckoner on the opposite page has been designed so that you always have a handy guide to keep.

We are also displaying conversion information by the foods that will be affected by the change to metric.

Remember, our staff are always there to help.

Same good value

Your food will not cost more as a result of the change to metric. Prices shown in kilograms look more expensive because a kilogram is around 2¼ times heavier than a pound (2.2 times heavier to be exact). So you can see that the price per kilogram is just over two times higher than the price per pound but the price of your food stays the same.

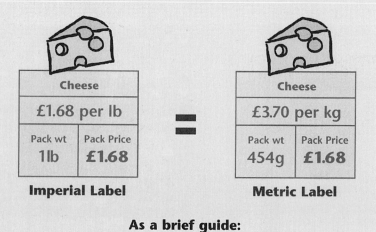

Cheese	
£1.68 per lb	
Pack wt	Pack Price
1lb	£1.68

Imperial Label

Cheese	
£3.70 per kg	
Pack wt	Pack Price
454g	£1.68

Metric Label

As a brief guide:

¼lb (4oz) = 113 grams	100 grams = 3.5oz
½lb (8oz) = 227 grams	500 grams = 1.1 lbs
1lb (16oz) = 454 grams	1 kilogram = 2.2 lbs

Figure 5.2 A Safeway leaflet on going metric

of the same product – such as decaffeinated coffee – and give their own verdict. In the December 1995 edition of *Independent Retail News* (a trade magazine which is read by many independent/symbol-group convenience-store retailers), a comparative test of own-label mince pies sold by the major cash-and-carry wholesalers and symbol-group operators – such as Londis, Spar, Mace, Booker and Nurdin & Peacock – was carried out.

activity

Your friend has asked for your advice on buying a personal stereo. What information would you advise them to obtain?

Customer care departments

Customer care is about providing what the customer wants, and this means giving consistent and reliable customer service, providing goods and services that work, responding quickly to customer queries and complaints, and making each customer feel like an individual. It means *solving* customer problems – not *creating* problems for them. Over the past ten years, customer care has become more important since many stores now stock very similar goods at similar prices. Each outlet uses its customer care and customer services operations to make itself different from its competitors.

Customer care is increasingly seen as the responsibility of *all* staff and not just those people who work on, for example, the customer-care or customer-services desk. Here are some examples of the work that people do in this area:

- deal with complaints
- listen to suggestions from customers
- deal with refunds, faults and the exchange of goods
- give out information and advice
- phone other stores to see if goods are available elsewhere

activity

(Note: this activity could be combined with others in this chapter to provide evidence of the full range of customer services offered by distribution outlets to a range of customers. You are advised to check the other activities before you begin this one.)

The group should divide into pairs to compare the services that are offered by the customer-care departments in a range of distribution outlets – e.g. convenience stores, department stores, specialist stores, wholesalers. Can you say why there are differences? Produce a set of notes on your findings.

Payment methods

(Payment methods are examined in detail in Chapter 12.)

Many outlets try to offer customers as many ways to pay as possible. Here are some examples (you will probably be able to find others):

- cash
- cheques – provided the customer has a cheque guarantee card
- credit cards such as those given by banks, building societies and large stores. These allow the card holder to spend up to an agreed amount (an upper limit) on credit. This means that they do not need to have money in their account but must be able to repay any money which is spent using the card. If bills are paid promptly, many cards are 'interest free' which means that interest does not have to be paid. Manufacturers, wholesalers and retailers which allow payment by credit card normally have to pay the company which issues the card 2% commission on all sales – i.e. £2 for every £100 of credit-card sales
- debit cards. With these cards, the customer must have money in their account before they can make a purchase. With Switch cards, for example, the money is debited from (i.e. taken out of) the customer's account and switched or transferred to the seller's account as soon as the sale is made
- interest-free credit. This makes the credit loan cheaper because the customer does not have to pay interest. (What effect will this have on sales?)

activity

What payment methods are offered by the outlets you have selected for the activity on page 127?

Refunds

If a customer buys a pair of shoes which fall apart when they are first worn, the customer can take them back to the shop where they were bought and obtain a refund, a replacement or even a free repair! The customer does not have to accept a credit note. Any notices such as 'No money refunded' or 'We do not accept responsibility for any loss or damage' (as often seen in dry cleaners) are generally illegal.

It is important for both retailers and wholesalers to have an effective policy for handling complaints and refunds. A positive policy will keep customers happy, keep their goodwill and hopefully keep them coming back to the store: new customers are very expensive to find.

activity

Continue the previous activity, comparing refunds policies.

After-sales service

This is the service which the seller provides after the goods have been sold. For example:

- Wholesalers give advice and help on displaying and promoting goods

- Computer companies provide helplines, support lines etc.: 'free to help you get more from your computer'
- Carpet companies provide 'free fitting and underlay'
- Garages provide a 'free courtesy car whilst yours is serviced'

These and many other examples of after-sales service are all intended to give the seller a competitive edge over their rivals. They are saying: 'Buy from *us*. We give you more.' (What other examples can you find?)

activity

Continue the activity above, comparing after-sales services.

Delivery

Delivery is a vital part of customer service, and is used as a major method of competition between businesses. Some businesses such as mail-order companies rely totally on the reliability of their delivery service in order to survive. Many retail outlets – and especially those which sell large appliances such as washing machines and freezers – provide 'free delivery' within a stated distance, whilst pizza home-delivery companies deliver in '30 minutes', and other businesses say: 'Allow up to 21 days for delivery.' Manufacturers and wholesalers deliver goods direct to retailers.

Businesses can either use their own transport or use a specialist delivery company. (The Body Shop, however, does both.) Here are some advantages and disadvantages of each method:

	ADVANTAGES	DISADVANTAGES
Using own transport	Greater control, and freedom to plan routes	Vehicles need to be serviced, taxed, insured and maintained. (What happens if they break down?)
Using a specialist haulage company	Reliable. Drivers and vehicles are always available.	Less control

activity

Using, again, the same outlets you investigated in the activity on page 127, find out their policies on delivery. For example, do they deliver to consumers/retailers? And do they charge for this service?

activity

A pizza company – e.g. Pizza Hut or Dominos – has opened in your local high street. Pizza Hut, for example, has a guarantee that if the pizza is not delivered within 30 minutes of the time the telephone order is taken, it will give £1 back to the customer ($3 in the USA).

Deliveries are made by motorcycle. Work out the limits or boundary of the delivery area that can be covered within 30 minutes and put this on a map of your local area. How might the limits be different if the Pizza Hut were in a rural area? Can you buy pizza by phone? Have they ever been late? And if so, what happened?

The physical environment

The physical environment of a retail or wholesale outlet covers both the internal selling space and the immediate external or outside area. Inside the outlets, customers want a comfortable temperature (are the shops in your local shopping centre always too hot? Is your local paper shop always cold? The authors were told 'It discourages the school children.' We pointed out it also discourages everyone else!), good ventilation, excellent hygiene and cleanliness, appropriate decoration, good lighting, accessible displays and shelving, good access for wheelchairs and prams etc (see Figure 5.3). These are all part of the 'hardware' of customer care. Many supermarkets and multiple stores design their premises and buildings so that they look the same and are immediately recognisable and familiar to consumers (Tesco is building new premises in what it calls 'cottage house style').

Externally, the outlet should be clean (if the outside area is not clean, how do you feel about the area which you cannot see?) and free from rubbish – there is legislation which prohibits rubbish from being left outside premises. There should be good access for customers and suppliers. Customers are increasingly demanding better physical conditions in which to spend their money.

Carry out a survey of the physical environment provided by your local distribution outlets. You could work in small teams. You will need to compare the facilities offered by different types of outlet such as large and small retailers, convenience stores, department stores, specialist shops and market stall holders. You should also include at least one wholesaler. You could look at cleanliness, the width of the aisles, heating, access for the disabled etc.

In-store facilities

With increasing competition, distribution operators need to offer a wider range of good in-store facilities in order to attract people into the store. Do your local stores provide any of these facilities:

- child-care facilities such as a crèche
- a children's play area
- public telephones
- 'hole in the wall' cash dispensers
- wide checkout points
- trolleys which can carry children

TESCO PLC

The personal approach

Our success rests on the skills and motivation of our people. Millions of pounds are invested in training each year because better trained staff make Tesco a better place to shop. The quality of our training has been recognised in a number of national awards.

Behind it all is a new attitude to serving the customer. Staff are trained not just to do jobs but to use their imagination and initiative – to bring their personalities to work and to find their own distinctive ways of making customers feel special.

66 I only get to Tesco once a week when my daughter takes me, so I have to remember everything or go without. The staff are ever so helpful. They'll always lift things down or offer to come round with me. I've got to know some of them really well. 99

Mrs Mary Yorke
Doncaster

Figure 5.3 Creating a comfortable shopping environment and friendly advice at Tesco

- help with packing the goods which have been bought ('bag packers')
- a gift-wrapping service
- umbrellas when it rains so that people can get to their cars without getting wet
- places for pets
- changing rooms where you can try on clothes before buying them?

Compare the in-store facilities that are provided by your local distribution outlets.

Complete charts like the two below by specifying the services which are offered to different types of customer by different types of outlet (you can also use other outlets).

Services provided by different types of outlet

	TYPE OF OUTLET			
TYPE OF CUSTOMER	CONVENIENCE STORE	DEPARTMENT STORE	WHOLESALER	MARKET STALL
Face-to-face				
Mail order				Will not provide a mail-order service
Trade★				
Adults				
Children				

★ Note: trade customers means other businesses, and these are often given a special service. For example, in our local car showroom which also sells spare parts, there is a separate counter/entrance for trade customers, who will get a trade discount (lower prices) because they are regular customers who buy in bulk.

Services provided to different types of customer

	TYPE OF CUSTOMER				
SERVICE	FACE-TO-FACE	MAIL ORDER	TRADE	ADULTS	CHILDREN
Information					
Customer care department					
Variety of payment methods					
Refunds					
After-sales services					
Delivery					
Quality of the physical environment					
In-store facilities					

METHODS FOR MONITORING CUSTOMER SATISFACTION

The level of customer satisfaction has to do with the extent to which customers are satisfied with the goods or services provided by a distribution operator. It is important for every business to be aware of what its customers think of its goods and services because satisfied customers are more likely to buy the product again or to tell their friends and family to buy the product (**word-of-mouth advertising**).

Here are four ways in which customer service can be monitored:

1 *Sales performance.* **Sales performance** refers to both the amount of goods sold and the trends in sales. For example, in January 1996, J Sainsbury were in the newspaper headlines not because it recorded large profits but because its profits had *failed* to rise.

2 *Feedback from staff and customers.* This can take the form of praise or complaints from customers by written or verbal means. Because sales staff come into direct contact with customers, they have a vital role in conveying information back to the management of the business, and the management, indeed, must encourage its staff to provide as much **feedback** as practicable. Staff should be willing and prepared to give information to management, and in return, management should have a system for rewarding those members of staff who have contributed to customer satisfaction – e.g. by promotion, special awards or special recognition.

   What information will management want feedback on?

   ● *The quality of the product or service.* Are the customers satisfied or dissatisfied?

     How often do you complain? Have you ever written to a tour operator or travel company complaining about the quality of the accommodation you received on holiday? (Very few 16- to 19-year-olds do complain, which is why they tend to be given the least attractive rooms in hotels and apartments.) Have you ever complained about the quality of the 'cappuccino coffee' at motorway services (which is usually cold and frothless!)? Companies should be very concerned if they receive complaints, and should take immediate action to correct them, by investigating the circumstances of the complaint and making sure that they do not happen again. (Why do you think that businesses need to care so much about complaints? How many businesses do you think take complaints seriously enough?)

     Many businesses rely on letters of praise from satisfied customers to sell their products

   ● *Prices.* Manufacturers, wholesalers and retailers will all need to know what their customers think about the level of prices for their products. They will also want to know how customers react to price changes. For example, if a wholesaler raises prices by 5%, by how much will the sales to retailers change? Or if a retailer *cuts* prices by 4%, by how much will sales to consumers change? It is equally important for a business to be aware of what prices are being charged by its competitors. Many retailers, for example, use low prices as a major method of competition, and many stores are now advertising 'If you can find this product cheaper locally, we will refund the difference in price.' (Can you name some local examples of this offer?) Sales staff are often in the best position to feed back sales/price information or indeed to make price changes to get rid of surplus stock. Shops will often cut prices at closing time to try to clear fresh or perishable goods

3 *A record of goods returned*. Keeping a record of goods which have been returned is a useful way of monitoring customer satisfaction and of highlighting where there might be problems in the organisation. Many distribution operators now have very sophisticated computer programs which form part of the Management Information System (MIS) for monitoring, tracking and dealing with complaints and 'returns'. Are you as a consumer aware of this?

4 *Customer questionnaires*. **Customer questionnaires** are increasingly being used by a wide range of organisations as a simple and useful way of finding out what customers think about the products and services which are provided. For example, questionnaires from Midland Mainline (train services), the Automobile Association (AA), Upper Crust (sandwiches), MFI (furniture retailers) were all given to the author in the same week! In Chapter 6 we examine how to construct questionnaires, and give examples of the types of questions that can be used to get the information the organisation needs.

1 Collect examples of customer questionnaires and display these on a notice board, with notes explaining the main features.

2 Make a short presentation to your group, using overhead transparencies, outlining the methods used to monitor consumer satisfaction. Put the information into a file headed 'Unit 2' as part of your evidence for this unit. Whenever you can, try to expand on the instructions given in the book – this is how you will get a distinction.

FORMS OF CONSUMER PROTECTION

The consumer is protected against, e.g., unscrupulous traders, dirty or unsafe goods, false descriptions on goods or short measures by a wide range of rules and regulations (many of which are Acts of Parliament), local and central government organisations, and voluntary agencies and associations. There is also an increasing amount of European Union (EU) legislation which helps consumers here. The consumer movement is now a major political force, with organisations like the Consumers' Association playing a leading role on behalf of consumers. Unlike the consumers of 50 years ago, the consumers of today cannot be ignored, and they are demanding better quality, fresher foods, green foods, 'cruelty free cosmetics' which have not been tested on animals, furniture which does not destroy tropical rainforest, clearer labelling with nutritional information, safer toys, a wider range of goods etc. They are no longer willing to be told 'Let the buyer beware' when they buy goods, but are demanding and expecting to be sold goods which are safe and fit for the purpose for which they are sold. **Consumer protection** has increased with the rise in consumerism.

Which? magazine, an independent consumer guide produced by the Consumers' Association

Contracts of sale

Whenever you go into a shop and buy an item – for example, a bar of chocolate – a **contract of sale** has been made. This can be written or verbal. In such a contract:

- a **seller** (this could be e.g. a retailer or wholesaler) has agreed to hand over or transfer a product to the
- **buyer** who in return agrees to pay a sum of money in exchange

There are certain assumptions underlying this process. For example, the seller will expect to get paid, and the buyer in turn can expect goods of a particular quality, quantity and price. These assumptions are called the 'terms and conditions of the contract'. If these terms or conditions are broken, then either side can go to court to sort out the problem.

Guarantees   A **guarantee** is a written document which states that a product will meet certain standards or specifications, and it is given by the company that makes the product. Usually, it only covers the first few months of the possible life of a product. With any guarantee, it is always wise to read the small print. As a consumer, you could gain or lose with a guarantee, so do not sign unless you are sure of what you are agreeing to. Here is an example of a guarantee from Amstrad:

Your telephone is guaranteed for a period of twelve months from the date of purchase. In the unlikely event of a fault please return it with a copy of the purchase receipt to your supplier who will exchange it. The guarantee does not cover damage caused by misuse, negligence (carelessness), excessive voltage, faults on the telephone line or lightning. Your statutory rights [these are what you are entitled to without the guarantee – for example, you can take the goods back and exchange them] are not affected by this guarantee.

Collect examples of guarantees, and attach these to a sheet of A3 paper together with extra notes explaining what the consumers are entitled to with these guarantees (make sure that you do not lose them and that you can take them off, because you may need them!)

The Trade Descriptions Act 1968 and the Consumer Protection Act 1987

These two Acts of Parliament make it illegal (a criminal offence) for a retailer, wholesaler or manufacturer to give a false or misleading description of a product or its price. Here are some examples which would be breaking the law:

- A false description of quantity: e.g. a street trader selling a '1 lb scoop of sprouts' when there are only 14 ounces. (How many should there be in this example? Also, if the sprouts were pre-packed, how would they be weighed?)
- False descriptions of country of origin and place of manufacture: e.g. a butcher selling 'fresh Welsh lamb' which is in fact defrosted lamb from New Zealand
- A false description of fitness for purpose and performance: e.g. Christmas trees being sold with the label 'Specially treated needles will not drop off' – and with needles which then drop off within 4 days!
- A misleading description of price: e.g. goods marked '£89 reduced from £129' which had not been sold at £129
- A misleading description of quality: e.g. a table marked 'genuine antique oak table', when in fact only the oak is antique and the table had been made the week before in Bermondsey, an area well known in London for antiques

The Sale and Supply of Goods Act 1994

This new Act came into effect on 3 January 1995, and it makes changes to the Sale of Goods Act 1979 and the Supply of Goods and Services Act 1982. The key features of the Act are:

- Any goods which are sold must be of satisfactory quality. A quality product is one that is reasonably fit for all the purposes for which it is sold, taking into account the price and the description of the goods. Satisfactory quality also includes the appearance and finish of the goods, whether there are any minor defects, and whether the goods are safe and durable. For example, if a person buys an electric kettle which includes the description 'Boils 3 pints of water in two minutes', it must be able to do this. However, if a person buys a cheap second-hand kettle, they should not expect top quality
- The customer cannot claim that the goods are of unsatisfactory quality if they:
  - did not see obvious faults when the goods were first bought
  - have just changed their minds and no longer want the goods
  - broke the goods themselves
  - were told there were faults but chose to ignore them
  - did not buy the goods themselves. If they were bought for the customer by someone else, the person who bought the goods must change them
  - were told by the salesperson that the goods might not be suitable but chose to ignore this advice

How the law protects the consumer

- The prices shown on goods must be clearly displayed and must be correct. Have you noticed that many stores have stopped pricing individual goods? (Over 9,000 stores now use bar-code scanners – compared with only 41 in 1982.) This makes it very difficult for people with bad eyesight to see any prices anywhere. Perhaps stores ought to provide those with less-than-perfect vision with free magnifying glasses!
- Correct weights and measures must be given. For example, a loaf of bread which is marked '800 grammes' must weigh 800 grammes, and a petrol pump which shows '10 litres' must have delivered 10 litres. Since Autumn 1995, all pre-packed foods must have their weights marked in kilogrammes.
- Since the UK joined the European Union, the size of many products has been standardised – e.g. for shoes, clothes and boxes of detergents (an 'E10' box weighs 4 kilogrammes and an 'E3' box weighs 1.2 kilogrammes)
- The prices of goods sold in a sale must be honest and true reductions, and must have been previously sold at the higher price shown, so that for example an electric kettle which is marked or labelled 'Reduced from £25.99 to £17.99' must have been sold before at the price of £25.99

SALES TACTIC FOILED

A new European law has been passed which will protect consumers from hard-sell over the telephone.

Shaun Spiers, the Labour and Co-op MEP for Bexley, Bromley and Greenwich, has given his backing to the law, but is unhappy that it does not cover banks and insurance companies.

The directive was approved by the European Parliament in Strasbourg last month and is deemed necessary due to the growth of international retailing.

Now the consumer will be protected from receiving misleading information from sales pitches on the telephone, in the post and through teleshopping on satellite. They will also be allowed a cooling off period in which they can cancel their orders.

Mr Spiers said: 'This is good news for consumers. You will now have legal protection from unfair selling techniques regardless of whether the salesman is calling from Paris or Peckham.'

activity

Why do you think all of the above legislation is needed?

The Consumer Association

The Consumer Association is an organisation which investigates complaints on behalf of consumers about poor services or goods. It also carries out comparative tests on a wide variety of products, using a star system to indicate which product is the best buy. The results are published in a range of *Which?* magazines – e.g. *Which?* itself, *Money Which* and *Which Car?*

The Ombudsman

The **ombudsman**, also known as the **Parliamentary Commissioner**, is a government official who has the power to investigate people's complaints against central or local government or its services. For example, if you live on a council estate with noisy neighbours and have tried everything to stop them making a noise such as complaining to the local council, you can as a last resort contact the ombudsman. The ombudsman has the power to order the council to pay you compensation.

The Citizen's Charters

The **Citizen's Charters** were introduced by the Conservative government to make public services more accountable (see Figure 5.4). Each Charter states the aims and objectives of the organisation to which it applies and lists 'what you can expect from us'. For example, there is a Citizen's Charter for Rail Services and one for further-education students.

activity

Obtain copies of the Student's Charter. Do you get what you are entitled to?

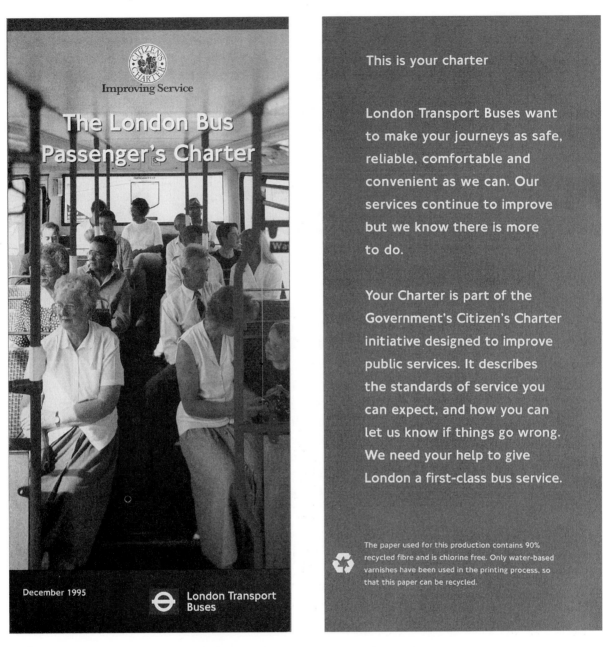

Figure 5.4 The Citizen's Charter for London buses

Trading Standards Departments

Consumer-protection acts are generally enforced by the **Trading Standards Department** of the local authority. This is what the Trading Standards Department of the London Borough of Bromley does: 'We make routine visits to some 6,500 commercial premises in the borough sampling and testing goods and services to make sure they meet legislation requirements on safety, quality, quantity, price and fair trading. We investigate all complaints.'

The Weights and Measures section of each Department provides advice on weights and measures to consumers and commercial premises. This includes routine visits to premises where goods are weighed and measured, such as shops, pubs and restaurants, and petrol stations.

Consumer advice is provided on a person's rights as a consumer or as a trader. Environmental Health Departments investigate unsafe or dirty shops and restaurants.

activity

Invite your local Trading Standards Department Officer to your centre to give a talk. Prepare a set of questions which you could ask. Write up the talk as a short article.

Telling customers about the consumer protection that is available

Many people do not know what their rights as customers or consumers are, and only a very small number will try to claim or enforce their rights if something goes wrong. Whilst every business will have its own objectives such as trying to make more profits or sell more goods, it is only in the last 30 years that distribution outlets have recognised that it can be more profitable to tell consumers about their rights. There are five reasons for this:

1 With the rise of consumerism and customer awareness, customers have become more demanding and businesses have been pushed into providing more information.
2 Businesses have recognised that complaints can have a positive effect by improving the quality of the services and products.
3 Satisfied customers are less likely to shop somewhere else.
4 Customer care programmes which give customers what they want can improve customer loyalty, which in turn improves profits.
5 Government legislation requires distribution operators to take a more active role in telling customers about their rights and about what they can expect – e.g. 'Our commitment to you'.

Any communication with customers about consumer-protection details – see Table 5.1 – must be easy to read and understand, and readily available.

activity

A survey carried out by the present authors showed that:

- most small/independent outlets, particularly stall holders and convenience stores, do not publish information about the consumer protection which is available
- only a small number of larger outlets had written material available
1 With your group, collect examples of ways in which different distribution outlets communicate details of the consumer protection which is available.

Table 5.1　Sources of information on customer protection

WHO COMMUNICATES	METHOD OF COMMUNICATION
Retailers and wholesalers	Posters, leaflets, bulletins, newsletters
Manufacturers	Packaging is frequently used to inform customers about their rights – e.g. 'Should you have a complaint about this product, please return to Customer Services'
Central and local government	The Office of Fair Trading, set up in 1973, publishes leaflets such as 'How to put things right'. The local council may have a telephone helpline/information desk. It may also publish leaflets
The media	Local and national newspapers and magazines frequently have articles on the theme of 'Know your consumer rights'. Radio and TV also have programmes – such as *Watchdog*
Independent agencies	The most important of these is probably the Consumers Association which regularly tests a wide range of products. The results are published in its magazine called *Which?*

2　Produce a leaflet on the forms of consumer protection which are available.

DELIVERING AND PROVIDING CUSTOMER SERVICE

Customer needs can range from very simple and basic needs such as food, drink, clothing, shelter and accommodation (physical needs) to the more complex need for friends and family (social needs). It is very important for operators to satisfy customer needs because this is the key way in which they can achieve:

- improved business performance. However this is measured, it must be the ultimate goal of every organisation. Giving customers what they need will improve trade and create more repeat business, and both profits and sales will increase
- improved customer and staff morale. Businesses which sell quality products in a quality environment invariably do better than their competitors. This is because staff in such businesses know that they are selling quality goods
- improved reputation. A retailer can improve its reputation by continuously providing quality goods and quality services. A business with a good reputation can expect an increase in sales and profits

In order to provide a good and effective customer service, an organisation must have a system which makes it happen, and everyone must take responsibility – whether they are managers, sales staff, warehouse staff, lorry drivers, checkout operators or shelf-fillers. The most valuable asset that any organisation has is the people who work in it, and the most important investment that an organisation can make is therefore to train its staff.

Match the customer need to the service and give examples by filling in the missing section in the table shown. (We have already done some to help you.)

CUSTOMER NEED	EXAMPLES OF CUSTOMER SERVICES, IN PARTICULAR OUTLETS, THAT MEET THE CUSTOMER NEED
Personal service	
Queries answered	
Product information	Information point, leaflets and properly trained staff
Quick service	Sufficient staff and checkout points
Variety of payment methods	
Attractive physical environment	
Access for wheelchairs	Access ramps and wide aisles
Money refunded	
Wide variety of products	
Good-quality products available when needed	
Delivery service	Delivery free within a 10-mile radius
Free replacement of faulty goods	

1 Make a checklist of factors which contribute to providing a good customer service – e.g. a pleasant manner, friendly approach.
2 Visit a range of outlets and, without buying anything, rate the staff on a 5-point scale, e.g.: 'Manner: excellent . . . good . . . satisfactory . . . fair . . . poor.

Communication

There are two methods of verbal or spoken communication:

1 *Face-to-face communication* where people are in direct contact and literally facing each other. This is personal, one-to-one

communication. Two examples are: a customer asks a shelf-filler 'Where is the cinnamon? . . . It's a spice'; a sales assistant asks a customer 'What size shoes do you wear?'

2 *Telephone communication*: e.g. a customer placing an order with a mail-order company.

A customer comes into a music store and asks you 'Have you got anything for my niece who is 13 on Monday?' Prepare a list of questions you could ask to find out what the customer wants. If the customer replies 'I do not know', what would you recommend?

Good communication is an essential part of customer service. Here is a 14-point plan for good verbal communication with customers:

1 Make the customers feel welcome.
2 Make the customers feel important.
3 Find out what the customer wants. Ask positive questions: e.g. 'How can I help you?' is better than 'Can I help you?' (with this last question, people can say 'No!')
4 Make positive statements – e.g. 'This coat is much better because it is waterproof and windproof' or 'Yes, the leather jacket is on sale at £44.99. We have reduced it by £45' (this is better than 'It was on sale at £89.99' because many people cannot subtract).
5 Dress smartly and look good: first impressions count, and appearance is very important. Do this even if it is a telephone enquiry: it will make your voice sound more attractive.
6 Be interested in what the customer wants, and be helpful.
7 Create a positive image. In particular, use positive **body language**, which is how people communicate without the use of words – here are some examples:
    - Using the eyes: do you look people in the eye when you talk to them? This is usually taken as a sign of honesty and openness. Or do your eyes shift around? This is usually a sign that someone is telling lies or has not done something which they should have done: e.g. 'Yes, I have nearly finished my assignment for element 2.1!' or 'Yes, the order will be with you in 24 hours!'
    - Using the face: always try to greet customers with a smile. It's a good way of exercising the facial muscles! And it is much better than looking sad or bored. What emotions or feelings do *you* show?
    - Using your head, hands and body: do you nod your head to agree?
8 Try to solve the customer's problems – offer alternative options, suggest it can be ordered and delivered etc. If you cannot solve a problem yourself, ask a colleague; this could be your line manager (for example, if you work in the bakery section of a large supermarket, this is likely to be the bakery manager) or someone on the same level as yourself.

9 Try to be flexible. Suggest other products they could buy, remembering that your job is to sell – e.g. 'Is there anything else?', 'Would you like the special waterproof polish which is recommended by the manufacturer?' (do sales staff in your shoe shop always say this when you buy new shoes?).

10 Be polite: try not to leave the customer waiting, and if you cannot serve them immediately, show them that you know they are there. You can do this by using body language – e.g. raising your finger, nodding your head or smiling.

11 Use appropriate language. For some people this could be very technical, whilst for others it could be very simple – e.g. 'This jacket is waterproof and breathable' or 'This jacket has an outer layer of proofed 100% nylon Pertex TX10i with an inner layer of hydrophilic coated PU. Fully taped Permatex.'

12 Use an appropriate tone of voice. This can mean varying the volume, speed, quality and pitch (high or low). Do you sound business-like, persuasive, soothing, honest? Try out these different approaches on your friends.

13 Be a good listener, and identify what the customer needs.

14 Be completely familiar with the product or service you are providing. For example, if you sell Portmeirion china, what designs and patterns do they have? Or if you are selling charity Christmas cards, you must know which charities you are supporting – e.g. is it the RSPCC, the RSPCA, or Oxfam?

What skills are needed to provide service to different types of customer? Complete this table.

TYPES OF CUSTOMER	CHARACTERISTICS	WHAT CUSTOMERS WILL EXPECT	SKILLS NEEDED
Trade	These are customers from other businesses who will usually have an account	Special prices for buying either in bulk or regularly. Also, credit facilities	
General public	Individuals and households	Products readily available at the right price and quality. Good service	
Familiar	These can be either trade or general public. They will be known to the salesperson. They are loyal customers	Continued good service. A friendly greeting	
Unfamiliar	These are customers unknown to the sales people. New customers are vital to the continuing success of a business. Sales staff should exceed customer expectations «so that new customers become familiar customers. This is called repeat business	Clear, correct information, and a positive response to queries. Personal attention. To be made to feel welcome	
Satisfied	These could be familiar or unfamiliar customers		
Dissatisfied	The dissatisfaction could be caused either by poor service or by poor-quality goods	Goods exchanged or money refunded. Complaint investigated	

Does the service provided meet legal requirements?

There are many laws, rules and regulations about the types of product that can be sold and the way service can be provided, and every distribution outlet will be affected in some way. You cannot be expected to know all the legal requirements. However, you must be familiar with health and safety legislation.

Invite the person responsible for Health and Safety in a large store to visit your centre. Find out what the store manager, security guard, sales assistants and customers have to do in the event of a fire.

You will find it helpful to know about the Trade Descriptions Acts 1968 and 1972, the Sale of Goods Act 1979 and the Sale and Supply of Goods Act 1994 because these set out what you can or cannot say to customers (see page 136). Always take care, and again do not claim something which the product cannot do. For example, if a stain remover claims to remove all traces of curry and spaghetti sauce off clothes, it must be able to do this or the customer will have a genuine cause for complaining. If the claims are untrue, this could lead to legal problems later.

What special regulations you will need to know about will depend upon the type of product which is sold and the method of selling which is used, and these regulations are all part of the product knowledge you will need to provide an efficient service. Here are some examples which you will find helpful (you will probably know of others):

Figure 5.5 Warning labels to be found on furniture

- Tobacco products cannot be sold to under 16-year-olds. Retailers can be taken to court if they do. If you sell tobacco products and are suspicious of a person's age, do not sell
- You cannot sell alcoholic drinks if you are under 18 (take care, therefore, if you are working on the checkout in a food outlet)
- If you work on a pharmacy counter selling medicines, you will need permission from your pharmacist to sell certain products. You will also need to ask the customer questions and advise them on certain points, such as 'Have you used this product before? It can cause drowsiness'
- If you sell food, you will need a hygiene certificate, and do not say that you have one if you haven't: you could be dismissed from your job for making false claims (telling lies). Most large stores are willing to train you for the hygiene certificate when you start working for them
- If you sell furniture which is likely to catch fire, e.g. from matches or cigarettes, make sure that the labels shown in Figure 5.5 are on the swing tickets (the card tickets attached to the product with plastic tags)

Figure 5.6 The BSI Kite mark

Figure 5.7 The BSI Safety mark

- If you work in an outlet selling mother and baby products, look for the BSI (British Standards Institute) Kite mark (see Figure 5.6): it means that the products – e.g. pushchairs, prams or carry cots – have been properly made and tested
- If you work in the lighting department of a retail or wholesale outlet, look for the BSI Safety Mark (see Figure 5.7): this is the safety symbol of the British Standards Institute
- If you sell electrical or gas appliances, look for the BEAB (British Electrotechnical Approvals Board) symbol or the British Gas Seal Of Approval, both (see Figure 5.8): mean that the appliances have been properly tested and meet set standards
- If you sell toys, beware that there are European Union regulations on toy safety which must be followed. If you are a consumer and think a toy is unsafe – e.g. a teddy bear has eyes which can be torn off and swallowed – contact the Trading Standards Officer at the local council (these are the people who will investigate you if you sell unsafe teddy bears). This regulation exists to protect both the consumer and honest and reputable traders
- Do not put 'Reduced price' labels on goods which have not previously been sold at the higher price shown on such labels

Figure 5.8 The BEAB symbol and the British Gas Seal of Approval

Self-test questions: Chapter 5

1 What are the customer services provided by different types of retail and wholesale outlet?
2 Describe four methods for monitoring customer satisfaction.
3 List three ways in which the law is used to protect consumers.
4 Describe two ways of informing consumers about the consumer protection that is available.
5 Give 10 features of good communication.
6 Make a list of customer needs. What customer services could be provided to meet these needs?
7 Why is it important to meet customer needs?
8 What criteria could you use to evaluate the quality of customer service?
9 Describe different types of customer.
10 Give three examples of legal requirements which have to be met when selling products.

Service with a smile

To achieve Elements 2.1 and 2.2, you will have to demonstrate that you have provided service to different types of customer. You can do this at a work-experience placement, at a part-time job where you deal with customers, or by dealing with customers at the centre where you study. If you use either your work experience or your job as evidence here, you must get permission from both your tutor and your employer. Alternatively, you could organise an event at your centre. Here are some examples which have proved successful:

- selling charity/centre Christmas cards
- selling T-shirts or mugs printed with the centre name or logo
- running a disco or party
- organising an open evening to show the work you have done for this course – you could invite friends, family, potential new students, employers

You must provide service to at least one dissatisfied and three satisfied customers.

Use the activities you have already completed for this chapter to produce a set of notes describing:

1 Customer needs and how these are provided for by a specific named warehouse, wholesaler and retailer.
2 The importance of meeting customer needs.
3 The customer services provided by three specific named distribution outlets.
4 How the customer services cater for different types of customer e.g. access for the disabled.
5 The methods which are used by these outlets to monitor customer satisfaction.
6 How these outlets inform their customers about the legal protection that is available to them (collect leaflets and notices and include these in your final report).

Investigating customer views

In this chapter, we will:

- compare the buying habits of customers
- describe methods for obtaining the views of customers
- look at the quality of survey data
- look at ways of improving customer service

We will cover Element 2.3, Performance Criteria 1, 2, 3, 4, 5.

THE BUYING HABITS OF CUSTOMERS

In this section we will look at why customers buy particular products. We have already described these kinds of goods – shown in Figure 6.1 – in Chapter 1. Here is a quick reminder of what they are:

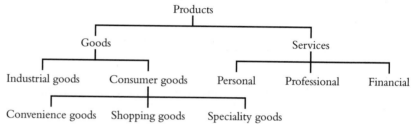

Figure 6.1 Types of product

- **convenience goods**: these are goods which are bought frequently, with the minimum of time and effort – e.g. the majority of groceries
- **shopping goods**: these are goods which are only bought after the consumer has compared a range of alternative options on the basis of price, quality, value for money etc. – e.g. electrical goods
- **speciality goods**: these are goods which the consumer will make a special effort to find and buy – e.g. a Rolex watch

(See Chapter 9 for a fuller discussion.)

activity

1 How frequently do you or your family buy: bread, milk, apples, potatoes, washing powder, toothpaste, flowers, CDs, dining-room furniture, CD players, sweets, floppy discs, magazines, shoes, shirts or blouses?
2 Put each good into the appropriate category – i.e. convenience, speciality etc.
3 How much do you or your family spend on each, e.g. daily, weekly, monthly? You could present the results as a simple chart as shown opposite.
4 Over the next 8 weeks, keep a record of which goods you buy in each category.

PRODUCT	FREQUENCY OF BUYING	AMOUNT SPENT — I.E. LEVEL OF BUYING	CATEGORY

Look at Table 6.1 which shows household expenditure, or how much people spent on goods and services in 1992. (The table is taken from *Regional Trends* 1994.)

Table 6.1 Household expenditure by commodity and service, 1992

	HOUSING	FUEL, LIGHT AND POWER	FOOD	ALCOHOL AND TOBACCO	CLOTHING AND FOOTWEAR	HOUSEHOLD GOODS AND SERVICES	MOTORING AND FARES	LEISURE GOODS AND SERVICES	MISCELLANEOUS AND PERSONAL GOODS AND SERVICES	AVERAGE HOUSEHOLD EXPENDITURE	AVERAGE EXPENDITURE PER PERSON
£ per week											
United Kingdom	47.4	13.0	47.7	16.4	16.4	35.3	42.9	40.9	11.9	271.8	111.0
North	33.0	13.1	44.7	19.7	15.9	30.5	37.4	30.6	10.6	235.5	95.1
Yorkshire & Humberside	40.9	13.0	44.9	18.0	16.0	27.6	32.7	36.8	11.3	241.2	100.8
East Midlands	47.2	13.2	46.1	16.4	17.3	36.3	45.6	37.7	13.0	272.8	107.5
East Anglia	46.7	12.4	49.8	15.1	16.3	44.4	44.6	35.7	12.6	277.4	112.0
South East	61.1	13.0	51.6	15.6	16.7	40.8	53.2	54.5	13.7	320.1	133.0
Greater London	59.7	12.4	51.2	15.7	17.7	37.6	44.3	44.1	13.8	296.4	130.2
Rest of South East	62.0	13.5	51.8	15.6	16.1	42.7	58.6	60.8	13.6	334.4	134.6
South West	51.6	12.2	46.1	15.1	13.9	37.2	40.6	42.7	11.2	270.4	114.1
West Midlands	41.2	12.8	45.4	15.3	15.0	28.5	39.0	28.7	10.7	236.6	94.4
North West	40.8	13.2	45.6	17.3	17.2	32.7	37.9	37.0	11.4	253.1	100.4
England	49.3	13.0	47.8	16.4	16.2	35.6	44.1	42.4	12.2	276.9	113.2
Wales	42.3	14.1	46.4	15.5	16.3	36.7	36.4	33.1	10.5	251.2	101.6
Scotland	35.9	12.9	45.9	18.2	17.2	30.9	32.7	33.7	10.4	237.7	98.3
Northern Ireland	27.1	15.2	50.2	16.5	20.5	34.4	44.2	25.9	10.6	244.6	88.9

1 Draw a pie chart or bar chart for your own region (Wales and Northern Ireland have already been done for you – see Figure 6.2 – so if you live in one of these regions, you will have to choose another region). What comments can you make? For example, which are the largest and smallest items, and can you say why? In Wales, for example, the average household spends £42.30 each week on housing, £46.40 on food etc. Compare these figures with those for yourself or your family.

2 What are the highlights or main features of the table? For example, which region spends the most on food, leisure goods, alcohol and tobacco, etc.? Which region spends the least?

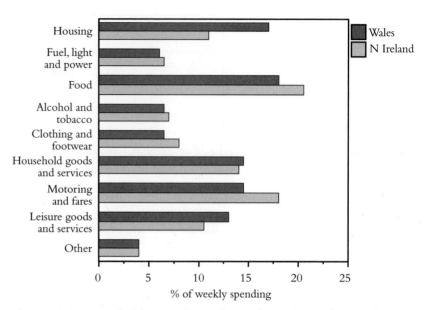

Figure 6.2 Household expenditure for Wales and Northern Ireland, 1992

CHARACTERISTICS OF CUSTOMERS

Age   Retailers pay considerable attention to the age of their customers because age is linked to income and lifestyle, and these affect what and how much people will buy. For example, primary-school children tend to buy impulse/convenience goods such as sweets, ice cream, lollipops, comics and football stickers, and retailers will therefore place and promote these goods on the lowest shelves in the shop. Although adults take little time to buy convenience goods, children are exactly the opposite and will spend considerable time comparing the merits of each product in terms of size, price, packaging (can this be used for something else?), whether there is a free gift or special offer, how long the product will last etc. Recently, Tesco took impulse/convenience goods such as sweets and chewing gum away from checkout points because parents had been complaining. J Sainsbury, on its part, now has an in-store kiosk, and in some cases a whole section devoted to cards, magazines, videos, books etc. (What do you think will happen to the small retailers which currently make a living from selling these goods? How often have you bought such items when you initially only intended to shop for your groceries?)

activity   To get an idea of how marketing people classify consumers by age, using a table like the one shown below put in what level of income you think these groups have and what products they might typically buy.

AGE GROUP	LEVEL OF INCOME – E.G. LOW, MIDDLE, HIGH	TYPICAL PURCHASES
Children up to 10		
Youths up to 19		
Young adults living on their own		
Young adults with small children		
Young adults with no children		
Middle-aged adults with children still at home		
Middle-aged adults with children moved away		
Retired		

House of Fraser customers cover a broad cross-section of the population but particularly high-income groups, women and people over 35. In the future, the population of the UK is expected to get older. What effect do you think this will have on House of Fraser sales?

Gender The gender of a person – i.e. whether they are male or female – influences both the types of goods and services which are bought by households and the level and frequency of buying. Even though there are an increasing number of one-person households, most large purchases are made by two or more people. There are obvious differences, for example:

- between women's and men's clothes shops. (How many of each are there in your local shopping centre? Compare your figures with those for The Glades and its French equivalent – see page 101)
- between goods which are made exclusively either for men or for women. However, this difference is disappearing with the increasing trend towards 'unisex' styles
- between the role of women and men in different families. (Who makes the decisions in your home?)

Within your group, what are the differences between the buying habits of the girls and boys?

1 Find out how much each group spends on average every month on clothes, entertainment, food and drink, toiletries, sport. You can add

other categories if you want to. Do girls and boys spend different amounts, or do they spend the same? Can you say why? Do parents and grandparents have the same pattern of spending?

2 Find out how often each group goes to shop or goes 'window shopping' (looking at the goods in the shops without actually buying them). Again, are there differences between the boys and girls? Can you say why?

3 Who do you go shopping with? For example, do you go shopping with boys, girls, boys *and* girls, on your own, or with your family, and which do you prefer? When do you spend most money?

Case study: supermarkets and customer loyalty

Here are the key findings from a survey done by Taylor Nelson AGB and reported in *The Grocer*, February, 1994:

- Every shop wants to keep its customers. The definition of a loyal customer is someone who spends 70% or more of their grocery budget (groceries are foods and household supplies such as washing powder) at one particular supermarket.

J Sainsbury came out top here, with 38% of its customers classed as loyal, with Morrisons, Tesco, Asda and Safeway (25%) in second, third, fourth and fifth positions respectively.

- However, the survey also discovered that, on average, 30% of a supermarket's customers also use another supermarket. For example, 39% of J Sainsbury's customers also use Tesco

Find out about and write notes on the following:

1 Do people you know use more than one supermarket to do their grocery shopping? Do you or your family use more than one supermarket, or are you loyal to one?

2 Which supermarkets are used by the people in your group?

3 How often do people go to the supermarket for groceries? 32% of Kwik Save customers go at least once a week. What image do you have both on Kwik Save and of other supermarkets?

4 How much do people spend on average each week on groceries (beware: they might not tell you!)? The Taylor Nelson survey above reported that J Sainsbury's customers spent the most.

5 Look at page 185. What effect do you think loyalty cards will have on the level and frequency of buying? In January 1996 Asda were accepting everyone's loyalty cards. Does your family have one?

(You can include cards given out by retailers such as BHS and C&A which give you a discount when you have bought over a certain amount.)

Ethnic grouping and culture

Have you ever been to a Chinese, Indian, Italian, Greek, Polish, French or English restaurant? All of these have their own particular style of cooking and eating. Chinese food is stir-fried quickly at high temperatures, and with Indian food, curry can be hot and spicy whilst kormas are creamy and delicately spiced. Italians eat varieties of pasta with fresh meat, tomatoes and aubergines. Language, religion, ethnic group and culture all affect what people eat and drink, and they can also affect the clothes people buy and the furniture they use. In many towns and cities, there are social clubs, TV and radio channels (which carry advertising directed specifically at the relevant ethnic group), banks, cinemas and shops which cater for the needs for people from a wide range of ethnic backgrounds. If you live in a large city such as Birmingham or London, you will find communities where the majority of people are Chinese, Greek, Italian, Caribbean or Indian. There will be retailers and wholesalers specialising and providing for the needs of all these groups.

Make a chart which shows any special events or festivals which these different ethnic groups have. For example, Chinese people also celebrate the New Year, but when do they do this? (Hint: take care – it's not on 31 December!)

Social class

Many businesses use what is known as the **A to E system** – see Table 6.2 – for classifying or grouping those consumers who use their goods or services. Have you or your family ever filled in a questionnaire which asked for your income, occupation, what newspaper you read regularly and what TV programmes you watch? The answers to these questions (which you do not have to reply to because most questionnaires are voluntary) will help the questioner to find out the social class to which you belong. Members of a particular social class tend to behave in similar ways and to buy similar products.

Table 6.2 The A to E system of social classification

SOCIAL GROUP	SOCIAL CLASS
A	Upper middle
B	Middle
C1	Lower middle class
C2	Skilled working class
D	Working class
E	Student

Here are how the questions appear on a questionnaire:

What is your occupation?

Professional		Manager	
Middle manager		Student	
Skilled manual worker		Retired	
Manual worker		Unemployed	
Office worker		Self-employed	

Can you link the above occupations with the A to E scale?

Which newspaper do you usually read?

The Guardian		Daily Mail	
The Times		Daily Mirror	
Daily Telegraph		Daily Express	
Independent		The Sun	
Financial Times		The Star	
None of the above			

1 Can you link these newspapers with the A to E scale?
2 If you want to confuse the questioner, you should tick both *The Sun* and *The Times* (newspapers). Why would this cause confusion?

Case study: Centre Court Shopping Centre, Wimbledon

Here is the profile (main features) of visitors to the Centre Court Shopping Centre in Wimbledon

- 78% of people came from the ABC1 group
- 76% had children under 16
- 60% used the Centre Court at least once a week
- 48% of people were shopping for fashion

- 70% were employed
- 79% came from a 3-mile radius (there are 390,000 people within a 15-minute drive of the centre)
- 35% came by car, 33% on foot, 30% by public transport

(Source: Centre Court Shopping Centre, Wimbledon)

1 What is the meaning of the term 'ABC1 group'? Who is included in it? Why is it considered important?
2 What can you say about the age of the visitors to the Centre?
3 What shops would you expect to find in Centre Court?
4 The majority of people came either on foot or by public transport. What does this tell you about car-parking facilities in the area? How much could these people carry home?

Geography   The town, region and country in which people live will all affect what people buy, their level of buying and their frequency of buying.

Table 6.3   The consumption of biscuits, tea, coffee and ice cream over one year in European countries

	BISCUITS – KG PER HEAD	TEA – KG PER HEAD	COFFEE – KG PER HEAD	ICE CREAM – LTR PER HEAD
France	7.0	0.1	3.1	6.0
Germany	3.3	0.4	4.6	5.5
Italy	9.8	0.2	3.0	–
UK	11.3	2.0	0.9	6.6
Belgium	8.1	0.2	6.3	6.8
Luxembourg	8.6	0.3	6.1	7.1
Netherlands	21.0	0.6	5.7	7.5
Denmark	9.9	–	6.6	9.7
Finland	3.3	0.2	10.3	11.3
Norway	1.8	0.2	8.6	12.1
Sweden	5.8	0.3	8.8	13.6
Portugal	3.4	–	2.9	–
Spain	3.8	–	1.7	5.2
Austria	1.2	0.2	8.7	7.7
Greece	5.0	–	3.2	3.9
Ireland	14.3	3.4	1.7	–

Table 6.3 (source: Euromonitor) shows the consumption of biscuits, tea and coffee as kilogrammes per (for each) person over a year in 16 European countries. For example, on average, each person in France eats 7 kilogrammes of biscuits in one year. Not everyone eats biscuits, so some people must be eating a lot more than this amount! The consumption of ice cream is shown as litres per person.

1 Draw charts (bar charts and pictograms work well) showing the figures.
2 What conclusions can you make? Give reasons for your answers. Do you consume more or less than other Europeans?

Lifestyle   A person's lifestyle refers to the way they live, what they eat, how they dress, the furniture they buy etc. The dictionary defines 'lifestyle' as the particular habits, tastes, attitudes and behaviour of an individual or group. Lifestyles are different in different countries, but they also vary between different areas of the UK. (What image do you have of someone from up north or down south?) Although many of the images we have of individuals or groups are **stereotypes**, they are used by businesses to advertise and sell their products – e.g. 'If the food is so good up north, why do northerners move south?' Lifestyles can even vary within the same town, and again can affect what people buy, how people buy, where and when people buy. (Do people in different parts of your area have different lifestyles? How do they differ?)

This table shows some of the changes that are taking place in lifestyles – i.e. lifestyle **trends**. Draw up a similar table and in each case, enter information both on how the change could affect people's buying habits and on how retailers might react.

CHANGE IN LIFESTYLE	EFFECT ON BUYING HABITS	HOW RETAILERS MIGHT REACT
Fall in birth rates		
Rise in one-person households when young people, divorced and separated people set up their own homes		
Greater concern for the environment	People want more environment-friendly products	
Rise in car ownership		
More women working		
Greater concern for fitness and health		
Greater concern for a healthy diet		
More people own freezers		
People want to use energy (gas, electricity, petrol) more efficiently		

activity   The size of the average household as measured by the number of adults in the family is falling (reported in *The European* of 14–20 October 1994). Table 6.4 gives some figures for a number of European countries. This trend has been caused by falling birth rates and more divorces (1 in 3 first marriages in the UK now end in divorce). The result is smaller families which use microwaves and convenience food.

COUNTRY	% OF ONE-PERSON HOUSEHOLDS, 1994 (AND 1981)
Sweden	40% (29%)
Germany	35% (30%)
Denmark	34% (31%)
UK	25% (22%)
Ireland	21% (17%)
Spain	10% (0.3%)

1 Give examples of other purchases which could be affected by this trend.

2 Give examples of how manufacturers/retailers could respond.

METHODS OF OBTAINING CUSTOMER VIEWS

The following are the main methods of obtaining customers' views on the quality of services provided by retail outlets:

- questionnaires
- personal interviews
- telephone interviews
- sample surveys

Questionnaires

The purpose of questionnaire interviews is to obtain *information* from people. Questionnaires can be used by any type of organisation. In the distribution sector, they can be used by:

- wholesalers, to find out what products retailers want them to stock
- transport companies, to find out what customers think about the reliability of delivery services
- retailers, to find out what customers think about the quality and range of customer services they provide

A **questionnaire** is a list of written questions arranged in a way which obtains the most information from the people who are questioned. The **interviewer** is the person who asks the questions. The **respondent** or **interviewee** is the person who answers the questions.

TYPES OF QUESTION

Although there are an unlimited number of questions which can be asked, they can be grouped or classified into two types of question:

1 **Closed questions.** These can be:
   - **Simple questions**: these are questions which have only two possible answers, such as 'yes' or 'no', 'male' or 'female' – e.g. 'Do you shop in the local high street?' 'Were you given this product as a present?'
   - **Multiple-choice questions**: here, the respondent has to choose one answer from a short list of possible answers. These are the

kinds of question which will be asked in the External Tests for the Intermediate GNVQ in Retail and Distributive Services. For example:

> 'Which factor most influenced your decision to buy the product?
>
> > Family/friends suggested it _
> > I saw it demonstrated _
> > It was good value for money _
> > I saw it advertised _'

- **Scaled questions**: with these questions, the respondent is asked to rate or rank their answers. For example:

> 'Please give your views on our goods and service:

	Excellent	Good	Fair	Poor
Value for money				
Variety of goods				
Speed of service				
Quality of display				

2 **Open-ended questions.** These are questions which the respondent can answer in any way they wish. They are very good for obtaining *qualitative* information – e.g. people's opinions. However, they are very difficult to *summarise* because with 100 people you could get 100 different answers. For example:

> 'Do you like shopping in your local high street? Give your reasons here:
>
> ....
> .... ,

HOW TO WRITE A GOOD QUESTIONNAIRE

Here are 10 rules for creating a good questionnaire:

1 Questions must be kept short.
2 Questions must be simple, with no long words which people do not understand. For example:

> 'What type of food shop do you use?
> Convenience store .... Chain store ....
> Multiple store .... Other ....

is not a good question because most respondents will not know what each type of store is (see page 171).

3 Always start by saying 'please' and end with a 'thank you': remember, people have used their time to answer your questions.
4 Try not to ask rude or personal questions which could annoy or offend people.

5 Make the questions easy to answer, for example by having boxes which people can tick.

6 Allow plenty of room for the respondent to write their answers: not everyone has small writing.

7 When you ask a question, always leave room for an answer which is different from the one you expected. For example, if the respondent says 'None of them', you can allow for this by putting 'Other (please give details)' as an option. For example:

'Where was the product purchased?
Argos .... Dixons .... Boots .... Mail order ....
Other (please give details ....)'

8 Make the questions easy to see and read: not everyone has perfect eyesight!

9 Always put in some questions which will allow you to *categorise* the person answering the questionnaire. For example:

'What age group would you put yourself in
15–25 .... 26–35 .... 36–45 .... '
What area do you live in?

These will allow you to summarise the data (from 7 above) with statements such as '80% of the 36–45-year-old age group bought the product in Argos' or 'Most 15–25-year-olds bought the product in Dixons.'

10 Make sure the questions are legal and do not harass people. For example, questions about ethnicity should be written:

Which ethnic group do you consider you belong to?

Figures 6.3 and 6.4 show two examples of questionnaires, the first produced by Consumerlink on behalf of Tefal U.K. and the second used by Eurostar.

1 What type of questions are used?
2 Why have they been used?
3 What do you think of the layout and style of the questions?

POSTAL OR WRITTEN QUESTIONNAIRES

The key feature of any **postal** or **written questionnaire** is of course that written answers must be given and the questionnaire returned to the person or organisation which distributed it. These forms of questionnaire cover everything from simple one-page questionnaires which can be distributed and completed in-store (MFI do this) to complex surveys which require considerable time and effort from the respondent (the person completing the questionnaire).

Advantages of postal questionnaires
● Every area can be covered
● They are reasonably cheap to send out

B **Please tell us about your purchase :** Tefal are keen to listen to their customers to learn about their changing needs. Your answers - and those of other customers - will be a great help to them.

3 **Did you receive this product as a gift?**

1 ☐ Yes   2 ☐ No

4 **Price paid (to nearest £) if known**

£|_|_|_| : 00

5 **Where was this product purchased? (Tick only ONE)**

1 ☐ Don't know, received as a gift   8 ☐ Co-op
2 ☐ Currys   9 ☐ Woolworths
3 ☐ Rumbelows   10 ☐ Other electrical retailer
4 ☐ Argos   11 ☐ Department store
5 ☐ Comet   12 ☐ Superstore/Supermarket
6 ☐ Electricity Board   13 ☐ Mail order
7 ☐ Boots   14 ☐ Other

6 **Where did you FIRST learn of this Tefal product? (Tick only ONE)**

1 ☐ Received as a gift   7 ☐ From a friend/relative
2 ☐ Television advertisement   8 ☐ From a salesperson
3 ☐ Radio advertisement   9 ☐ Store demonstration
4 ☐ Newspaper advertisement   10 ☐ On shelf in store
5 ☐ Magazine advertisement   11 ☐ Other
6 ☐ Magazine article

7 **What are the THREE most important factors influencing your choice of this Tefal product? (Tick only THREE)**

1 ☐ Did not choose   10 ☐ Durability
2 ☐ Tefal reputation   11 ☐ Safety features
3 ☐ Colour   12 ☐ Easy to use
4 ☐ Style/appearance   13 ☐ Special offer
5 ☐ Previous experience of Tefal products 14 ☐ Friend/relative recommendation
6 ☐ Value for money   15 ☐ Salesperson
7 ☐ Product packaging   16 ☐ "Which?" report
8 ☐ Special features of product   17 ☐ Other
9 ☐ Quality

8 **Is this product . . . (Tick only ONE)**

1 ☐ . . . a replacement for an old model?
2 ☐ . . . an additional purchase to one you already use?
3 ☐ . . . the first purchase of this type of product?

9 **What was the brand name of the model you are replacing? (Tick only ONE)**

1 ☐ Not replacing   8 ☐ Kenwood
2 ☐ Braun   9 ☐ Sunbeam
3 ☐ Rowenta   10 ☐ Moulinex
4 ☐ Morphy Richards   11 ☐ Tefal
5 ☐ Swan   12 ☐ Philips
6 ☐ Russell Hobbs   13 ☐ Other
7 ☐ Hoover

10 **Which ITV channel do you watch most often? (Tick only ONE)**

1 ☐ Thames/London Weekend   8 ☐ Anglia
2 ☐ Central   9 ☐ Grampian
3 ☐ Granada   10 ☐ TSW
4 ☐ Yorkshire   11 ☐ Border
5 ☐ HTV   12 ☐ Scottish
6 ☐ TV South   13 ☐ Channel
7 ☐ Tyne Tees   14 ☐ Ulster

C **Please tell us about yourself:** Tefal would also like to know more about you as a person - it helps when designing new products and planning advertising. Knowing more about you also helps Consumerlink and other responsible organisations to ensure that, if you choose to receive information, it will interest you.

11 **Which of the following are you likely to buy in the next twelve months?**

1 ☐ Large screen TV   10 ☐ Vacuum cleaner
2 ☐ Satellite receiver   11 ☐ Freestanding cooker (GAS)
3 ☐ Video   12 ☐ Freestanding cooker (Electric)
4 ☐ Camcorder   13 ☐ Built-in oven/hob
5 ☐ Midi/Hifi   14 ☐ Fridge/freezer
6 ☐ Hifi separates   15 ☐ Personal computer
7 ☐ Dishwasher   16 ☐ SLR camera
8 ☐ Washing machine   17 ☐ Electric shower
9 ☐ Tumble dryer   18 ☐ None of these

12 **Which of the following newspapers do you read REGULARLY?**

1 ☐ The Sun   7 ☐ Independent
2 ☐ The Star   8 ☐ The Guardian
3 ☐ Daily Mirror   9 ☐ Daily Telegraph
4 ☐ Daily Mail   10 ☐ The Times
5 ☐ Daily Express   11 ☐ Daily Record
6 ☐ Today   12 ☐ None of these

13 **Is the person whose name appears above?**

1 ☐ Male?   or   2 ☐ Female?

14 **Your date of birth:**

|_|_| |1|9|_|_|
Month   Year

15 **Partner's date of birth:**

|_|_| |1|9|_|_|
Month   Year

16 **Marital status:**

1 ☐ Married   3 ☐ Divorced/Separated
2 ☐ Widowed   4 ☐ Single/never married

17 **Occupation:**

	You	Partner
Professional/senior management	1 ☐	1 ☐
Manager in business	2 ☐	2 ☐
Administrator/clerical	3 ☐	3 ☐
Manual	4 ☐	4 ☐
Housewife	5 ☐	5 ☐
Student	6 ☐	6 ☐
Retired	7 ☐	7 ☐
Other	8 ☐	8 ☐
Self-employed/business owner	9 ☐	9 ☐

18 **Please indicate the ages of ALL children living at home:**

☐ None
☐ Under 1   ☐ 5 yrs   ☐ 10 yrs   ☐ 15 yrs
☐ 1 yr   ☐ 6 yrs   ☐ 11 yrs   ☐ 16 yrs
☐ 2 yrs   ☐ 7 yrs   ☐ 12 yrs   ☐ 17 yrs
☐ 3 yrs   ☐ 8 yrs   ☐ 13 yrs   ☐ 18 yrs
☐ 4 yrs   ☐ 9 yrs   ☐ 14 yrs   ☐ 19 & over

068440 2122203 01.188.10.3925735 - INDEX 01/l3R

Figure 6.3 An extract from Consumerlink's questionnaire for Tefal

- Because people can complete the questionnaire in their own time, it can be very long and detailed
- When people do not have to give their own names, they are usually more honest

Disadvantages of postal questionnaires

- Most people throw questionnaires into the bin, so that very few are returned
- Respondents cannot ask questions
- People may need an incentive before they reply – e.g. 'If you reply within 10 days, your name will be entered into a great free competition' (does anyone ever win these!)

Q2	What is the **main** purpose of your trip....?	(13)
	Business meeting	1
	Commuting to/from regular place of work	2
	Attending a sporting/other special event	3
	Travelling to/from holiday, short-break	4
	Visiting friends, relatives or a second home	5
	Other reason	6

Q3	What were your main reasons for choosing EUROSTAR for this trip? (maximum of 3 reasons)	(14)
	The times of the trains were convenient	1
	The stations were conveniently located	2
	Price	3
	The quality of the on-board service	4
	To guarantee arriving on time	5
	To sample EUROSTAR	6
	To be able to work during the journey	7
	To be able to relax during the journey	8
	I don't like flying	9
	I don't like ferries	0

C3   The service on board (excluding the catering service)

	not at all satisfied ... your score ... completely satisfied	(211-217) no opinion
The staff are welcoming and efficient	1 2 3 4 5 6 7 8 9 10	☐
The train manager is accessible if needed	1 2 3 4 5 6 7 8 9 10	☐
The immigration officials are polite	1 2 3 4 5 6 7 8 9 10	☐
I can get information and communicate with staff *in my preferred language*	1 2 3 4 5 6 7 8 9 10	☐
The announcements are clear and easy to understand	1 2 3 4 5 6 7 8 9 10	☐
The announcements are sufficiently informative	1 2 3 4 5 6 7 8 9 10	☐
Overall, how satisfied are you with the service on board (excluding the catering service)?	1 2 3 4 5 6 7 8 9 10	☐

Do you have any other comments about the service on board (excluding the catering service)?

(skip 218-222)

Figure 6.4 Extracts from Eurostar's questionnaire

Personal interviews   A **personal interview** is one in which the interviewer will interview or question the interviewee *face-to-face*. There are two types of personal interview:

1 **Structured interviews**: when the interviewer will follow a set plan and only ask those questions which have been worked out before the interview.

2 **Unstructured interviews**: when the interviewer will decide on the questions *during* the interview. This is a very difficult and skilled job.

Most people will use structured interviews, particularly when the interview is being carried out in a street or shopping centre.

Advantages of personal interviews

- Both structured and unstructured interviews can be held
- Interviewees can ask the interviewer if they do not understand a question
- There is a good rate of response because many people feel important when they are being interviewed
- The interviewer can see and hear the body language and can therefore change their approach to the person accordingly

Disadvantages of personal interviews

- Interviewers need to be trained, which can be very expensive
- People need to be chosen carefully, otherwise the survey may not give a true picture of the topic being investigated
- Complex or difficult interviews can take a long time
- Some people always say 'no' (what do you do in this case?)

Telephone interviews

Businesses are increasingly carrying out interviews on the telephone. For example, computer companies ring their customers to find out about the quality of the service they have received.

Advantages of telephone interviews

- They are quick and easy to carry out
- Every part of the country can be covered
- People can speak directly to an employee of the business
- There is a reasonable rate of response (this concerns the number of people who are willing to answer questions)
- The interviewers can all be in one place

Disadvantages of telephone interviews

- People may be out or not answering the phone
- The interviewer cannot see the person and so cannot see the respondent's body language
- They may be expensive
- Not everyone has a phone, so some people will never be surveyed

activity

Write notes describing all the above methods of obtaining customer views.

Sample surveys

A **sample** is a small part of the population which has been specially selected so as to be representative of the *whole* population. It is the smallest number that can be selected which will still give reliable results (it would be too expensive to survey the whole population). A good **sample survey** will be:

- cheap and easy to carry out
- sufficiently large so that the results which are obtained will mirror or reflect the complete population
- small but accurate and reliable – able to provide the data that is needed
- free from bias. This means that the results of the sample should be a true reflection of the population. For example, a survey designed to find out people's views on the quality of service offered by a particular retailer would be biased if only children were questioned. A range of people should therefore be interviewed to get reliable results.

TYPES OF SAMPLE

- **Simple random sample**: here every person has an equal chance of being selected as part of the survey, although only a small number will actually be chosen
- **Stratified sample**: here the population is divided into **strata** – i.e. levels or layers – according to certain criteria, and males and females, for example, are then chosen from each strata to make up the required number
- **Systematic sample**: here people are chosen systematically. For example, every seventh person is selected

How to obtain information using questionnaires and interviews

A **survey** is a method for gathering statistical data. The following steps show how to carry out a survey:

STEP 1   IDENTIFY THE TOPIC THAT NEEDS TO BE INVESTIGATED

This topic could be a problem that a business is trying to solve – e.g. 'Why are so few teenagers buying our clothes?' Or perhaps someone has an idea that they want to prove or disprove (sometimes called a **proposition**) – e.g. 'I think few teenagers buy our clothes because they are old-fashioned.'

STEP 2   PLAN THE SURVEY

Here are some of the factors that will have to be looked at when planning a survey:

- What questions should be asked? It is always wise to try out or test questions *before* a survey is carried out to make sure they work
- What interview method to use – e.g. personal or telephone

- Where should the survey be carried out? This will depend upon the topic that needs investigating. For example, if it is a survey to obtain customers' views on a particular retail outlet, the best place may be outside the shop in question; and you could ask people who leave why they use the shop
- When should the survey be carried out? For example, if you want to find out the age of people who use a particular shop, you will have to carry out the survey at various times, because if the survey were carried out at 10 am only, you might conclude that the shop is mostly used by the elderly and by people with small children. (What might you conclude if the survey were between 3.30 and 4 pm?)
- If a questionnaire is used, should people fill in the questionnaire themselves or should this be done for them by the interviewer? (What do you think are the advantages and disadvantages of each method?)
- How many people should be questioned?
- How should the people be chosen, and who should be included in the survey?
- When does the survey have to be completed? Surveys are normally carried out to solve problems which are urgent or important, and every survey will have to be completed by a specific deadline
- How much will it cost to carry out the survey? Do we have enough money?
- How can we make sure that the data which is collected is fair and accurate?

When you gather evidence for Element 2.3, you will need to consider all these factors when you carry out a survey of customers' views.

STEP 3   CARRY OUT THE SURVEY

The purpose of a survey is to obtain the data you need to solve the problem you have identified. This data will later be analysed and turned into information. Here is some data:

    25   18   36   09   11   27

If you were told it is the winning numbers in next week's National Lottery, it would become very valuable information!

It is never easy asking people 'Please would you mind spending a few minutes of your time answering a few questions?', particularly when you have to stop people in the street or shopping centre. Here are some suggestions which will improve your chances of getting people to stop (which in itself is a positive response):

- Always try out your questions first on your family, friends or colleagues to make sure they work. This will save trouble later when you have to question people you do not know

- Find out if permission is needed to interview in a particular place. You cannot normally interview inside shops, railway stations or shopping centres
- Carry an official card or letter which says who you are
- Politely tell people the purpose of your survey
- Dress smartly: people do not want to be stopped by scruffy-looking students
- Always be polite: say 'please' and 'thank you'
- Try to stay bright and cheerful, and always smile
- Do not smoke, eat or chew gum, or bring a dog
- Choose a pleasant and convenient place to stop people
- Be patient, and do not take negative responses such as 'Sorry, I haven't got time' personally

STEP 4   ANALYSE THE QUESTIONNAIRES

Once the questionnaires have been returned, they need to be *analysed*.

The replies to each question first need to be totalled. This will be much easier if you have used closed questions (see page 157). For example, the question 'Do you shop in the local high street?' might have produced the result: 27 people said 'Yes' and 3 people said 'No'. This result is better shown in terms of *percentages*. To find one number as a percentage of another, the formula is:

$$\frac{\text{part}}{\text{whole}} \text{ or } \frac{\text{the number replying yes or no}}{\text{the total number of replies}} \times 100 = \frac{27}{30} \times 100 = 90\% \text{ replied yes}$$

The question 'Why do you shop in the local high street?' could produce 30 different answers (because 30 here was the total number of people questioned), which could be very difficult to analyse. It would have been much easier to analyse the replies if the question had been multiple choice. (When the GNVQ External Tests were first introduced, there were some open-ended questions. Now, all the questions are closed questions which can be marked by machine. Machine marking is both quicker and cheaper.) Thus:

> 'Why do you shop in the local high street?
> Good transport facilities: 9 people (or 30%)
> Good parking facilities: 12 people (or 40%)
> Wide range of shops: 6 people (or 20%)
> Good value for money: 3 people (or 10%)'

would be easier to analyse.

When interviewing, it is always better to choose a simpler, rounder number – such as 20 rather than 19. Thirty is an excellent number of people to interview or give questionnaires to because it is said to be a 'large sample', which means that the results which are obtained will generally be more reliable and will therefore give a good indication of how most people would reply.

A CHECKLIST FOR EVALUATING THE QUALITY OF THE SURVEY DATA

1 Is the data complete – i.e. are *all* sections of the population represented?
2 Is the data reliable and accurate? For example, if people were questioned at another time, would the results be different?
3 Have enough people been questioned?
4 Is the survey free from bias – i.e. were people properly selected?
5 Were all the deadlines met?
6 Were the 'right' questions asked, and was the right data obtained to find solutions to the original problem?
7 Would another method have produced more reliable results?

Self-Test Questions:
Chapter 6

1 Describe the main characteristics of consumers.
2 How could a consumer's age affect what they buy?
3 What is the A to E system of social classification?
4 Name four changes in lifestyle. How have they affected buying habits?
5 Give the advantages and disadvantages of two methods of obtaining customer views.
6 What are the features of a good questionnaire?
7 What is sampling?
8 Why might a sample be unrepresentative or biased?
9 What criteria could be used to evaluate the quality of survey data?
10 What customer services are offered by the library at your centre and how could they be improved?

evidence
indicators

THE CUSTOMER IS ALWAYS RIGHT

Here is a rough draft of a questionnaire that could be used to find out what improvements in customer service are needed. It will need to be refined and worked on before it is suitable for use with the general public.

	EXCELLENT	GOOD	FAIR	POOR
Quality of delivery service				
Access for wheelchairs				
Access for pushchairs				
Availability of products				
Variety of products				
Quality of products				
Variety of payment methods				
Concern for the environment				
Friendliness of staff				
Staff knowledge of products				
Quality of in-store facilities				

1 Construct the questionnaire.
2 Test out the questionnaire and carry out the survey on customers with different characteristics – age, gender etc. – which will have to be included as part of the questionnaire. (Note: it is much easier to actually carry out the survey than it is to invent answers which you think will fit!)
3 At least three different retail outlets must be included.
4 Describe what other methods could have been used to obtain customer views.
5 Use a checklist to evaluate the quality of the survey data you have obtained.
6 Using the results of the questionnaire, produce a report which identifies the improvements needed in the customer services offered by three different outlets.

UNIT 2 QUALITY AND SERVICE TO THE CUSTOMER END TEST

When two answers are required
  a = 1 and 2
  b = 2 and 3
  c = 3 and 4
  d = 1 and 4

1 Which of these customer services are most likely to be provided by a small corner shop?
  a customer-care department
  b a range of in-store facilities
  c simple payment methods
  d a baby changing room

2 Which *two* of these services would be most appreciated by customers of a mail order company?
  1 attractive staff uniforms
  2 good restaurant facilities
  3 a variety of payment methods
  4 well-trained staff

3 Which *two* of these in-store facilities are likely to be of most help to young parents?
  1 baby changing facilities
  2 specially designed trolleys
  3 more sweets at checkout points
  4 narrower aisles between shelves

4 Which of these services is most likely to be available to customers of an outdoor market stall?
   a a good physical environment
   b free delivery
   c personal service
   d a wide range of payment methods

5 Which of these methods of monitoring customer satisfaction is likely to give the widest range of opinions?
   a a record of complaints
   b customer questionnaires
   c a record of praise received
   d a record of goods returned

6 Which of the following would break the Trade Descriptions Acts?
   a blocking a fire exit
   b paying females and males different wages
   c displaying expensive goods on shelves
   d giving a false price

7 Which of the following tests goods and publishes the results?
   a Consumers' Association
   b Ombudsman
   c Citizen's Charter
   d guarantee

8 A promise from the seller of goods to the buyer to repair or replace a good if it breaks down within a stated time is called
   a consumerism
   b Ombudsman
   c guarantee
   d Citizen's Charter

9 Which two of these would be the most suitable methods for a local jeweller to communicate the protection that is available to consumers?
   1 advertising on national television
   2 providing in-store leaflets
   3 displaying in-store posters
   4 advertising in the local library

10 Which two of the following would meet customer needs for a comfortable physical environment in an out-of-town superstore?
   1 wider checkout points
   2 more attractive countryside

3 large outdoor stock rooms
4 better heating and ventilation

11 Which is the best method of providing a more personal service in a self-service store?
   a issuing free advice leaflets
   b introducing a continuously staffed advice point
   c installing televisions
   d playing music in the store

12 Customers in an independent store expressed a need for more information about the products. Which two of the following are the best methods of achieving this?
   1 giving out advice leaflets
   2 placing an advertisement on television
   3 using the local radio station
   4 improving the labelling of goods

13 The main reason for a business to meet customer needs is
   a to attract new competitors
   b to improve its reputation
   c to increase its costs
   d to increase administration

14 A customer in a shop asks for information about a product. However, the sales assistant is new and does not know anything. What should the sales assistant do?
   a use body language
   b refer the customer to an appropriate colleague
   c suggest they write for a catalogue
   d suggest that the customer go elsewhere

15 A sales consultant in a mail-order company requires retraining to deal with the public. Which training course should they take?
   a using body language
   b developing non-verbal skills
   c improving telephone technique
   d effective face-to-face skills

16 Customers complain that they do not feel welcome in the store. What are the two most likely reasons for this?
   1 a lack of personal attention
   2 impolite staff
   3 too many products on display

4 there are no other customers about

17 Which would be the most useful way of
    evaluating the quality of a delivery service?
    a counting the number of deliveries made on
       time
    b counting the number of vehicles
    c counting the number of drivers
    d counting the number of items carried

18 A wholesaler sells entirely to the same group of
    retailers on a regular basis. These customers are
    called
    a dissatisfied customers
    b unfamiliar customers
    c trade customers
    d the general public

19 Which of the following is a legal requirement
    when selling shoes?
    a there must be a large variety on display
    b they must be sold in a plastic bag
    c they must be fit for their purpose
    d a range of sizes must be available

20 Which of these retail outlets would most often
    be found on a local shopping parade?
    a a specialist retailer
    b a niche retailer
    c a fashion shop
    d a convenience store

21 Which of these retail outlets is a person likely
    to visit most often? An outlet which sells
    a shopping goods
    b speciality goods
    c convenience goods
    d industrial goods

22 A small local shopkeeper wants advice on the
    cheapest method of obtaining customers' views.
    Which of these methods would you suggest?
    a a telephone survey of all customers
    b personal interviews with every customer
    c a questionnaire posted to all customers
    d a questionnaire given to customers in the shop

23 Which *two* of the following customer services
    are most likely to be provided by an
    independent corner shop?

1 a customer-care department
2 a specialist advice desk
3 personal help and advice
4 straightforward payment methods

24 Which *two* of these customer services are most
    likely to be provided by a large high-street
    department store?
    1 cash payment only
    2 a variety of in-store facilities
    3 free delivery for large items
    4 ordering goods by computer

25 A wholesaler wants to carry out a survey of its
    customers. Which of these methods is most
    likely to give an unbiased result?
    a choosing customers from one area
    b choosing customers at 9 am in the morning
    c choosing customers who spend more than
       £1,000
    d choosing a random sample of customers

26 A transport business is going to survey its
    customers. Which of the following instructions
    could lead to a biased result?
    a a wide geographical area will be covered
    b a wide range of customers will be interviewed
    c customers from different ethnic groups will
       be interviewed
    d a total of 10 people will be interviewed.

27 A mail-order business has been receiving an
    increasing number of complaints about its
    customer service. Which *two* of these methods
    are most likely to lead to improvements?
    1 name badges for all staff
    2 telephone training for staff
    3 more efficient processing of orders
    4 better wheelchair access for customers

28 Customers have been complaining that the
    deliveries from a local business are always late.
    Which *two* of the following are most likely to
    improve the situation?
    1 new delivery vans
    2 more friendly staff
    3 a better product range
    4 better administration of orders

For the answers, see p. 344 at the end of the book.

C   H   A   P   T   E   R   7

Investigating the retail sector

In this chapter, we will:

- describe different types of retail outlet
- look at how retailers attract customers
- look at recent trends in retailing
- consider the use of technology in retailing
- consider employment protection and legislation in retailing

We will cover Element 3.1, Performance Criteria 1, 2, 3, 4, 5.

In Chapter 1, we saw that the retailer is the link in the supply chain selling goods or services to the final consumer. The retailer may be a specialist retailer, or a wholesaler or manufacturer selling direct to the public.

Whoever is performing the retailing function, the services provided may include:

- selling small quantities (breaking bulk)
- a local supply of a variety of goods/services
- the displaying of goods/services
- a delivery service
- credit facilities
- an after-sales service
- an exchange of goods (e.g. Marks & Spencer will exchange goods or provide a refund)

TYPES OF RETAIL OUTLET

There are many different types of **retail outlet**, and we can look at retailers in a number of different ways. They may be seen in terms of:

- the range of goods they sell – according to whether they are specialist, general, niche or department stores
- whether they are large or small: they may be a corner shop, a superstore, a hypermarket
- who owns them: they may be independents or part of a chain (multiples)
- those with shops and those – such as mail-order companies and door-to-door sales companies – without shops
- their method of attracting sales – e.g. offering discounts with 'no frills', offering high-quality goods, offering high-quality service

Figure 7.1 is taken from Appendix I. It shows how retailers are classified in the official figures.

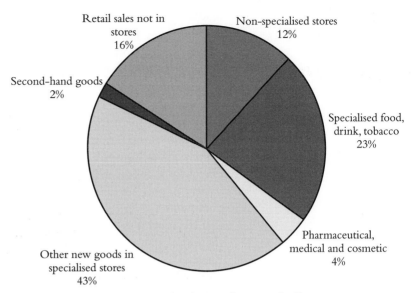

Figure 7.1 Businesses involved in each type of selling

A number of different terms are used to describe retail outlets. Notice that some retailers fit into more than one category.

Specialist retailers are those which primarily sell one product category. They may sell: clothes, shoes, books, records, fishing tackle, car parts, toys or bicycles. Some, like the delicatessen or the off-licence, may specialise in food or drink. Well-known specialists include Mothercare and Dixons. Such shops will usually be positioned in a busy shopping area to take advantage of passing trade. Since specialist retailers concentrate on a limited range of goods, they are in a position to offer expert advice on their particular product: people may ask 'Can you recommend a dry white wine?', 'Do you have brake pads for a 1982 Ford Fiesta?' New specialists include video-hire stores such as Blockbuster Video.

Some specialist retailers carry a very wide range of stocks, and look rather like the traditional department stores described below. Lillywhites, the sports specialists, for example, has departments for football, cricket, golf, skiing, keep fit and so on.

Niche retailers cater for a very specialised, and therefore limited, market. Since relatively few people will be interested in their goods, these retailers will need to have either a large profit margin on each item (antique dealers, for example) or access to a wide market. A specialist stamp shop may, for instance, advertise in collectors' magazines to let those interested know where they are. Customers may be willing to travel to get a specialised service not available elsewhere, or alternatively they may use mail order. Such outlets do not rely on passing trade, and therefore may not need expensive 'shop window' sites in busy shopping centres.

Examples of niche retailers include: shops selling items from various eras – e.g. 'The 60s shop' and the Roaring Forties (as featured in the Yellow Pages TV advert) – antique-fireplace shops (usually called 'Great Grates') and even The Christmas Shop open all year round at London Bridge.

General retailers sell a number of different product groups. These retailers may be small scale – e.g. the local corner shop – or large scale – e.g. a department store or a variety chain store such as Woolworths. Local corner shops need to stock a wide range of products in order to make a living from the limited area that they serve. New technology, especially in food packaging, has made it possible for them to sell a variety of goods without the need for specialised knowledge or equipment (other than perhaps a freezer). Modern packaging means that the retailer simply needs to store goods in an appropriate way and then display them effectively. Modern methods of preparing and freezing foods have extended their shelf-life, and this allows even shops with a slow turnover to stock them.

Convenience stores serve a local area with food and everyday household items such as razor blades and shampoo. These stores include the small corner shop run by the owner, independent shops operating as part of a voluntary group such as Spar or Londis, and multiples such as M&W and One Stop – both of which operate a chain of branches over the South of England. Petrol-station forecourt shops are also classified as convenience stores.

Case study: One Stop convenience stores

Figure 7.2 A One Stop convenience store

It is a mistake to think that all convenience stores are small businesses. One Stop, owned by Portsmouth & Sunderland Newspapers, runs a chain of 116 convenience stores. The group began in Hampshire, but plans to expand into the

Midlands in 1996.

One Stop's sales are made up of:

newspapers and magazines	16%
tobacco	24%
confectionery	16%
lottery	4%
groceries	30%
alcohol	7%
others, including fresh flowers	3%

A pharmacy section is being introduced to new shops.

Eight One Stop stores currently have scanners; half of all stores will have scanning by the end of 1998.

Growing trends are:

- On-site bakeries usually 'bake-off' (bake on the premises using bread, cakes and pastries supplied by Country Choice)
- 'Eating on the hoof' with microwaves, hot-drinks dispensers
- Alcohol
- Pharmacies supplied twice a day by Unichem
- Fresh and chilled food is taking over space from packaged groceries
- Videos are being phased out due to competition both from specialists and from cable and satellite TV companies

The style of One Stop shops is based on the service-station look. The pharmacy is designed to serve the local community and also to bring in extra customers who will then buy other goods. CTN (confectioner, tobacconist, newsagent) goods are sold from the counter, whilst the rest is self-service. A 'rustic' image is given by displaying speciality breads in wicker baskets; daily specials are written up on chalk boards.

Profit margin across the range is 24% – i.e. goods sold for £1 will have cost 76p, leaving 24p gross profit. Shop-running costs still need to be paid before the owners make a **net** (or **final**) **profit**.

A newly opened store will probably serve an estate of 6,000 homes. It will have an area of 2,500 square feet and employ 21 staff, including one pharmacist. Opening hours are Mon–Sat 6 am to 12 midnight, Sunday 8.30 am to 12 midnight. Pharmacy hours are 8.30 am to 6.30 pm.

1 What does the name 'One Stop' suggest? (What is 'one-stop shopping'?)
2 Why do people go to a convenience store rather than to the supermarket?
3 What percentage of the sales are CTN (confectioner, tobacconist, newsagent) goods?
4 How is One Stop attempting to draw in a wider range of people?

Department stores have many different departments under one roof (see Figure 7.3), each catering for a different range of goods – one for kitchenware, one for women's clothes, one for toys and so on. In a sense, these stores are a collection of specialist shops found in one building, operated by one owner. Frequently, individual stores are branches of national groups, such as Debenhams, The John Lewis Partnership, Selfridges and The House of Fraser.

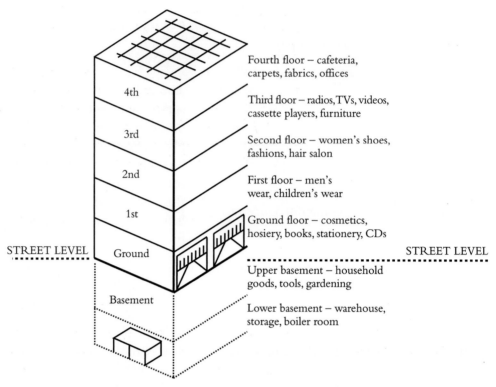

Figure 7.3 A diagram of a department store

The original department stores developed at a time when people were getting easier access to buses and trains. These were big stores offering a greater variety of goods and services than the local shops. Two new shopping ideas developed:

- 'one-stop shopping' – covering all types of goods, and also services ranging from banking to hairdressing
- the idea of 'browsing': looking at goods without being pressed to buy

Today's department stores are still situated in large shopping centres, and continue to provide quality goods to a mass market. They continue to offer services such as hairdressing, booking agencies and banking. Standards of service, and therefore staff costs, are very high.

activity

Identify a department store near to you.

1 On which floor is the cafeteria? Why do you think this is?
2 Where is the store situated? Why is this? (Notice how many customers these stores need – see page 181.)
3 In what way is a department store different from a shopping mall or a shopping arcade?

Independents (there are almost a third of a million of these) consist of those shops not owned by a larger organisation. They include:

- the local corner shop/general store
- specialist local shops involved in a wide range of trades
- voluntary retail cooperatives. These are independent retailers who have made an agreement to buy most of their goods from a particular wholesaler. Where these chains operate under a brand name, they are known as 'symbol independents'. Examples include Spar (see Figure 7.4), Londis and Happy Shopper (linked with Nurdin & Peacock).

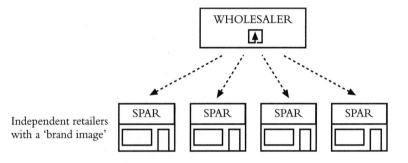

Figure 7.4 How Spar works

Both the wholesaler and the retailer benefit:

1 The wholesaler is guaranteed large regular orders from the retailers in the chain, rather than many small pieces of business from a wide range of retailers. Advantages are:
   - less paper work
   - fewer but larger deliveries
   - being able to order more efficiently
   - being able to develop own brands
   - more efficient working, which allows saving in cost and lower prices to retailers
2 The retailers gain the benefits of belonging to a large organisation, including:
   - stock at reduced prices
   - regular deliveries
   - help with modernising the shop
   - local, and possibly national, advertising
   - remaining independent – still their own boss
   - still being able to provide much of the local friendliness and service associated with small retailers

Multiples are shops which have a number of branches in different locations but are owned by one company. They may be regional (Partners, the stationery firm, for instance, has branches mainly in the Midlands) or nationwide (like W H Smith, Boots the Chemists or

Marks & Spencer). Multiples generally choose high-street or shopping-precinct locations, and they are easy to recognise because all branches have the same image and similar stocks, though there *are* regional differences. All the main decisions are made at head office.

There are:

- **small multiples** – retailers with 2–9 outlets
- **large multiples** – retailers with 10 or more outlets

Sometimes, one company owns a number of different multiple groups. For example:

1 British Shoe Corporation owns:
   - Dolcis
   - Saxone
   - Lilley & Skinner
   - Freeman, Hardy and Willis

2 Sainsbury owns:
   - Sainsbury's – supermarkets
   - Savacentre – hypermarket
   - Texas – DIY
   - Homebase DIY
3 W H Smith owns:
   - W H Smith – stationery
   - Virgin Our Price – tapes/CDs
   - Waterstones – books

For 1 and 2 below, you can use either the company annual reports or *Who Owns Whom* published by Dun and Bradstreet. You should be able to find these in your local reference library.

1 In February 1996, Sears was the largest high-street retailer in the UK. Which companies does Sears own?
2 Which well-known retailers are owned by:
   - The Kingfisher Group
   - Storehouse?
3 Give three benefits that an independent retailer would get from joining a voluntary retail cooperative group.
4 There are more Spar shops in the European Union than any other single 'brand'. Why in this case is Spar not classed as a multiple, whilst Marks & Spencer is?

Superstores are outlets with over 25,000 square feet of single-level selling area. Many superstores (see Figure 7.5) sell groceries, though there are also some Do-It-Yourself (DIY), electrical and furniture stores. Examples include:

Figure 7.5 J Sainsbury superstore (36,000 square feet) at North Cheam

- groceries – Tesco, Asda, Sainsbury, Waitrose
- DIY – Homebase and Texas (Sainsbury), B&Q
- furniture – MFI

Hypermarkets, which originated from a continental idea, are a combination of supermarket and discount warehouse. They sell a number of different product groups – not only food but also clothes, household goods and garden furniture. Although similar to superstores, they are larger, having over 50,000 square feet of single-level selling area.

The investment is huge – perhaps £10 million for a site before building begins. A typical location would be on a ring road outside a town. La Cité at the Channel Tunnel terminal outside Calais is a good example (see page 101). Other Continental examples include Casino, Carrefour, Mammoth and, in this country, some Asda stores and Savacentre (run as a joint venture between Sainsbury and British Home Stores).

Discounters are retailers who specialise in competing purely on price. Kwik Save, Aldi and Netto all operate in the grocery trade. Traditionally, these paid little attention to display, often leaving goods in boxes on the floor. Variety was also restricted as stocks were bought on the **80/20 principle** – that is, since 20% of the goods provide 80% of the profits, it is best to concentrate on that 20%.

Discount warehouses sell **consumer durables** (those goods bought by consumers that remain useful over a considerable period of time, e.g. cars, washing machines, CD players). Examples include:

- Comet (part of the Kingfisher group), which stocks over 2,000 lines of electrical and household goods
- Argos, which sells a wide range of personal goods chosen from a catalogue in the shop
- Toys Я Us which sells toys, children's bicycles etc.

Discounters keep prices down by:

- bulk buying – this is cheaper
- concentrating on fast-turnover goods
- operating on lower profit margins
- offering a minimum of personal service – this keeps staff costs down
- 'no frills' – fairly basic stores
- self-service

Case study: lower than cost

In its early days, Kwik Save kept prices so low that some were even below cost. Profits were made, not on selling goods, but on investing the takings and earning interest. It worked like this: goods were bought on credit from the supplier and were then sold in the shop for cash. This cash was then *invested* until it was time to pay the supplier.

Local shops could not match these prices, and a number were put out of business.

1 What is the main difference between a superstore and a hypermarket?
2 In what ways has the popularity of the motor car since the 1950s helped the development of large shops?
3 How can discounters offer lower prices than their competitors?

Stall-holders are retailers operating from a market or street stall. Overhead costs are usually low, and as a result so are prices. A disadvantage for the customer is that it may not be possible to find the retailer in future if there is a problem with the goods. Goods sold may include: clothes and shoes (possibly seconds or unfashionable lines), fruit and veg, CDs and tapes, batteries, tools and fast food.

Other small-scale retailers without shops include:

- itinerant (door-to-door) sellers
- mobile shops (e.g. fish and chip van, ice-cream van)

Non-store retailers sell to the growing number of **home shoppers**. They include:

- mail-order firms such as Littlewoods and Freemans, who produce catalogues showing a wide range of goods from electricals to clothes and soft furnishings. The 'Other 9%' shown in Figure 7.6 includes:
- Mail-order advertisements, in newspapers and on day-time television (frequently for goods only available from a warehouse near Plymouth)

Note that mail order has recently moved up-market: the 'Innovations' mail-order catalogue, for example, is distributed inside the *Sunday Observer* newspaper, whilst some retailers such as Next, Habitat and Mothercare have specialist mail-order catalogues to target the young and well-off

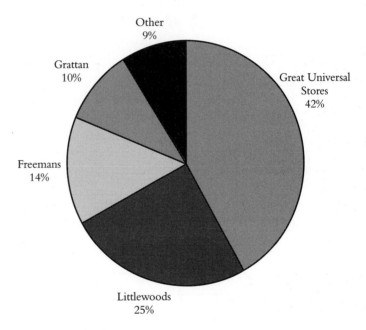

Figure 7.6 The market share of mail-order retailers

- **On-line shopping** which is made possible by linking home computers via a telephone line (see Figure 7.7) with one of the various on-line service providers which allow access to the Internet. It was estimated that by January 1996, one quarter of 'Net users had purchased goods in this way. Developments to make on-line payment by plastic cards more secure will increase the popularity of this method

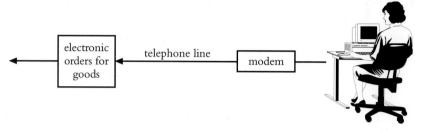

Figure 7.7 On-line shopping

- Home shopping via **TV shopping channels** is another recent development

1 Name local examples of retailers from each of the following categories: specialist, niche, general, independent, multiple, department store, superstore, hypermarket, convenience store, non-store.
2 What sort of goods does each sell?
3 Draw up a table like the one shown. There may be several boxes to complete for each retailer. (Use abbreviations – e.g. G = general, m/o = mail order). Add your own local examples to the list.

NAME OF RETAILER	SPECIALIST, GENERAL, NICHE	CONVENIENCE STORE, DEPARTMENT STORE, SUPERSTORE, HYPERMARKET	INDEPENDENT, MULTIPLE	MARKET STALL, SHOP, MAIL ORDER	MAIN PRODUCTS
Dixons					
Asda					
Local Spar shop					
B&Q					
Habitat					
Freemans					
Tie rack					

4 What is 'on-line shopping'? At the moment, what is holding this back?
5 Draw a sketch map of a local shopping area. Identify the different types of retailer.

HOW MANY SHOPS ARE THERE?

Napoleon once said 'England is a nation of shopkeepers'. This was still true in 1945 when there was one shop for every 60 people in the country! Some recent figures are shown in Appendix I.

activity

1 About how many people are there per shop today? You can calculate this from the figures on page 345. Assume that the population is 55 million.
2 The 'threshold' population is the minimum number of customers needed to ensure that a business can survive. Some examples are shown in the table.

RETAILER	CUSTOMERS REQUIRED
Local grocer	350
Small multiple store	20,000
Marks & Spencer	50,000
Sainsbury's	60,000
Department store	100,000

Why, in this case, do we find shops so close together?

WHAT DO RETAILERS SELL?

In Chapter 1, we saw that retailers provide a commercial service. They are the final part of the supply chain which takes goods to the consumer.

Remember that goods can be classed as:

- primary products – these are natural goods
- secondary products – these are manufactured goods

Remember also that goods can be classified as:

- **consumables** (goods used up quickly)
- **durables** (long-lasting goods)

activity

1 Draw up a table like the one shown below.
   - Enter five primary and five secondary goods that a retailer might sell
   - Tick each off as a consumable or a durable
   - Name local retailers who will sell each product
   - Into which category of retailer do each of these retailers fit (multiple, niche etc.)?

TYPE OF GOOD	CONSUMABLES	DURABLES	LOCAL RETAILERS	TYPE OF RETAILER
Primary goods: 1 2 3 4 5				
Secondary goods: 1 2 3 4 5				

2 Draw up a second table as shown (one example is given):

TYPE OF RETAILER	NAME	OWNER (IF PART OF A CHAIN)	EXAMPLES OF PRIMARY GOODS SOLD	EXAMPLES OF MANUFACTURED (SECONDARY) GOODS SOLD
Independent grocer				
Superstore	Waitrose	John Lewis Partnership	milk, meat, potatoes	biscuits, tissues
Hypermarket				
Stall-holder				
Mail-order firm				
Specialist independent				
Specialist multiple				
Niche retailer				
Department store				

HOW DO RETAILERS COMPETE?

We can buy similar products from a range of shops. Why do we shop where we do? There may be a number of reasons. If it is difficult to get out and about because there is no transport, or if we have very little time, then we may simply go to the local shop – there is no choice. This may apply to old people, the disabled and parents with small children. The majority of people, however, are able to shop around, and in recent years competition between retailers has been fiercer than ever before.

Retailers need to consider a number of factors when trying to get our custom:

- price
- quality

- display
- variety
- access
- service
- payment methods
- loyalty discounts
- after-sales service
- the number of outlets they need
- ethical issues
- *Price*. Often, price is associated with quality – notice, for instance, the advertisement 'Stella Artois – reassuringly expensive'. However, where a retailer sells established brands at lower prices than the opposition, then price becomes one of the most powerful selling points: the brand guarantees the quality, and the price attracts the customer.

  The John Lewis Partnership, the owner of department stores and the Waitrose supermarket group, has a reputation for quality, but its motto 'Never knowingly undersold' shows that it is also aware of the importance of price.
- *Quality*. Unless the price is unreasonably high, retailers will generally find it easier to sell a good, quality product. People want a bargain rather than something cheap. In food retailing, quality may refer to lifestyle features such as 'low fat', or 'organically grown'. With clothes, symbols such as the Woolmark may be important.

  Where money is not a consideration, quality may be the most important selling point. The London stores of Harrods in Knightsbridge and Fortnum & Mason in Piccadilly are relatively expensive. Their selling point is quality of goods and of service.
- *Display*. Retailers may use a number of displays to present an image and draw the customer inside. This is effective where there is a high volume of passing trade, and is especially important in main shopping centres. Window dressing is a specialised skill, and since it can be expensive, it is used only at the quality end of the market. Liberty's, for instance, will use specialised window dressers, the local boutique will dress its own windows as effectively as possible, and other shops may not consider displays important at all, choosing instead to use posters advertising special offers for the week. Similarly, inside a shop, the retailer may try to present goods in an attractive manner, or, like Aldi and Toys Я Us, simply 'pile 'em high and sell 'em cheap'.
- *Variety*. Stores such as Kwik Save have built their success entirely upon low price and selling fast-moving lines. They will not attract shoppers looking for variety and choice in the same way as, for instance, Tesco, Sainsbury, Safeway or Asda. Aldi stocks 600 lines, Tesco 17,000.

  Especially where they are considering spending a large amount of money (perhaps on a CD player, a bicycle, a three-piece suite or a car), shoppers will want a variety to choose from. The more expensive the product, the further people will be prepared to travel.

- *Access*. One of the main functions of the retailer is to provide a local supply of goods. If shops are not accessible, the customers cannot reach them. For specialist shops selling perhaps shoes or clothes, a busy high street, a shopping mall or a pedestrian precinct may be an ideal location. A superstore which relies on car owners who will make large 'one-stop' purchases needs to have easy access by road and large car parks; an out-of-town location may be the answer here. For a small convenience store selling everyday items, 'being accessible' may mean being within walking distance.

You may have seen red routes – areas on major roads where parking is restricted. The traffic flows more quickly here, but retailers along the way have found their trade badly hit as they are no longer accessible to motorists.

Access may also be improved by 'child-friendly' stores (e.g. as in Figure 7.8), stores catering for the old or disabled so that, for instance, aisles are wide enough for wheelchairs and difficult steps and awkward shelves are avoided, and late night or Sunday opening. 'Armchair shopping' by mail order is accessible to many people who have not the means or the time to get out. This was first introduced in the USA by Sears-Roebuck as a way of bringing choice to those living in remote areas miles away from the nearest town. Today, people with busy lives may find mail order through catalogues or the weekend papers a convenient way of shopping. A modern extension of this idea is 'on-line' shopping mentioned above.

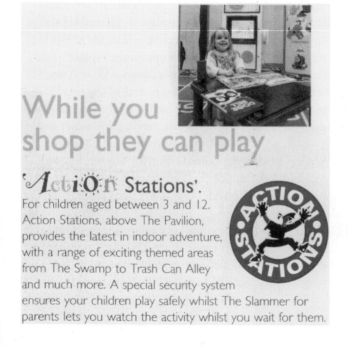

Figure 7.8 Facilities for children at Lakeside shopping centre

- *Service.* Having cut prices as low as they can, many retailers are now improving customer service as one way of getting ahead of their rivals. As the Department of Trade and Industry's (1995) report *Ingredients for Success* puts it, 'the competition may copy the product but they can't copy the people.'

  Service may include: advice, the 'personal touch', trolleys for wheelchair users, special parking places for disabled and those with children, and staff assisting customers to carry awkward items. Despite the increase in 'cash and carry' shopping at superstores, delivery is still important for bulky goods such as furniture and carpets.

- *Payment methods.* A retailer who accepts a wide variety of payment methods will attract more customers. Possible payment methods include:
  - cash: this is the usual method for small purchases, since plastic cards and cheques cost the retailer money
  - immediate payment by other means such as cheque, credit card and debit card. Plastic cards are growing in popularity
  - credit terms, where the agreement is usually to pay a deposit immediately and the balance in instalments over a number of months or years. Retailers selling consumer durables such as fridges, televisions, furniture and cars may find that it is necessary to allow credit since relatively few people are able to pay the whole amount immediately. How many people could buy a new car for cash? In January 1996, the electrical store Colourvision sold around 45% of its goods on credit.

  Small retailers normally insist on cash. Larger retailers, however, will frequently accept a variety of payment methods.

- *Loyalty cards* are a recent introduction in retailing. The customer presents the card when making a payment, and points are added based upon the size of the purchase. When the points reach a certain level they can be used to get discounts on future purchases. These cards are based upon the idea that it is easier to keep existing customers than to attract new ones. They are an up-to-date way of giving vouchers.

Multimedia Time Machines 95

APR 0% * **INTEREST FREE CREDIT**

Interest Free Credit is available subject to status. Written quotations are available on request. Be sure you can afford the payments before entering into a credit agreement.

Case study: the supermarket war

The four leading supermarkets and their out-of-town superstores are becoming more dominant; between them, Sainsbury, Asda, Tesco and Safeway control 80% of the retail grocery market. Despite a change in government attitude to out-of-town shopping, 54 new superstores were opened in 1995, and as many again in 1996. There has been some price cutting, but 'launching a price war would be the retail equivalent of nuclear war' says Verdict Research.

Tesco took market leadership in early 1996 partly because of its loyalty cards (see Figure 7.10 and 7.11).

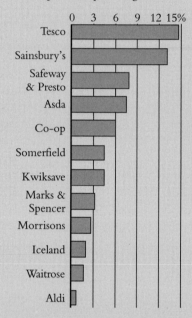

Market share
The superstores' percentage share

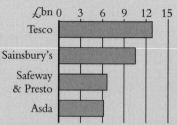

Sales
Overall sales in grocers total £59.2bn
These are the top four:

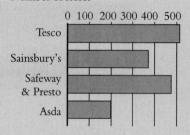

Outlets
Number of stores

Figure 7.10 The Tesco Clubcard

Figure 7.11 How Tesco has taken a decisive lead in market share

activity Discuss the main ways in which the major supermarkets compete. Provide examples to support your ideas.

- *After-sales service* is important with consumer durables. Korean manufacturer Daewoo ('That'll be the Daewoo') launched its car sales with a promise of free after-sales service for the first three years. It will also collect and return the car and provide a replacement car until the service is complete. Such offers are important selling points for goods which need regular (and usually costly) maintenance. Many computer retailers provide a free on-site warranty for the first months after purchase.
- *The number of outlets.* Consumers buying expensive consumer durables where after-sales service is likely to be important are attracted to well-known names with many retail outlets. They feel that the organisation will not disappear overnight, and realise that servicing will be convenient if there is a local branch.

  Some retailers such as Marks & Spencer guarantee to change any unwanted purchases, or to refund money, with no questions asked. This offer is more attractive because there are branches around the country: the customer can go to the nearest branch even if the goods were not purchased there.
- *Ethical issues.* As well as being genuinely concerned about the environment and human and animal rights, retailers are aware that the way they treat these issues will also affect sales. The Body Shop, for instance, has built its reputation on environmentally friendly products, whilst Shell, on the other hand, has received criticism for its policies in Nigeria. We also deal with ethical issues in Chapter 11 (p. 310) when we look at how retailers choose their suppliers.

Case study: how did Tesco compete?

At the beginning of 1996, Tesco had become the single largest grocery retailer. Below are some of the methods they used to compete with rival groups:

1 Price and value for money:
   - New deal – low prices on everyday products including brands such as Nestlé and Kellogg's, and fresh foods such as milk and apples
   - Value lines – 'Tesco Value' own brand offers low prices on over 100 family basics such as bread, toilet rolls and baked beans
   - Promotions – special offers on quality items. These change each week

2 Quality:
- Tesco's 'Quality Guarantee' means that any product will be exchanged or money refunded with no questions asked

3 Choice and variety:
- In most stores, Tesco's offers 17,000 different items (Netto offers around 600, Sainsbury around 20,000). These goods are selected from all around the world, although the 'Best of British' campaign is designed to promote home-produced goods – for example, over 100 British cheeses are available

4 Customer service: originally, the supermarkets were able to cut prices by cutting out customer service. Recently, customer service has been reintroduced as a means of competing with rivals.
- Customer panels have been introduced to let Tesco know what the customers think. One result has been that impulse goods such as sweets have been removed from store checkouts
- 'One-in-Front' service – where there is more than one person queueing in front, a new checkout will be opened
- 'First Class Service' – staff are encouraged to use their initiative to help customers. This improves the store's image
- Better in-store facilities including: bank ATMs (automatic teller machines), nappy-changing and bottle-warming facilities, customer service desks in all superstores, and wine experts in stores advising customers what to buy to drink with their meal

5 Store design: different types of store have been designed to match different customer shopping patterns:
- Superstores offer a wide range of goods

and surface-level parking; often these stores are located on the edge of town, or on development sites within cities
- Compact stores are scaled-down superstores for areas for which a superstore is not possible
- Metro – high-street shops designed for town-centre shoppers
- Express – combines a petrol forecourt with a convenience store stocking 1,400 product lines

6 Opening hours: in line with other retailers, Tesco stores now open on Sundays and on some Bank Holidays. There is also an experiment with late-night opening until 10 pm.

7 A responsible, caring image: a 'green' image is now a selling point. Tesco has devised a number of campaigns to show that it is a responsible company:
- Healthy Eating campaign – products designed for nutritional value
- Natural choice – crops used by Tesco are produced with minimal use of fertiliser or chemical sprays
- Computers for schools – Tesco provided new computers for over 10,000 schools in 1994 – see Figure 7.12

Figure 7.12 The Tesco Computers for Schools campaign

- Fund-raising for children – Tesco raised over £1 million for the Save the Children Fund in 1994
- Recycling – packaging is being designed so that it can be recycled. Some superstores have recycling collection areas
8 Loyalty cards: retailers know that it is easier to *keep* customers than to find new ones. Loyalty cards are an attempt to encourage shoppers to come back again.

The Tesco Clubcard gives one point for every £5 of purchases after a minimum of £10, and has played an important part in making Tesco the market leader. Competitors have responded with: Safeways ABC card and Sainsbury's Reward card. Asda announced in December 1995 that it would honour loyalty cards from its competitors – Tesco is the main target here (see page 186).

1 How does Tesco compete with the discounters such as Kwik Save, Aldi and Netto? Which policies are aimed at Asda, Safeway and Sainsbury?
2 How is Tesco improving accessibility?
3 Figure 7.13 shows two other examples of loyalty cards. Can you name three others? What is the thinking behind loyalty cards?

Figure 7.13 Loyalty cards for Safeway and Dillons

Visit the major supermarkets in your area. Check how they compete under the following headings:

- Prices of selected major brands
- Prices of own brands
- Means of payment accepted: cash, cheque, debit cards, credit card
- Do they have a loyalty card?
- Other concessions (e.g. money off if plastic bags are returned)
- Variety of goods
- Ease of shopping (cramped, spacious, easy to find goods?)
- Customer service:
  - facilities: toilets, parking, disabled access, nappy-changing rooms
  - staff (service, friendliness)
  - queues
- surroundings (pleasant etc.)

You may find it useful to design a matrix by using a spreadsheet or the table facility on a word processor.

Niche retailers may have very little competition. However, with electrical sales, Do-It-Yourself shops or groceries, it is a different matter. Here, there is likely to be some competition in the area from larger operators, and the small shop is unlikely to be able to match their prices or variety.

1 Look at the table below which compares a small convenience store with a supermarket. How do small retailers survive?
2 Supermarkets now offer services which until recently have been offered mainly by small retailers. What are these?
3 How could joining a voluntary retail cooperative help the independent retailer?

BENEFIT TO CUSTOMERS	SMALL RETAILER (CONVENIENCE STORE)	LARGE RETAILER (SUPERMARKET)
Personal service	More likely to offer a friendly personal service. Customers may be known to the retailer, so may be allowed some small credit occasionally. Probably self-service, few queues	Service will be efficient but impersonal. Self-service, but there may be queues
Convenience	The shop is local and therefore convenient – especially if few items are required in a hurry	Not convenient for a few items: travelling and queueing mean that it is only worthwhile if a fair number of items are required. Will have easy parking and access
Hours	Will be open 'all hours' probably every day	May open seven days a week. Also, later opening is being tried (Tesco will open until 10 pm)

BENEFIT TO CUSTOMERS	SMALL RETAILER (CONVENIENCE STORE)	LARGE RETAILER (SUPERMARKET)
Payment methods	Usually cash, though exceptions may be made for well-known, loyal customers – may take a cheque. Unlikely to have Switch or credit-card facilities.	Requires immediate payment, but will accept: cash, cheque (with cheque card) or debit card (such as Switch)
Product range	Tries to stock a wide range of items, but has a restricted choice – one brand of cat food etc. (Stock ties up cash, and there is the risk of being left with unsold goods.) May not have bread or milk left in the afternoon.	Will have a wide range of stock, including own brands. High turnover makes this possible
Quality	Usually branded goods. May suffer from being in the shop a long time	Good quality – quick turnover ensures freshness
Price	Generally higher prices. Low turnover, limited funds and restricted storage space means that bulk-buying and special discounts are not available. A reasonable mark-up is needed to make a satisfactory profit on the low volume of sales. Sells at manufacturer's recommended price.	Bulk buying means that cost of stock is lower, and high sales turnover means that satisfactory profits can be made with low mark-up

Case study: the National Lottery – helping small shops compete?

The National Lottery was launched by Camelot on 14 November 1994. In the first year, two-thirds of the adult population bought tickets, spending a total of £4.4 billion. Most of the regular players are people on low incomes or pensioners. On 27 January 1996, one of the 'roll-over' weeks, sales of tickets reached £8 million per hour.

The tickets are sold at 20,000 shops, of which 5,100 are convenience stores and 8,400 CTNs (confectioner, tobacconist, newsagents) – this is one product which has the same price and quality wherever it is bought. Camelot believes that the Lottery was 'the best news for convenience stores and the independent retailer for years'.

On the other hand:

- Local Chambers of Commerce report that shops with no Lottery machine find business down by as much as 25% over the week, with a 60% drop on Saturdays
- Much of the Lottery spending is not new money but simply a switch from 'treats' such as chocolate
- Whereas a Lottery ticket gives a 5% profit margin, other goods give a higher margin. If Lottery spending competes with these goods, the retailer may be worse off

In February 1996, the National Heritage

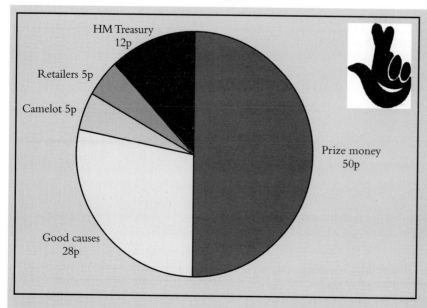

Figure 7.14 The National Lottery: where each £1 goes

Select Committee met to look at the way the Lottery was operating. Among those giving evidence were representatives of retail organisations who urged the government to force Camelot to be more open in its dealings with retailers. In particular:

- The Association of Convenience Stores (ACS) asked for an increase in the retailers' cut, and it also asked Camelot to disclose how it chooses its retail outlets
- SIR (Society of Independent Retailers) pointed out that where sales fell below £3,000 per week, Camelot had the power to remove lottery terminals

activity

1 The average retailer takes around £4,000 per week from sales of Lottery tickets (£4.4 billion/20,000 retailers/52 weeks). How much of this does the average retailer actually keep?

2 If a customer buys a Lottery ticket instead of spending £1 on sweets, how does this affect the retailer? (See page 345 for the profit margin on chocolate.)

3 Is the National Lottery good for the small retailer? Give points for and against.

4 How much money does a retailer make from:
    - £2 spent on chocolate
    - £10 spent on Lottery tickets?

5 What is the function of bodies such as SIR and ACS? (See the section on retailer representatives later in the chapter.)

Case study: competition in DIY retailing

The traditional idea in DIY (do-it-yourself) is that price is crucial because there is little customer loyalty and it is difficult to make your own cans of Dulux paint, packets of nails or doors different from those of your competitors.

In general, prices are kept low by buying in bulk and by keeping down costs. This means larger stores, and out-of-town sites if possible. Strangely, one of the most successful DIY stores in 1995, however, was Wickes, one of the smaller ones. How did they do it?

- *Variety*: Wickes does not believe that it is important to carry a lot of choice: it carries only 4,000 lines. However, says chairman Harry Sweetbaum, 'We have everything you need to build a house, but we don't have five ranges of paint like B&Q does'
- *Own brands*: 90% of the goods are own-brand (see Figure 7.15). Although Wickes stocks a narrower range, it sells more of each item than its larger rivals
- *Number of outlets*: there are around 100 Wickes stores, whilst B&Q has nearly 300.

Figure 7.15 Wickes's own brand of paint

However, Wickes is pushing ahead with plans to open 20 new stores a year.

Although planning permission for out-of-town stores is now more difficult to get

Figure 7.16 A B&Q advert promoting a caring image

(see page 197), Wickes is getting the go-ahead because it sells the 'heavier' products such as timber, sheds and conservatories. These are less likely to compete with town-centre shops

- *Price*: Wicks realises that DIY customers of the 1990s are more price-conscious than they were 10 years ago. It is able to keep prices down by selling a lot of its limited range of own-brand goods

Wickes has thus been successful recently partly because it is well suited to the price-conscious DIY customer of the 1990s who puts value for money ahead of variety of choice.

B&Q – a caring company

One of Wickes's main rivals is B&Q, a much larger chain. B&Q has 300 outlets across the country, which means that nationwide advertising for the company is worthwhile – 'Don't just do it – B&Q it!'

B&Q grew in the 1980s when the boom in housing meant that customers wanted a wide variety of products. Today it still offers a wide choice at competitive prices, but in recent years it has begun to compete through its 'image'. The company has recognised that people are now concerned about the environment. B&Q has therefore recently advertised itself as a caring company (see Figure 7.16).

At the time of writing B&Q is thinking of buying Wickes.

B&Q has placed full-page advertisements in the 'quality' press.

1 Name three 'quality' newspapers.
2 Why does B&Q feel that it is worth aiming at these particular readers, rather than the readers of the 'tabloid' press? Try to give two different reasons. (Remember that the aim of advertising is to sell more products.)
3 Wickes is smaller than B&Q. How does it manage to compete so successfully?

RECENT TRENDS IN RETAILING

Over the last 20 years, retailing has changed as a result of the following developments:

- the continuing effect of the abolition of resale price maintenance in 1964 (see below)
- the development of the 'motor car economy'. This has led to 'one-stop' shopping where families buy all of their supplies at one shop. It is worth travelling further to do this
- own branding – large retailers have developed own brands often made for them by leading manufacturers
- new technology at the checkout, and in the packaging and preserving of food – this has speeded up the checkout process and reduced delivery times from suppliers
- faster transport links across the world, which has made available a wider range of goods

- the growing sophistication of customers and a general rise in the standard of living, which has led to fierce competition in the high street
- new technology in the home, which may cause a revolution in shopping methods in the future

The following trends have emerged as a result:

1 *The growth of discounting.* Large-scale retailers can get 'economies of scale' which allow them to operate more efficiently and to sell at a discount. For instance, they can obtain stocks more cheaply by buying in bulk. In turn, they can pass these discounts on to the consumer in the form of lower prices at the checkout.
2 *The trend towards larger shops.* Discounting attracts customers away from the smaller retailers – look at Figure 7.17.

(a)

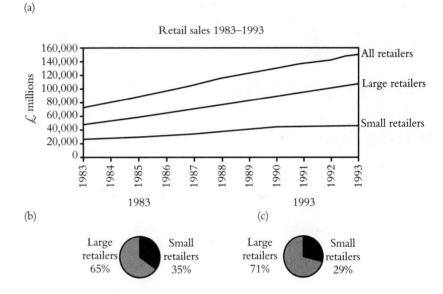

Figure 7.17 (a) retail sales 1983–93, showing the widening gap between large and small retailers; and the share of the retail trade in (b) 1983 and (c) 1993

3 *The end of all resale price maintenance?* Shops have not always been allowed to cut prices. Instead, for many years retailers were compelled to sell at the price set by the manufacturer. The Resale Prices Act (1964) changed this. Now, manufacturers could suggest a 'recommended retail price', but in practice shops could sell at any price they wished. The effect was that the larger retailers immediately began to cut prices, and the smaller retailers suffered as a result. The growth of the supermarkets, the superstores and hypermarkets, and the decline of the smaller shops were a direct consequence of this.

There were two exceptions:

- Booksellers agreed to maintain standard prices. This 'net book agreement' remained in effect until 1995 when it was broken by Asda who sold John Le Carré's *Our Game* at a discount price in their stores. Since then, book discounting has become common
- Chemists also agreed to maintain the price of non-prescription drugs such as aspirin. At the time of writing, Asda is also trying to break this agreement

There is a fear that discounting in books and drugs will lead to the closure of small bookshops and chemists, just as it led to the decline of the small neighbourhood shop.

Case study: the Net Book Agreement

In October 1995, the Net Book Agreement (NBA) broke down when Asda, the supermarket chain, began to sell books at discounted prices – *Our Game* by John Le Carré was one of the first. The NBA had prevented price competition between booksellers by forcing them to sell at the price set by the publishers. This Agreement, along with that on certain medicines, had survived the abolition of resale price maintenance in the 1960s because it was thought to be in the public interest. Supporters said that:

- it would keep smaller bookshops in business because there could not be any

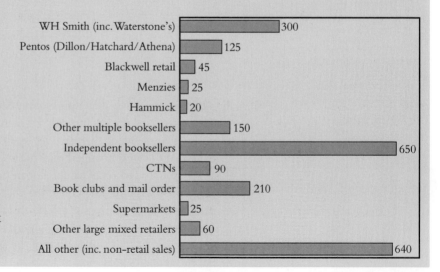

Figure 7.18 The UK book market in 1995 – turnover in £ million

Retailer	Turnover (£ million)
WH Smith (inc. Waterstone's)	300
Pentos (Dillon/Hatchard/Athena)	125
Blackwell retail	45
Menzies	25
Hammick	20
Other multiple booksellers	150
Independent booksellers	650
CTNs	90
Book clubs and mail order	210
Supermarkets	25
Other large mixed retailers	60
All other (inc. non-retail sales)	640

price-cutting

- it would guarantee that a wide variety of books would be published, as without the Agreement publishers would concentrate on bestsellers only

Opponents believed that the Agreement simply kept book prices high.

The end of the Net Book Agreement reduced book prices but did not lead to the increased growth in sales needed to compensate for the lower prices. W H Smith, the single largest bookseller selling 1 in every 4 books, decided to play tough. They asked publishers for a 48% discount on prices, a 60-day credit period, and for books to be on sale or return.

The likely effects of the collapse of the NBA are:

- Independent booksellers will be forced out of business
- Small publishers may also fold
- Booksellers with buying power will demand special deals so that they can offset the new low selling price

4 *Out-of-town shopping.* The growth in car ownership over the last 30 years has meant that more people are able to travel further to shop. They are prepared to do this if they can get a wider variety of goods at lower prices than are available locally. The car is necessary not just to get to the store but to carry home the large amount of purchases that are necessary to make the journey worthwhile.

The original out-of-town idea (as already mentioned) began with the continental hypermarkets. The idea was copied in the UK from the 1970s onwards with stores such as Savacentre (a joint development between Sainsbury and British Home Stores). Out-of-town sites became popular because land is cheaper, and there is car-parking space and less traffic congestion.

Case study: out-of-town shopping

In the 1980s, the property and consumer booms led to a surge in new shopping developments, many of them in out-of-town locations. In particular, there were:

- large shopping malls which encouraged large retailers to move from their traditional town-centre locations to these new purpose-built sites. The main ones are:
  - Merry Hill Centre near Dudley, the largest in Europe. 4.5 million people live within 65 minutes' drive
  - MetroCentre Gateshead – the second largest
  - Meadowhall outside Sheffield
  - Lakeside, Thurrock (see Figure 7.19)
- superstores built on the edge of town by large food retail chains such as Sainsbury and Tesco. In the 1980s, 70 of these new food superstores were built each year, many on 'green field' sites

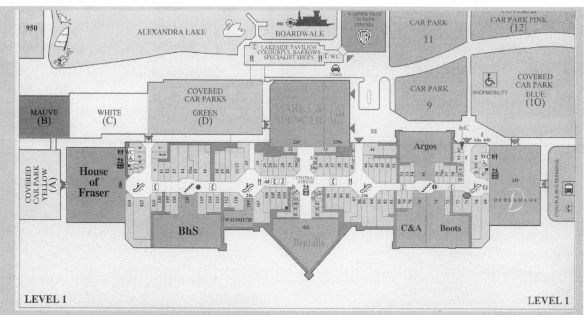

- 250 retail parks, mainly housing carpet and DIY 'sheds'

As a result of this, the UK has many more shopping centres than anywhere else in Europe (see Figure 7.20).

Between them, the four shopping malls mentioned above attracted 437,000 customers on one Saturday in December 1994. Not only shoppers, but also the larger stores are moving out to them.

By 1996, out-of-town shopping took 27p in every £1 spent, whilst high streets have less than 50p. The real losers, however, are the smaller local shops.

Sunday trading has pushed the shopping malls up the league table for numbers of customers. Oxford Street in London, for years the leading shopping centre in the country, is now in 4th place after Merry Hill, Meadowhall and Metro Centre. Of the traditional town centres, only Eastergate in Chester can now compete.

The future?
In 1993/4, the government decided that the

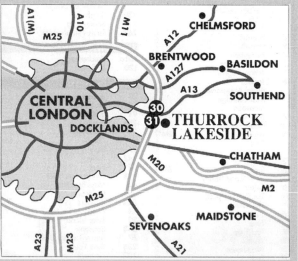

Figure 7.19 Lakeside shopping centre: location on map, and centre layout

trend must stop. They were concerned about the increased use of cars that out-of-town shopping relies upon, as well as about the drastic effect upon town centres.

- New developments will no longer be allowed if they are likely to harm town centre shopping. Each application has to

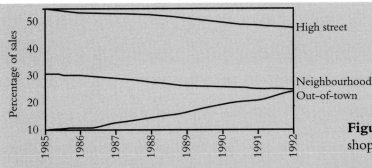

Figure 7.20 The effects of out-of-town shopping: share of retail sales by location

explain why it cannot be done *nearer* to town. Nevertheless chains such as Currys and Halfords have plans to move more branches out of town

- Out-of-town sites will still be allowed for more bulky items (carpets and furniture, for example) which cannot be sold in cramped, expensive high streets
- Only three more malls have planning permission: Cribbs Causeway near Bristol, Brayhead Glasgow and Bluewater Park near Dartford. However, there are unlikely to be any more regional centres like Merry Hill
- The supermarkets are moving back to the high street, often with smaller stores such as Tesco Metro. Local authorities, backed by Boots and Marks & Spencer (who own property in most high streets), are working to bring life back to town centres

5 *In-town shopping centres.* Town-centre developments include shopping arcades with pedestrian precincts, a variety of shops, pleasant surroundings and usually a multi-storey car park linked by a lift. Examples include the Arndale Centre in Manchester, at the time, the largest covered shopping area in Europe. The Glades at Bromley is typical of the many smaller developments (see page 101).

6 *Non-store shopping.* Mail order has grown significantly over recent years. Today, it has a turnover of more than £4 billion a year. Although the large catalogue companies dominate the market (see page 179), a number of other companies, including Habitat, Next, Argos, Mothercare and some garden suppliers, have also developed mail-order sales.

    On-line shopping via computer (as already mentioned) is a new but growing area.

7 *Own brands.* Manufacturers, and in some cases wholesalers, have had branded goods for many years. The idea is to give the product a distinctive image and make it recognisable to the consumer – e.g. Heinz beans, Perrier mineral water, Colegate toothpaste. A lot of money has been spent in turning these into household names. A relatively recent development is the emergence of retailers' own brands: Winfield paint (Woolworths), Jonelle scarves (John Lewis), Tesco beans.

(Interestingly, own-brand cigarettes are never given the same name as the retailer that has developed them – e.g. Tesco's own brand is Benington. Why is this?)

Originally, own brands were regarded as inferior as well as cheaper. More recently, however, many have become brands in their own right. Marks & Spencer, which has a reputation for quality, sells 98% St Michael own-brand goods.

8 *Multi-packaging*. There is a trend towards selling several items in one package. Complementary items multi-packaged include: the 'bundling' of free software (worth several hundreds of pounds if bought separately) with a new computer, a bar of chocolate taped to a jar of coffee, a comb with shampoo, bacon with eggs and Sharwoods' Chinese New Year package of black bean curd and noodles.

Larger multiples encourage customers to buy in bulk by selling multi-packs: four tins of beans, eight cartons of fruit juice and so on. To some extent, this goes against the traditional idea of the retailer breaking bulk, and reflects the trend towards consumers stocking up on major shopping expeditions every week or so.

9 *Specialisation*. With a general rise in consumers' disposable income, there has been a growth in specialised retailers catering for diverse tastes. Some of these goods are unusual and are highly priced. Examples include 'Fired Earth' a company specialising in a wide range of ceramic tiles imported from around the world – Sock Shop and Tie Rack.

10 *Customisation*. One of the effects of mass production has been the standardisation of products, of which **branding** is a particular example. However, recently, retailers have become aware that they can cater for individual needs by mixing mass-produced components to the customer's requirements – e.g. 'Make your own pizza from our wide variety of toppings', or 'Have your jeans shortened while you wait.' Many retailers selling personal computers will similarly put together a package to suit the customer – e.g. an extra disc drive, an extra 4Mb of RAM, a sound card and so on.

1 What is happening to the total value of retail sales?
2 What is happening to the value of sales of:
  i large retailers
  ii small retailers?
3 What is happening to the small retailers' share of total sales?

1 What has caused the decline of the high street and neighbourhood shops?
2 Give two reasons why the government has decided to refuse planning permission for new out-of-town developments.
3 How is the high street 'fighting back'?
4 On a map, mark and label the four large shopping malls. Which motorways would you use to get from: Exeter to Merry Hill; South London to Lakeside; Durham to the Metro Centre; Barnsley to Meadowhall?
5 Mark and label the three proposed shopping malls. Which motorways serve these?

Changes in opening hours

With both men and women at work in the week, shops have tended to stay open longer in recent years:

- Many have abandoned the mid-week 'half-day closing' (Sheffield Wednesday FC was formed from a team of shopworkers who played on their half day off)
- Late-night shopping is common
- Sunday trading is now legal for all shops. Previously, the situation was confused. Many small traders did open and were allowed to do so under local bye-laws – unless a member of the public complained. The large retailers, however, were not allowed to open. Reports suggest that Sunday trading has not increased total trade, but merely spread existing trade over seven days.
- Many of the stores offering mail-order business can be contacted until late at night
- The licensing laws introduced in World War I restricted the sale of alcohol to lunchtimes and evenings. These laws have recently been relaxed. Public houses and off-licences are now allowed to operate throughout the day, seven days a week.

European Standardisation

One aim of the European Union (EU) is the 'harmonisation' of standards between the Member countries. EU laws are affecting retailers in a number of ways:

- VAT (value-added tax) has for some time been levied on most goods
- Standards of hygiene required by the EU has meant a change in equipment and working practices in the food industry
- Most recently, the UK has introduced metric measures for prepacked goods – although loose goods (such as fresh fish or potatoes) can still be sold under the old imperial system. A bottle of beer must be labelled as, e.g., '568 ml', but the same measure bought on draught in a public house can still be sold as a *pint*

The Conservative government has resisted some EU proposals, including the introduction of a minimum wage – which many smaller retailers feel would make it difficult for them to employ staff. (This issue is dealt with below under the 'employment' section).

Case study: D Day – the European harmonisation of measures

1 October 1995 became known as 'D' (decimal) Day. From this date, retailers were required by European law to label products with metric measures rather than the traditional imperial measures. There was some criticism that the government did not give the event enough publicity. However, many larger retailers did provide customer information to help shoppers with the change. Figure 7.21 shows an extract from the Tesco leaflet 'Changing to metric'.

During the next few months Tesco will start to convert products that are currently sold by imperial weight (pounds, ounces) into metric quantities (kilograms, grams etc). This is necessary to comply with changes in the law to meet European requirements.

You may have already noticed that many goods sold in sealed containers, such as bottles and tins have been labelled in metric for some time. For example wines and spirits are sold in litres and centilitres, with tea, coffee and cereals sold in kilograms and grams.

WHEN WILL THIS HAPPEN ?

During the next few months, many pre-packed products which are individually priced according to their weight will start to be packed and weighed in metric units.

WHICH PRODUCTS WILL CHANGE ?

All pre-packed products including meat, poultry, bacon, fish, cheese and fruit and vegetables will change.

WHAT CHANGES WILL I NOTICE ?

ON THE PACK: Pre-packed products in our fresh food areas will show the metric weight and price.
ON THE SHELF EDGE PRICE LABELS: The label will show both the price per kg and the price per lb for these products.

WHICH PRODUCTS ARE NOT CHANGING ?

All products purchased 'loose' from our service counters, eg Delicatessen, meat counters, fish counters will continue to be sold in imperial quantities as will fruit and vegetables that you select and pack yourself.

HOW CAN I COMPARE PRICES, IF SOME PRODUCTS ARE METRIC AND SOME IMPERIAL ?

The shelf edge price labels for pre-packed products will show the price per kg and the price per lb, so that you can make a comparison between different areas of the store such as the Delicatessen counter or the fish counter.

Also please use this conversion card to help you, or ask any member of our staff for assistance.

TESCO
CONVERSION CHART
METRIC TO IMPERIAL

50g	1.8oz	900g	1lb 15oz
100g	3.5oz	1kg (1000g)	2lb 3oz
200g	7oz	2kg (2000g)	4lb 6oz
250g	8.8oz	3kg (3000g)	6lb 9oz
500g	1lb 2oz	4kg (4000g)	8lb 13oz
750g	1lb 10oz	5kg (5000g)	11lb
800g	1lb 12oz	10kg (10000g)	22lb

CONVERSIONS SHOWN ARE APPROXIMATE

Figure 7.21 An extract from a Tesco leaflet on going metric

activity

1 A greengrocer selling loose fruit and vegetables will not be affected by the change: true or false? Explain your answer.
2 What are the metric equivalents of 1 lb 10 oz; 4 lb 6 oz? What are the imperial equivalents of: 500 g; 2 kg; 3.5 kg?
3 Cheese which formerly cost £0.90 for 7 oz will now be labelled as £__ per kg (fill in the price in pounds).
4 Dr Pepper is normally sold in 440 ml cans. In a special offer, it is sold in cans containing 13.5% extra. How much is in each of the new cans?
5 In which metric units are the following measured: petrol, timber, instant coffee, prepacked oranges, orange juice, biscuits, curtain material, sausages?

The use of technology

BAR CODES

Most packaged products are now identified by an individual product number supplied by the manufacturer. To enable this to be read by machine, the number also appears in the form of a **bar code**. Large retailers use a **laser scanner** to read the bar codes on each of the products that a customer has chosen. The shop's computer will have been programmed with the price (and often a description) of each stock item so that a till receipt can be automatically printed. Bar-code readers may be fixed or hand-held, and are clearly much faster than keying in numbers by hand.

Bar codes will normally have 13 digits, though suppliers of smaller products may use 8-digit codes. A 13-digit bar code would be composed as shown in Figure 7.22.

9 780748 722037

First 2 digits = country identifier – e.g. 50 = GB, 40 = Germany   Next 5 digits = manufacturer   Next 5 digits = product   Final digit = check digit

Figure 7.22   An example of a 13-digit bar code

The manufacturer numbers are allocated by the numbering authority of each country.

Bar-code readers are becoming more common, but the large retailers are still the main users. Retailers without bar code readers may use their own, simpler numbering system. Often, labels are fixed *over* the bar codes, perhaps containing a 4-digit code which is keyed into the cash register by hand.

EPOS (ELECTRONIC POINT OF SALE)

This refers to the technology that uses scanners to read bar codes. It is not just EPOS's increased speed at the checkout that is important: stores also use the system to provide valuable management information (see Figure 7.23). In addition to using the reading to print the customer receipt, the computer will store the details of each sale. This can be used to: analyse sales from a particular till, analyse sales at a particular time of day or week, and update stock records, so that goods can be reordered as necessary.

EFTPOS (ELECTRONIC FUNDS TRANSFER AT POINT OF SALE)

Many customers pay by plastic card – either debit card or credit card (see page 328). EFTPOS allows the electronic movement of funds from the account of the customer or the credit-card company to the retailer's account. The customer's card is 'swiped' through a machine which reads the electronic stripe on the back of the card, and a voucher is printed for the customer to sign. If the card is valid and the signature matches, then the transaction is completed.

On Switch debit cards, EFTPOS allows customers a 'cashback' facility in £10 multiples up to £50. This is similar to withdrawing money from a cash machine. A customer requiring £20 cashback is billed for an extra £20 which is then paid to the customer from the till.

By 1993, EFTPOS accounted for around 30% of sales at Sainsbury's.

EDI (ELECTRONIC DATA INTERCHANGE)
This system allows orders to be sent to suppliers electronically – i.e. from computer to computer. The speed and accuracy of the service

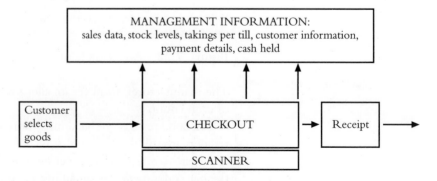

Figure 7.23 How EPOS provides instant information

makes it cheaper than telephone, post or fax. In addition to orders, information such as sales forecasts and stock levels can also be sent in this way.

Advantages of being able to send orders so quickly are:

- It is less likely that the retailer will run out of stock whilst waiting for deliveries
- There is no need to stockpile – which could lead to waste
- Goods are in better condition

Also:

- EDI can be used across the world at any time of day or night
- Suppliers' documents such as invoices and statements can also be sent in this way. There is less paper, less post to sort and, since details go straight to the computer, no need to key in information

1 What advantages does scanning bring to the store? What advantages does scanning bring to the customer?
2 By 1996, 75% of groceries will pass through scanning systems. Does this mean that 75% of grocers will have scanners?

FUTURE DEVELOPMENTS

In the USA, trials have begun on **self-service checkouts**. A bill is generated which the customer takes to a cashier responsible for several checkouts. In Holland, experiments are under way to do away with the checkout altogether. Instead, customers will scan their own goods. In England, Safeway has already introduced a similar system in some stores. Hand-held scanners allow customers to log the price of goods as they are put into the trolley. An itemised bill is produced which is paid at an express checkout. This service should be available to loyalty-card holders in all of their stores by 1998.

The terminals in outlets such as McDonalds and some Bass public houses use a **touchscreen** which makes transactions easier for the operator. There is a key for each possible sale, so that there is no need to type in details from a keyboard. This system is useful where a limited range of goods is sold.

EMPLOYMENT PATTERNS

The distributive trades – retailing and wholesaling – make up the second largest single industry in the UK employing over 2.5 million people. Retailing alone is the biggest service sector employer, with 1 in 8 of the working population and almost half a million shops.

When looking at employment in retailing, we must remember that:

- many small retailers are self-employed and may not employ staff at all

- the larger retailers employ staff in a wide range of roles. As well as the staff we see in the store, there are accountants, buyers, personnel officers, marketing managers and so on. We discuss the role of different departments on pages 268 to 271. Figure 7.24 shows the levels of employees found in larger retail organisations

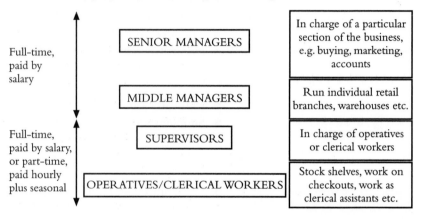

Figure 7.24 Grades of staff in large retail organisations

Staff FULL-TIME WORKING

Depending upon the nature of their work, full-time staff will be paid either a monthly salary or a basic wage, with additions for overtime hours worked. Managers will be engaged on full-time contracts, although in some cases these may last for a fixed period only (perhaps one year or two years). Supervisors and clerical staff will also normally work full-time. Checkout operators and staff performing manual duties such as shelf-stacking would once have been full-time, but this is changing.

PART-TIME WORKING

Increasingly, retailers are taking on part-time staff to perform the relatively unskilled operations in the warehouse and shop. Part-time staff have a number of advantages for the employer:

- they can be employed to fit with changing levels of demand
- they are relatively cheap to employ as they do not qualify for all of the rights of full-time staff

SEASONAL WORKING

In certain trades, demand changes with the seasons. In a seaside resort, the summer period will be busy, whilst in the toy trade, Christmas will be the peak time. Retailers may cater for increased demand by paying overtime to existing staff. However, employing temporary staff may also be the answer. These may be employed on a full-time or a part-time basis, but for a limited period only.

Some general trends in employment are:

- Flexible working practices: it is becoming usual for retailers to employ staff on terms which enable them to vary weekly hours according to market demand. Burtons, the high-street tailors, has introduced zero-hour contracts which enable it to call up shop staff only when they are needed. Burger King, the retail fast-food chain, hit the headlines when it was reported that an employee at one of its outlets was asked to clock off when the restaurant was empty and clock on again when customers came in
- Employment is becoming less secure: in common with the rest of industry, retail employees are no longer sure of 'a job for life'. This is true at all levels of the organisation as competition and new technology changes the way in which jobs are carried out
- There is more part-time working – especially by women. Much shop work is relatively unskilled, and the small amount of training required makes it ideal for part-time workers. This suits the employer who gains more flexibility with staffing, whilst some employees – students for example – find that working part-time – perhaps evenings or weekends – fits in well with their other commitments
- The 7-day-a-week opening is a mixed blessing. Depending upon the employer, it may mean an opportunity to earn more money or unwelcome shift work and the loss of a Sunday at home.

Read the extract on Sunday trading on page 208. Is it to be welcomed? What do you think?

EMPLOYMENT PROTECTION AND CONSULTATION

Contracts of employment

Many of those engaged in the retail sector are self-employed – often as small shopkeepers working, perhaps, in partnership with members of their families. Many small retailers need to work very long hours in order to make a living.

Employees, on the other hand, must have a **contract of employment** setting out the terms and conditions of their job. The magazine *Retail Newsagent* included this outline of the contents of a contract of employment in an article on staffing:

Sunday trading

Sunday Trading legislation allows retail organisations to trade for up to six hours on a Sunday. The frequency of Sunday Trading at your branch/store will depend on local trading conditions.

Working on a Sunday is voluntary for all members of staff who were recruited before 26 August 1994. Staff recruited after this date who are required to work on Sundays may choose to opt out of Sunday working but need to give three months' notice.

Details relating to your individual hours of work and payment for Sunday working will be discussed with you at the appropriate time.

Due to historical differences in trading conditions and legislation in Scotland, separate arrangements exist for employees working in Scotland as distinct from the remainder of the United Kingdom. In Scotland, Sunday is a normal working day and employment contracts will reflect this. All employees working in Scotland will be contracted to work over seven days (Monday to Sunday), and will receive normal rates of pay for any hours worked on a Sunday.

(Source: Burton Menswear staff manual*)*

CONTRACT OF EMPLOYMENT

Once an employee starts work, and therefore implicitly accepts the employer's terms and conditions, he or she is legally entitled to 'written terms' – in other words a contract. This must be given within two months of the start of employment and applies to all employees, part and full-time, providing their employment lasts for at least one month. The document must include the following points:

- Names of both the employer and the employee
- The date employment began and, if different, the date upon which the period of continuous employment began
- Rate of payment, plus how and when it is to be made
- Hours of work, including arrangements for overtime
- Holiday entitlement and pay – and how

holiday pay will be calculated if employment ends
- Entitlement to sick leave and relevant pay
- Details relating to pension schemes
- Notice required for termination of employment from each party
- Employee's job title or brief description of the work
- For temporary staff, include the period the job is expected to continue, or the termination date if the term is fixed
- Either the place of work or, where the employee will be required to move around, an indication of this and the employer's address
- Details of any relevant collective agreements which may affect the terms of employment
- There must also be a note of disciplinary and grievance procedures, including:
  (i) The name of the person to whom the

employee can apply regarding any grievance relating to his or her employment or any disciplinary action

(ii) How an application should be made

(iii) Any further steps which follow from making an application

(Source: Retail Newsagent, *6 January 1996)*

activity

1 Which employees are not entitled to have a contract of employment?
2 'Collective agreements' are negotiated by trade unions. What do you think this term means?
3 Who are the 'parties' to the contract?
4 Why do you think it is important to mention 'arrangements for overtime'?
5 When do you think an employee takes out a 'grievance procedure'? Think of an example.

Representative groups

Representative groups may include:

- **Trades unions**: The main unions for retail employees are: USDAW (Union of Shopworkers Distributive and Allied workers), GMB (General, Municipal and Boilermakers Union) and the Transport and General Workers Union (TGWU). The unions will represent the interests of their members by:
  - bargaining with employers for better wages and conditions of work
  - providing help and advice – they may for instance defend a member in a court case or at an industrial tribunal (a court dealing with complaints under employment law)
  - providing facilities for adult education, leisure and sports
  - acting as a pressure group. For instance, they may put pressure on Parliament to change the law – for example, unions are in favour of the minimum wage.
- **ACAS** (Arbitration, Conciliation and Advisory Service) may be brought in when employers and trade unions have a disagreement that they cannot resolve
- **Professional bodies**: many employees in managerial positions will belong to professional bodies such as the Institute of Marketing or the Chartered Institute of Management Accountants (CIMA). These provide qualifications and information, and lay down guidelines for standards in the profession
- **Staff associations**: where employees do not have a trade union, they may be represented in the workplace by a staff association. This will provide a forum through which employees can voice their concerns. It may also provide benefits such as leisure facilities and social activities

- **Pressure groups** representing various retail interests include:
  - ACS (Association of Convenience Stores)
  - SIR (Society of Independent Retailers), a pressure group for independents

  These last two groups gave evidence at an enquiry into the National Lottery held in February 1996 by the National Heritage Select Committee

Legislation

Laws affect employees in the retail trade in a number of ways:

- Health and safety in the workplace: the Health and Safety at Work Act 1974 (HASAWA) sets out the need for safe working conditions. It is the responsibility of the employer to set and maintain suitable working conditions, whilst the employee in turn must help by working in a safe manner
- Equal opportunities in recruitment and at work: acts of Parliament cover matters such as discrimination on the grounds of sex (Sex Discrimination Act 1975 and 1986 and Equal Pay Act 1970), race (Race Relations Act 1976) and disability (Disability Discrimination Act 1995)

  There are no laws dealing with ageism – i.e. not taking on older employees. However, some chains – such as B&Q – have a policy of encouraging older people to work for them
- Dealing with payments and related matters: as well as paying the employee, the employer must deduct the correct income tax (often called PAYE, or pay as you earn) and National Insurance Contributions (NIC). These must then be sent to the Inland Revenue. The employee must be given a pay slip showing the gross pay earned, the deductions for PAYE and NIC, and the net pay received
- Wages and salaries: at the time of writing, wages and salaries are not controlled by law, but are set by agreement between the employer and the employee. Sometimes, a rate of pay is set nationally for a particular job by agreement between the employer and the relevant trades union. This situation may change, however. The Labour Party has promised to introduce a minimum wage, in line with European Union policy, if it wins the next general election. Many small shops, however, believe that they would not be able to pay more in wages, and would have to lay off staff.

Case study: the minimum wage

At present, there is a debate about whether there should be a minimum wage in the UK. Since 70% of retail workers earn less than £4 per hour (see Table 7.1) this debate is very relevant to the retail sector.

What do retailers think?
Small retailers, who usually employ non-union staff, do not want a minimum wage. The Association of Convenience Stores (ACS), for example, believes that this would lead to job losses in over 80% of its stores.

Table 7.1 Some examples of shopworkers' pay

SUPERMARKET	JOB	HOURLY RATE	TRADE UNION
Tesco	Checkout ops	£4.27	USDAW
Sainsbury	Checkout ops	£3.90	USDAW
	Senior ops	£4.50	USDAW
Somerfield	Checkout ops	£3.49	USDAW
Presto	Checkout ops	£3.85	USDAW
Morrisons	Checkout ops	£3.65	USDAW
Kwik Save	Checkout ops	£3.75	USDAW
Asda	Checkout ops	£3.67	GMB
Convenience stores	Checkout ops	£3.30 average	Usually none

Rates as at January 1996

What does the UK government think?
In 1989, the Member countries of the European Union drew up the Maastricht Treaty. The Conservative government in the UK has, so far, felt unable to accept certain sections of this treaty; in particular, the government disagrees with the idea of a minimum wage. Indeed, in 1992, it abolished the wages councils which had set minimum wages for those employees (including many shopworkers) who were not represented by trades unions. The government believes that if employers are forced to pay higher wages, this will 'price workers out of jobs' – i.e. they will become too expensive to employ.

What does the Opposition think?
The Labour Party has suggested that it will introduce a minimum wage if it wins the next election. Although no figure has been agreed, £4.15 per hour was suggested at the 1995 Labour Party conference. This figure is half the median male earnings (£8.30 per hour). They point out that their net profits are very low (between 1p and 3p in the pound – those of the larger stores such as Sainsbury's are 8p).

A survey of 928 convenience stores showed that:

- a £4 minimum wage would increase average convenience-store wages by 20%
- average reduction in profits would be 35%
- 13% of independent convenience stores (the smaller ones) would close
- 30% of convenience stores said that they would need to raise prices to pay for the increased wage bill

What do the trades unions think?
Generally, the trades unions want a minimum wage – including USDAW, who represents shop and distributive workers, and the TGWU who supports transport workers.
Convenience Store magazine (January 1996) quoted an USDAW spokesperson as saying: 'Those who pay less than £3 an hour don't deserve to be in business – we know of instances of convenience stores paying less than that. They charge exorbitant prices – they should be able to pay reasonable wages.'

1 There are 32,000 convenience stores in the UK. If 80% laid off just one member of staff, how many staff would lose their jobs?
2 Why are wages so low in small convenience stores compared to the average wage?
3 If convenience stores were forced to close or to raise their prices, which section of the population would suffer most?
4 Explain the difference between **median** earnings and **mean** earnings. Why is the median used as a basis for the minimum wage? (Think of the wide variety in rates of pay for different jobs.)
5 Who do you agree with? Do you think that there should be a minimum wage? (Try to keep up-to-date with this debate – information about it will appear in the newspapers from time to time.)

Self-test questions:
Chapter 7

1 Explain the terms: convenience store, superstore, hypermarket, independent, multiple.
2 Name three primary and three secondary products which may be sold by retailers.
3 Name five different ways in which retailers may compete. Give examples.
4 Give two examples of changes to opening hours which have affected retail employees in recent years.
5 Give one example of how European standardisation has affected retailers.
6 What is the meaning of the abbreviations EPOS and EDI? Explain these two innovations.
7 Describe the government's attitude to out-of-town shopping since 1993. What is the reason for this change?
8 Give two examples of seasonal peaks in trade. What type of retailers might benefit from each?
9 Name five pieces of information which should be stated in a contract of employment.
10 How might the introduction of a minimum wage affect retail employees? Give one benefit and one possible disadvantage.

PART 1

Choose *three* different goods, at least one a manufactured good and one a primary good. Produce a report to describe:

- the various types of retail outlet selling each of the goods. You should identify a number of actual outlets. You may wish to use a table similar to the one on page 101
- the ways in which the various retailers selling each product compete with one another. Give actual examples – you may wish to include an appendix containing press cuttings or advertisements as evidence
- the use made of technology by each of the retail outlets. Explain the features of the technology used and how these benefit each retailer
- any trends which have affected the retailing of the three products over recent years. Identify also any current trends. Again, you may include press cuttings etc. in the form of an appendix

PART 2

Select *two* contrasting retail outlets from those mentioned above – this work will be more effective if you choose large retailers. For each, provide notes on:

- patterns of employment. You will need to contact each organisation to find out to what extent staff are: full-time, part-time or seasonal. You will also need to explain what factors have influenced these employment patterns and whether there is a particular trend
- forms of employment protection. Write a brief description of the legislation which employers must be aware of when employing staff. Identify also the main features in a contract of employment
- consultation. Explain the ways in which the employees are consulted by the employer. You may mention the role of: works councils, trades unions and staff associations

Investigating the retail environment

In this chapter, we will:

- consider elements of store design
- look at different types of store layout
- look at how the internal layout and ambience of a store can affect customer behaviour

We will cover Element 3.2, Performance Criteria 1, 2, 3, 4, 5.

Customers are interested in getting the right goods at the right price. However, with so much choice around, a retailer must do more than just stock and display goods. It is necessary to create a whole selling environment in which customers can be persuaded to buy. This chapter looks at how the various retailers attempt to do this.

ELEMENTS OF STORE DESIGN

Stores are designed to achieve two main purposes:

1 to attract customers into the store. Customers are attracted into a store by its external appearance. This can appeal in various ways: perhaps by the shop window display, perhaps by signs which show what the store is selling, or simply by its general appearance. Where the store is part of a chain of stores, the architecture, the lettering and the logo all help to give it an identity. Every branch of Woolworths, The Body Shop and Habitat shares the same distinctive image which is instantly recognisable. The customer knows what to expect.

2 to maximise sales from these customers once they are inside. The design and decor inside the store will be carefully planned. Customers are tempted to buy where there is an atmosphere which they find attractive, a store layout which enables them to find the goods, and displays which present those goods effectively.

The larger organisations spend a good deal of time and money in building up a 'brand' image. Both the store facade and the interior decor are designed to reinforce this.

The store facade

First impressions are important. The facade should identify the store and distinguish it from others, and it should also tell the customers exactly what is inside – i.e. whether it is a chemist or a shoe shop, whether it is for young people, whether it is a convenience store etc.

When designing the store facade, a retailer must pay attention to:

- the shop name and logo
- the fascia

- the shop front
- the window display

THE SHOP NAME AND LOGO

Figure 8.1 Some well-known retail names and logos

Where a large retailer has developed a strong image, then the name is sufficient to trigger off the right associations: John Lewis 'Never knowingly undersold', 'Boots the chemists', 'Dewhursts the butchers' and so on. Notice the 'The' becomes an important word in a shop name: '*The* Body Shop', for instance, is far more effective than just 'Body Shop' as it implies that there is no serious competition.

Retailers also spend a lot of money on the appearance of their names, since the lettering and the logo give them a distinctive trade mark (see Figure 8.1).

Small independents have a different problem. They are not well known and therefore need to make an immediate impact, particularly when they are in a parade of often competing shops. They may need to put up a sign explaining exactly what they sell, or alternatively to think of a name which gives the right impression – see Figure 8.2.

J F HAKE Fishmonger	*CRESCENT MINI MARKET* Off-Licence Newsagent Grocer *OPEN ALL HOURS!*

NORTHERN LIGHTS (Aberdeen) LTD All your electrical needs

Figure 8.2 Examples of signs for small independent shops

activity

1 Some retailers have established such a strong image that the name itself tells us what is inside the store. Complete the table using the answers given.

SLOGAN	RETAILER	PRODUCT LINE(S)
The wonder of		
.... everyone's favourite ingredient		
Don't just do it .... it		
I'll see you in		

Answers: B&Q, Courts, Woolworths, Sainsbury's groceries, variety of goods, furniture, DIY.

2 Provide a suitable sign for independents selling each of the following: young fashions, tapes/CDs/videos, health foods, anything else that appeals to you. You need to make it informative and eye-catching but simple. Try to think of a suitable trading name.

Case study: fascias

One solution to shop-front design for the independent trader is to use a **branded fascia** – see Figure 8.3 for an example. There are many branded fascias available, but the problem is that those produced by manufacturers represent a particular product rather than the shop, and may therefore give a misleading impression. A Fosters or Carlsberg fascia may give the impression that the shop is an off-licence when in fact it is a convenience store. According to Alan Toft, director of the Federation of Wholesale Distributors:

'There are two schools of thought. Some wholesalers believe that any professionally designed fascia is better than an anonymous, old fashioned shopfront. But there is a considerable body of opinion in wholesale circles which believes the front of the shop is the most valuable platform a local retailer has and they should therefore guard it jealously. A fascia should tell the local community the shop is a convenience store and not a confectionery, or cigarettes or brewery outlet only.'

Fascias are supplied free both by manufacturers and by wholesalers. The idea is to support independent shops as well as to advertise the supplier. Fascias cost the supplier around £1,500 each, and generally need servicing around twice a year.

Manufacturer's fascias
The tobacco industry once had a monopoly on fascias, but now has a voluntary agreement with the government that all those advertising tobacco should be taken down by the end of 1996. (Are there still any in your area?) These are being replaced by fascias advertising the likes of Heineken, Mars, Coca-Cola and *Auto Trader*. Coca-Cola has an agreement to take over from Rothmans the tobacco company, and *Exchange and Mart* is considering taking over from Gallaher tobacco.

Wholesalers' fascias
The large wholesaler Nurdin & Peacock issues 'Happy Shopper' fascias to retailers who stock N&P own labels exclusively and at least 300 product lines. There is also a one-off charge of £100. Wholesalers such as Spar and Londis also supply fascias to retailers in their groups. Spar has over 16,000 fascias in 17 countries.

Most independents seem glad to have this free help in making their shop look more professional. However, their main importance may be in attracting passing trade; the locals already know what the shop sells.

(Adapted from Convenience Store Magazine, *January 1996)*

Figure 8.3 A branded fascia

1 Why are wholesalers and suppliers keen to support retailers by providing costly fascias free of charge?
2 In what sense is the success of the independent retailer important to wholesalers and manufacturers? (Clue: think of the supply chain. Think also of own-brand goods.)
3 Which cigarette brands are produced by Gallaher and which by Rothman? Which products are produced by Tetley-Carlsberg?

THE SHOP FRONT

The **shop front** can be either **straight**, **recessed** or **open** (see Figure 8.4).

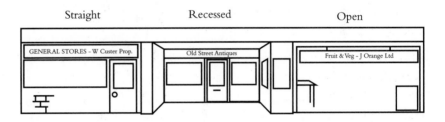

Figure 8.4 Straight, recessed and open shop fronts

A straight front is used by the majority of shops. It allows passing shoppers a clear, unrestricted view. The disadvantage is that shoppers pausing to look into the windows may cause an obstruction on the pavement.

A recessed front draws shoppers from the pavement towards the windows and allows them to pause and look at the goods without causing an obstruction. A disadvantage is that it also attracts people who just want to shelter from the rain.

Open fronts are used by shops in indoor shopping precincts where bad weather and retaining heat are not considerations. This style is also used by high-street shops selling fresh produce such as fruit and vegetables and fresh fish. This style is a combination of a shop and a stall. The advantage is that there is extra space for customers – which is important if queues form – and that it is easier to bring in new stock (important for fresh food, which is delivered each day). It is also possible to extend the display onto the pavement. Since customers do not have to walk through a door, they are more likely to browse around. However, security may be a problem, and there is a greater risk of pilfering.

THE WINDOW DISPLAY

Window displays are important because they advertise the shop – even at night when it is closed. Displays vary depending upon the exact message they wish to send, but the aim is the same: to attract 'passing trade'. The expertly designed window of a department store announces 'This is quality', whilst the list of special offers glued to the window of the cut-price grocery store says 'This is a bargain.'

Shops will pay more for a prime position on a high street simply because here the shop window will be seen by more people.

Inside the store – creating the right atmosphere

There is a great deal of psychology involved in selling. This goes beyond the obvious need to display goods in a clean environment. The larger organisations in particular have a clear aim when they design their stores; the various forms of wall decoration, floor patterns, ceiling tiles, lighting arrangements are all carefully planned to achieve the desired effect. The idea is to carry the image presented by the shop front through into the store itself so as to create a positive buying environment.

Dimensions: sight, sound, smell, touch

The large retailers are well aware that they can manipulate the shopper by appealing to the various senses. We take in messages not just with our eyes but also with our ears and nose, and by feeling and touching. Some of this is common sense: if a shop is freezing cold, we won't stay in it for long. However, retailers also use some quite sophisticated techniques to actually persuade us to buy things.

SIGHT

Of all the information we receive about our environment, 80% comes from what we see. The most obvious way of attracting shoppers is therefore by displaying goods in an attractive manner in clean surroundings. However, the image presented by the shop itself is also important. Depending upon what we are buying, we might need clear or subdued lighting or a well-lit food-hall. We may be happy to buy cut-price groceries or electronic goods from a bare warehouse, but we may be more inclined to buy sophisticated clothes, ceramics, glasses or perfume in a more intimate setting, perhaps with a lower ceiling and a carpeted floor. Some years ago, research even suggested that floor patterns were important in setting a customer's mood. The theory was that lines (like the cracks in the pavement) made customers feel anxious and thus inhibited buying.

Clearly, price is a big factor in any buying decision, but often there is little to choose between shops. Recently, retailers have been attempting to compete by providing better customer service – this includes providing pleasant surroundings. The new supermarkets, for instance, are well–lit and spacious, and have waiting areas with seats and large potted plants. The large shopping malls such as the Metro Centre at Gateshead, the Arndale Centre in Manchester and the Lakeside at Thurrock provide a pleasant total shopping environment which benefits all of the retailers located there.

Be aware, when you next enter a shop, of how the decor is used to give a desired effect. Particularly in the larger stores and those concerned with fashion, the colour schemes, lighting, style of fixtures and fittings, and size and shape of the selling area are all designed to make an impression upon the customer. Tricks include hiding pipes and wiring by putting wooden slats across the ceiling (few people look directly upwards) or painting ceilings in a dark colour which appears to reduce the height of the store.

1 Red (the colour of aggression) is the favourite choice of motorists for new cars. Which colours do you feel best convey a relaxed/restful atmosphere, a vibrant/exciting atmosphere? What sort of shops would use these?
2 Which shops need a feeling of space, and which need a cosy/intimate atmosphere?
3 Why are high–street locations more expensive than locations elsewhere? Which retailers need a high–street location? Which retailers are free to choose the cheapest locations in the country?
4 In which shops do you see the different lighting effects shown in Figure 8.5.

Figure 8.5 Some do's and don't's of lighting

SOUND

Public address (PA) systems can be used both for music and for announcements.

Music

The following conversation was overhead some years ago (in the 1970s!):

Question: 'What's that new hairdresser like?'
Answer: 'Not bad: they play Hendrix.'

Music can clearly help to create an image which will appeal to particular customers.

Not all shops use music – the supermarkets and department stores, for instance, tend not to – but some of the large shopping centres do. Opinions vary as to whether or not background music is helpful to the retailer. For example:

- The local independent shop may just have the radio playing because the staff like it. The choice ranges from own tapes to pop-music stations and even football commentaries on Saturday. There is no selling theory behind this, and indeed there may be little effect on trade as customers tend to be local and to use the shop simply because it is convenient
- Larger stores such as the Continental-style hypermarkets will have carefully selected tapes. This 'muzak' is designed to relax shoppers, to make them feel secure and to 'smooth out' the shopping experience. The music is not intrusive and is hardly memorable, and frequently it is purely instrumental since words may distract customers
- Clothes boutiques frequently have loud 'popular' music playing. This announces clearly that they cater for a certain kind of customer: the young and fashion-conscious. The music is often played into the street to attract potential shoppers: if you like the music, you'll probably like the clothes. Some shops such as Top Man in London's Oxford Street have gone further with banks of TV monitors showing music videos. The stars on the screen may even directly promote sales by wearing clothes like the ones on display. There is lots of evidence that music changes our mood. If we feel good when we try on clothes, then we are more likely to buy
- Record shops may use music and video in a similar way – as a sort of audio shop window

Announcements: The public address system

The PA system is often the most effective way of getting messages to people in large stores:

- *Staff announcements.* These are important to the retailer but can be annoying to customers. Now, at least among the larger shops, there is some attempt to pass these messages – e.g. 'Would the duty manager please report to till 5?' – carefully without intruding upon the shopper's mood. One possible scenario: the music fades down (which may be the first time that we are aware of it), and an electronic chime (gentle but distinctive) attracts the attention of staff. The voice is clear and polite. The music fades up again

- *Customer announcements.* Where promotions or special offers are available, the PA system may be used to draw the customers' attention to these. This is particularly so in superstores and hypermarkets where the selection is so large that shoppers may otherwise not be aware of them
- *Health, safety and security announcements.* These may include: notices about lost children or about the need to evacuate the store if there is an emergency

Unwanted sound

The **acoustics** of a shop are important. People can generate a lot of noise, and this can create an uncomfortable atmosphere. Shops may use ceiling tiles and floor cushioning to absorb unwanted sounds. Similarly, double glazing will keep out the noise of the traffic.

For discussion:

1 Can you think of any local shops which play music? What do these shops sell? Can you see any connection between the music and what the shop is trying to achieve?
2 Suggest when music may, and when it may not, help to sell.

SMELL

'That smells good. Shall we get some?'

Newly baked bread or fresh coffee beans have their own particular aroma. Shops can make the most of this when tempting us to buy. The new trend for baking on the premises through bake-out (see page 222) provides not only fresh bread but also the *smell* of fresh bread (see Figure 8.6). (Strange that France, the land of genuine fresh bread, is presently going wild over English white sliced!)

Essentially, smell persuades us that we have the genuine article. With some items, indeed, the smell is the whole point, and we therefore need to sample it: the smell of joss sticks, the smell of soap, the smell of perfume, even the smell of flowers.

Unwanted smells

Some smells would not help with sales, and every effort is made to keep these away from the sales area. Examples might be cooking (as opposed to baking) smells, petrol fumes, body odour. The flow of smell must be carefully controlled. Ventilation will remove what is not wanted whilst allowing a flow of what is desirable.

Figure 8.6 An advert promoting in-store baking

1 Why do you think that shops no longer allow smoking on the premises? (Give two reasons.)
2 Name three occasions when smell may help, and three occasions when it may hinder, buying. Which shops need to be particularly aware of this?

TOUCH

In some shops it is vital that the customer can touch the goods because some goods need to be tried on or tried out: a shop selling guitars, a furniture shop and shops selling clothes or shoes are examples. At other times, touch can both tempt and reassure the customer. It is well known, for instance, that with clothes and fabrics, quality can be *felt*. Touch may answer the following questions: How thick is the material? Does it feel 'warm'? Is it soft? Is it 'cool'? Does it 'feel right' when we put it on? Are these shoes comfortable?

Temperature is also an important consideration. A shop should be comfortable – neither too hot nor too cold. In itself, this will not *make* us buy, but the wrong temperature may *prevent* us from buying, perhaps by forcing us to leave the shop.

HYGIENE FACTORS AND MOTIVATORS

You will notice that for each dimension above, we have outlined those factors which will persuade people to buy and those which will put people off. These are known as **motivators** and **hygiene factors**.

- Hygiene factors: these are necessary, but are not in themselves sufficient. We will be discouraged if they are not there, but they alone will not actually persuade us to buy. For instance, a shop must be clean otherwise we will walk out, but cleanliness alone will not sell the goods
- Motivators: as long as the hygiene factors are present, motivators will persuade us to buy. For example, there may be a bargain discount or a promotion on an exclusive perfume

1 Give some examples to complete the tables shown (the first one is done for you).

DIMENSION	HYGIENE FACTOR	MOTIVATOR
Sight	Shop and staff must look clean and tidy. Dirty floors, scruffy staff etc. will put people off	Goods are clearly and attractively displayed, posters show how delicious food will look when it is prepared, signs show special offers, the decor of the shop puts customers into the right mood to buy
Sound		
Smell		
Touch		

2 Which senses would you use to carry out the tasks shown in the second table (there may be more than one)? For each task, give an example of what exactly you might do.

AIM OF RETAILER	SIGHT	SOUND	SMELL	TOUCH
Communicate information about a special offer to customers in the shop				
Attract customers in from the street				
Give an impression of high quality				
Give an impression of cleanliness in the shop				
Suggest that the bread is fresh				

Case study: designing the modern store

Energy efficiency at Sainsbury's

Since the 1970s, fuel costs have risen sharply. Store design has needed to take account of this so as to conserve energy in the use of heating, lighting, air conditioning and refrigeration systems. Sainsbury stores built in the mid-1990s use only 60% of the energy used by similar stores built 10 years earlier.

This has been achieved in a number of ways:

- Refrigerators and freezers produce heat (feel the back of your fridge at home). This is recycled for use in the store's air-conditioning system and to provide hot water for cooking, washing and cleaning
- bakery ovens are a more obvious source of heat. Depending upon demand, they may run from 8 to 15 hours a day at 230 °C. The excess heat is used to heat the bakery itself
- Lights help to heat the air in the sales area. New stores use fluorescent lights which use 20% less energy
- Building Energy Management System. This is a computerised system which takes account of factors such as opening and closing times and the temperature outside the store. It uses this information to calculate the most efficient start and stop times for extractor fans, chiller units and ovens. It controls temperature in the sales and other areas of the store and controls lighting during both trading and non-trading hours. Any faults are reported directly to head office

(Source: Sainsbury)

1 Why was it necessary for Sainsbury's to design stores to save energy?
2 Which particular fuel price rose in the 1970s?
3 In what ways could a small independent shop use energy more efficiently whilst still maintaining an appropriate temperature throughout the shop?

Types of store layout

Retailers are concerned to maximise the use of the sales floor. They can measure how efficient they are by calculating the sales per square foot or square metre. For instance, a convenience store reported that 'over Christmas sales were £22 per square foot', and in 1995 MFI's annual report stated that sales per square foot had increased by 9% over the year. This was achieved by reducing delivery times, so that stores were able to use their space for selling rather than for storage.

The store layout will vary considerably with the type of shop, but the basic idea is always the same: to get the customer to see and buy as much as possible. A number of different layouts are used depending upon the type of shop. The main layouts are:

- the **grid-iron** pattern
- the **free-flow** pattern
- the **boutique** pattern

THE GRID-IRON PATTERN

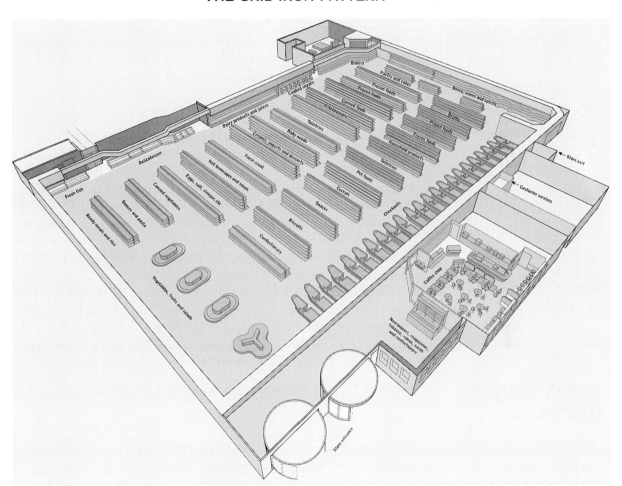

Figure 8.7 A grid-iron layout at Sainsbury

This pattern is favoured by supermarkets – see Figure 8.7 – and convenience stores as an effective way of selling high volumes of low-value goods. Long rows of parallel fixtures channel customers through the shop from entrance to checkout, which are often at different ends of the store. Where the store is very long, there may be a way of crossing from aisle to aisle at various points, but the general idea is to take the customer past as many goods as possible during the shopping expedition.

This layout makes efficient use of the available floor space. It can appear predictable and unexciting, but because the store is likely to be selling essential food, this is not really a problem.

Within the grid iron system typical of the grocery store, retailers choose the position of goods on the shelves according to whether the goods are **demand lines**, **impulse buys** or **promotional lines**.

- Demand lines are those goods most frequently bought. It has been found that in most types of business, 20% of the goods offered are responsible for 80% of the sales. These 80/20 goods (also called **Pareto goods**) are normally spread around the shop to encourage shoppers to visit every part of the store. It is also usual to place these goods near the entrance to encourage immediate interest from the shopper.

   As a rule, best-selling items are usually displayed at eye level ('eye level is buy level'), with related items above or below. This is because customers tend to look up and down rather than from side to side

- Impulse lines are goods that are not on the shopping list but which the customer might still be persuaded to buy. They include chocolate bars and magazines. These are placed where the customer will be reminded to buy them as an afterthought, possibly near the checkout where queuing gives the customer time to make a decision

- Promotional lines are special offers such as three for the price of two or cheap Guinness during the World Cup. They should be spread throughout the store but not too close to demand lines or they will simply replace these in the shopping basket. The idea is to keep the customer interested and to avoid 'flat spots' along the shelves

Sainsbury explains the positioning of its goods as follows:

Nowadays, fresh produce comes first, followed by pasta, soups, tinned food and biscuits. Perishables are stored in chillers along the walls because that's the best area for controlling their temperature, and the meat aisle is always in the middle as people like to browse when choosing their Sunday joint.

Non-food items come next, and frozen food goes towards the end because if it were near the entrance, it would defrost by the time customers leave the store. Wine is against the end wall so that people can take their time finding a bottle to go with the meal they've just chosen.

(Source: Sainsbury's 1995 Annual Report)

THE FREE-FLOW PATTERN

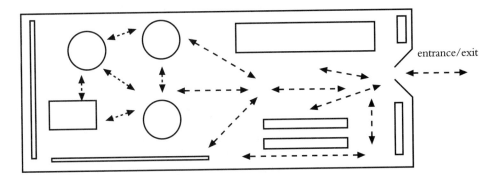

Figure 8.8 The free-flow layout

This pattern is favoured by department stores and by fashionable clothes shops selling higher-value goods. Here, fixtures are positioned in an irregular manner to enable shoppers to move from one to the other at will (see Figure 8.8). The idea is to surround the customer with merchandise. There may be a number of checkouts positioned on islands in various parts of the shop floor.

Although it is a less efficient way of using floor space than the grid-iron system, this type of layout *is* nonetheless appropriate for higher-value goods: it is appealing to the eye and encourages the customer to browse.

THE BOUTIQUE PATTERN

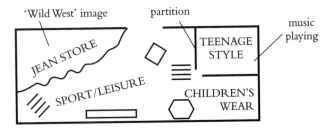

Figure 8.9 The boutique layout

This is a variation on the free-flow pattern. Here, departments or sections are arranged to give the appearance of speciality shops (see Figure 8.9), and are targeted at specific customers. For instance, in a department store there may be separate sections on the same floor catering, perhaps, for different age groups. In this way, there are 'shops' within stores, with special displays and their own identity. Sometimes, these may be concessions run by outside companies – the 'General Store' operates in this way.

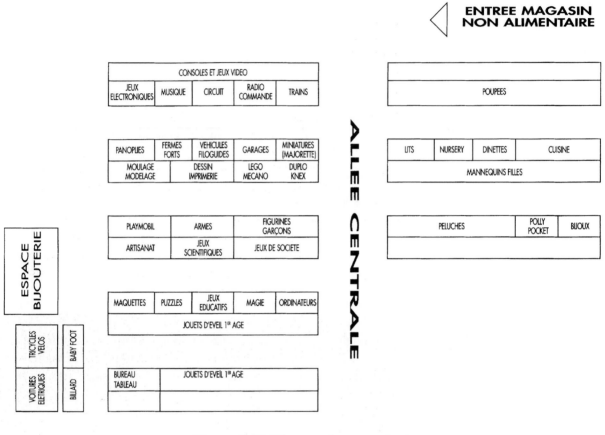

Figure 8.10 The store layout at Auchan

1 What type of store layout do Sainsbury and Auchan use? Why is this?
2 Copy the Auchan plan (see Figure 8.10) and label this in English (use a French dictionary if necessary).
3 Which of your local shops use the free-flow pattern? What do these shops sell?
4 Where are impulse lines displayed in your local convenience store?

Display techniques

When goods were kept behind the counter, people used to buy what was on their shopping list. Today, with goods on open display, we frequently buy extra items which we had no intention of buying when we entered the shop. There is no doubt that sales can be affected by the way in which the merchandise is presented.

In considering how to display goods, the retailer has to ask:

- Where should the different goods be placed?
- How should the different product lines be grouped?

Different displays include:

- open
- theme
- lifestyle
- coordinated
- classification dominance

- **Open displays**: department and fashion stores using free-flow or boutique layouts attempt to surround the customer with a variety of choice. Within the display, similar items may be grouped together – all shirts together, all pullovers together and so on. Alternatively, *related* items may be grouped – e.g. coordinated ranges of clothes, matching outfits
- **Theme displays**: these centre around a particular theme (see Figure 8.11(a)). In August, the shops are full of 'Back to school' displays with calculators, school bags, pens and notebooks. In July, they feature 'on the beach' displays with suntan lotion, sunglasses, towels and swimming costumes

(a)   (b)

Figure 8.11 Examples of (a) a theme display and (b) a coordinated display

- **Lifestyle displays** try to identify the goods with a particular type of person, image or lifestyle. This is a technique used in advertisements where the goods are shown in a particular context: the car driver is young, stylish and powerful – Haagen Dazs ice cream is not just for children, and so on. Some shop displays copy this technique with either real or mock-up props. Examples include motorbikes in clothes boutiques and furniture displayed in mock-up rooms

- **Coordinated displays**: sometimes, a display may include a number of related items, all of which are for sale – possibly a table with cutlery, plates, wine glasses and the appropriate lighting. Other examples might be the child's bedroom with bunk beds, coordinating wallpaper, bedcover and pillow cases, or the garden furniture with sunshade and barbecue (See Figure 8.11(b).)
- **Classification dominance displays** show that the retailer is dominant in a particular product area. John Lewis, for example, sells a wide variety of goods, but is a specialist in fabrics. This will be reflected in window displays where models may have fabric, rather than clothes, draped around them. Other examples may be:
  - a sports shop specialising in skiis or football shirts
  - a DIY shop specialising in power tools

  Displays may be designed to emphasise this dominance

Security and store layout

The trend towards displaying goods openly and encouraging customers to examine merchandise brings security risks. Nevertheless 'shrinkage' (the polite word for theft of stock) can be minimised by thinking about store layout. Points to avoid are:

- expensive merchandise near the door (unless it is secured)
- the till too near the door
- 'blind spots' where customers cannot be seen – there are advantages in not having centre shelving too high

A shop should have:

- mirrors/security cameras so that the aisles can be seen
- loop alarms which will be triggered if stock is moved (for non-self-service shops)
- good security lighting during closing hours

HOW DO RETAILERS AFFECT BUYER BEHAVIOUR?

A retailer must be aware that there are different types of **buyer behaviour**. This behaviour will vary with:

- the particular needs of the buyers: are they in a hurry? Do they have a clear idea of what they want?
- the type of goods. Shopping for convenience goods tends to be a routine exercise, a chore even – it is necessary but hardly exciting. Shopping goods, on the other hand – e.g. CD players, clothes and computers – are more expensive and require more thought

The retailer must cater for the buyers' needs but will also attempt to influence their behaviour so as to make the maximum number of sales. We have seen that store design, choice of decor, store layout and types of display all play their part here.

The retailer may focus on a number of different aspects of buyer behaviour:

1 *Speed of shopping.* Sometimes, a customer is in a hurry. Usually, this applies to shopping for convenience goods, particularly food. Perhaps the need is to get something for tea or to get the shopping done before the children get out of school. Stores ideally wish to slow down the speed of shopping but they must allow for the quick shopper otherwise this trade will simply go elsewhere. Queuing is the main problem, and recent attempts to deal with this include:

- fast checkouts – perhaps cash only, one basket only, or no more than eight items. Tesco's 'one in front' policy has reduced queues by 45%. Here, a new checkout will be opened if there are more than two people in a queue
- CTN (confectioner, tobacconist, newsagents) sections at the entrance to supermarkets – no need to go through the whole shop to buy a magazine or chocolate
- food shops specially designed for busy fashionable shopping areas. Tesco Metros, for instance, cater for shoppers in busy town centres – areas like London's Oxford Street. These customers will not have a car available to carry away a trolley full of goods, and may also be laden with goods from other shops. The range of goods caters for quick shopping – enough for the evening meal rather than a bulk buy for the week.

2 *Shopping duration.* Where possible, the retailer will try to slow down the speed of shopping. Self-service enables customers to choose their own speed, but the store layout may well encourage more purchases than were originally intended. One technique is to place some demand goods (see page 226) near the entrance to get the shopper interested. The idea is to start the customer buying and encourage browsing across the whole range of merchandise. Slower shopping generally means that more goods will be purchased because the various techniques of: store layout, positioning of impulse buys, attractive displays, special offers and even use of smell are all given a chance to work.

Shopping tends to take longer for expensive items. Goods such as clothes, CD players or a new multi-gym are usually bought after much thought and consideration. In this case, the retailer may encourage the customer to make a buying decision – 'This offer is only while stocks last' is one method.

The new shopping malls present such a variety that shopping becomes an event to be enjoyed. A pleasant day out – or two!

3 *Unplanned (impulse) purchases.* These are additional buys made on the spur of the moment – perhaps inexpensive 'treats' such as sweets. These sales are made by the thoughtful positioning of goods on the

shelves. Traditionally, these have been placed at checkouts, but more recently supermarkets in particular have changed this: they now appear on the ends of rows in the main store or in the small CTN shop in the foyer. To some extent, this change has been forced onto retailers – in 1994, for example, Tesco (as already mentioned) removed sweets from the checkouts because its customers asked it to.

4 *Excitement.* One way of making shopping an exciting experience is to use music and video in clothes and music shops, to set up demonstrations in computer stores and to create *movement* in the displays in toy shops. Similarly, Christmas lights and fountains (see Figure 8.14) in shopping malls add to the shopping experience.

5 *Movement through the store.* We have already seen that retailers will use store layout to control the flow of customers through the shop. With convenience goods, they should pass all such goods before they leave, whilst with shopping goods, the customer should be able to choose from the surrounding displays.

AN INVITATION TO STAY

Why not treat yourself and your fellow passengers by turning your one day shopping trip into a relaxing break. Lakeside Shopping Centre has teamed up with the Stakis Dartford Bridge Hotel to bring you an exclusive group discount. For the price of £22.50 (compared with a standard price of £34.00) two people can make use of a twin or double bedded room with en-suite facilities, enjoy a full English breakfast and make full use of the Club Tropics Leisure Centre.

The hotel is a mere 5 minutes by coach from Lakeside so why not spread your shopping trip over two leisurely days, or in addition to your shopping trip enjoy the Essex and Kent countryside and other local attractions. Even Christmas shopping may no longer be an event that is put off until the last minute, but instead a well-earned break to look forward to all year.

(Source: Lakeside Shopping Centre)

SWEET FACTS

- The confectionery market is worth £4.7 bn in sales and 815,000 tonnes in volume. This is equivalent to every Briton spending £7 and eating over one kilogramme per month
- The confectionery market is bigger than the biscuit, breakfast cereal, ice cream and tea markets combined
- Mr Average Briton eats 148 bars of chocolate every year
- £135m was spent on advertising confectionery in 1995
- Enough Cadbury's Dairy Milk is sold each year to cover 430 football pitches
- A survey conducted in 1995 found that nine out of 10 people could recognise the Milkybar Kid, but only six out of 10 could put a name to the Chancellor
- 17,000 Smarties are eaten every minute in the UK
- Britons eat four times as much confectionery as the Italians

(Source: Retail Newsagent, 6 January 1996)

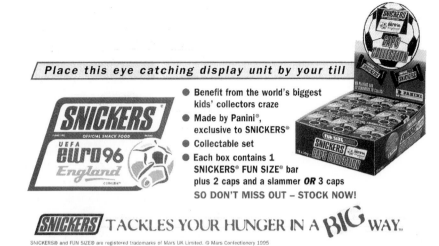

Figure 8.12 A Snickers advertisement for retailers

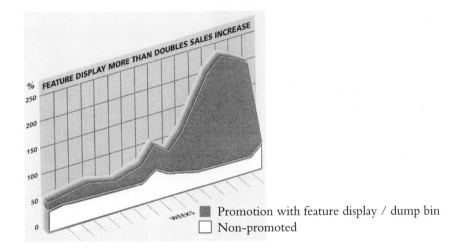

Figure 8.13 A typical impulse sector promotional increase

1 Where does the advert in Figure 8.12 suggest is the best display location?
2 What does the chart in Figure 8.13 show about the effect of displaying and not displaying sweets? How does this suggest that shop displays affect buyer behaviour?
3 What is a 'feature display'? Can you give an example?
4 Where are sweets displayed in supermarkets? Why is this?

Figure 8.14 Making shopping an exciting experience at Lakeside

Case study: how supermarkets influence buyer behaviour

Store layout and design

- The entrance is at the opposite side to the exit
- Customers have to pass most of the displays on the way to the checkout
- The grid-iron pattern is used. This is the most efficient use of space

The positioning and display of goods

- Fruit and vegetables are positioned near the entrance. This gives an immediate impression of freshness – like an open-air market
- Goods which go together, such as meat and gravy, or wine and corkscrews, may be displayed together. This encourages impulse 'add-on' buys
- Rewards, such as soft drinks, wine and beer are offered at the end of the shopping trip. By now customers have the buying habit and may buy on impulse
- Fresh meat and fish are positioned at the back of the store. Carcasses can be moved in without the customers seeing

- Crisps and confectionery are placed at intervals to keep children interested. Bored children distract their parents

Positioning and display for fast sales

- Some suppliers allow stores discounts if they display their goods on shelves 130–135 cm from the ground. 'Eye-level is buy-level': these sell more rapidly
- Special discounts – 'three for the price of two' etc. – are used to introduce customers to new goods or to clear old stock
- An end-of-aisle site may sell more than five times as much as a mid-aisle position. Goods are displayed more prominently here

Own brands

- Own brands are profitable. They take advantage of advertising used by the major companies by using similar colours. Own-brand cola, for instance, usually has a red label
- Basic own-brand foods may have deliberately plain labels. This gives the impression of 'no frills, just value for money' (Why pay for a fancy packet?)

The senses

- Colours are carefully chosen to be restful but fresh: shop decor must not distract the buyer. Each chain has its own distinctive colour scheme to make the customer feel at home
- Fish and meat sold along the aisles is vacuum-packed. It looks good, but looks nothing like an animal: there is no smell and no blood
- Sudden noises can be distracting, but silence too can be unsettling. Stores aim for a controlled background noise, either soft music or the hum of machinery
- Certain types of lighting can reduce the eye-blink rate from 32 to 14 times per minute. The customer becomes relaxed and is more easily persuaded to buy
- Unpleasant smells are drawn away (another reason for fresh meat and fish to be at the back). On the other hand, fresh smells such as baking bread are pumped around. The main value of in-store bakeries is the smell and 'wholesome' image they give to the store, rather than the profit they make

Learning more about us

- Security cameras give stores valuable information about buyer behaviour – the routes that buyers take, where they stop and look, and so on
- Plastic cards used at the checkout tell stores about their customers. A major benefit of loyalty cards is that stores can identify their customers and their shopping habits. They can send vouchers to customers who they think will be interested

Visit your local supermarket and draw a plan of the store layout. Look for examples of the features mentioned above, write these down and label them on your plan.

Recent trends in shop design

We have seen that retailers are constantly studying customers' shopping habits. Recently the large chains have designed shops in a range of styles to try and appeal to the different shopping patterns.

Figure 8.15 shows the range of shop designs used by Tesco. Each of the four is designed to cater for a different shopping pattern.

1 Give *two* differences between the Superstore and the Compact store. Are they likely to be found in different locations?

2 How are the needs of town-centre shoppers using the Metro shops likely to be different from the needs of the Superstore shoppers? Give at least *two* differences.

3 Read the article on page 238 from *The Guardian* newspaper and the information on Shell Select Shops.
   Is the research good news for small independent retailers or for large multiples such as Tesco and Shell? Explain your answer.

4 What type of goods are sold at Shell Select and Tesco Express stores? What type of store layout is used?

5 What are the benefits of combining petrol-station forecourts with convenience stores from the point of view of the retailer and the shopper?

6 Tesco says that it will 'maintain a presence in the high street'. How are high-street shoppers described in the Guardian article? Which type of Tesco stores cater for the high-street shopper?

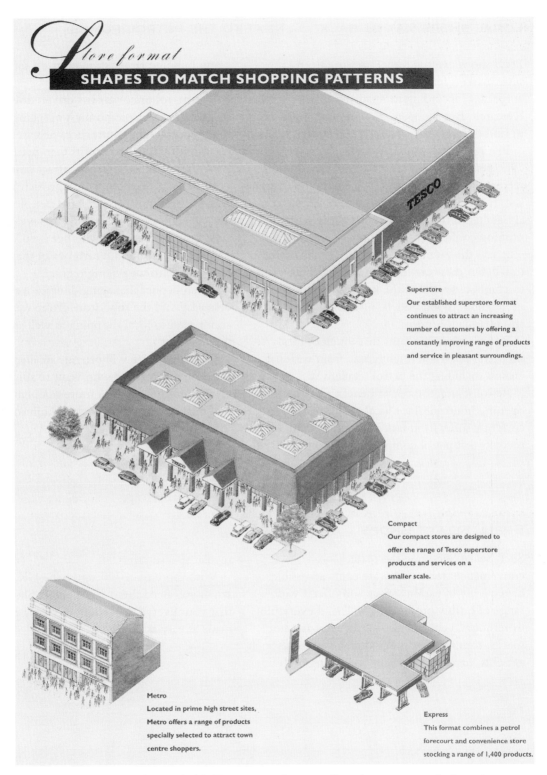

Store format

SHAPES TO MATCH SHOPPING PATTERNS

Superstore
Our established superstore format continues to attract an increasing number of customers by offering a constantly improving range of products and service in pleasant surroundings.

Compact
Our compact stores are designed to offer the range of Tesco superstore products and services on a smaller scale.

Metro
Located in prime high street sites, Metro offers a range of products specially selected to attract town centre shoppers.

Express
This format combines a petrol forecourt and convenience store stocking a range of 1,400 products.

Figure 8.15 Tesco store formats: four shapes to match shopping patterns

LOCAL SHOPS MAY BE BACK . . . NEXT TO THE PETROL PUMPS

Local shops, wilting under pressure from supermarkets for 30 years, could stage a comeback, according to retail consultants Verdict Research. But shoppers are more and more likely to find them on petrol station forecourts.

In a report published yesterday, Verdict says: 'The perceived wisdom is that neighbourhood retailers are under threat on all fronts and that it is only a matter of time before they disappear altogether. Our research shows clearly that nothing could be further from the case.'

It says the number of local shops may continue to fall, but these are likely to become bigger and to combine several of the key activities required of neighbourhood outlets, including post office and pharmacy services.

But the research warns that much of local shopping provision might come from national chains, including the petrol retailers.

Petrol station forecourts benefit from the long opening hours ideal for local shops, but they currently suffer from lack of space. Verdict predicts that petrol companies will therefore begin building larger shop units on their forecourts.

The petrol price war has driven down profit margins on the basic business of selling fuel, and the report says forecourt shops are, in some cases, contributing more to profits than petrol sales, which act as a loss leader to attract customers.

But Tesco's Express format, which has led the way in combining grocery and petrol retailing, is not yet achieving required profit levels. Verdict says: 'It is not yet clear whether even Tesco can squeeze the required return out of the shop under the current pricing regime.'

Tesco deputy managing director Terry Leahy yesterday said the superstore group remained committed to local shopping as well as its out-of-town format.

He added: 'We will provide smaller town stores aimed at those who want to shop for convenience foods on a more frequent basis. We will maintain a presence in the high street.'

(Source: The Guardian, *3 February 1996)*

SHELL SELECT SHOPS

Shell Select Shops are the perfect local convenience stores. They are easily accessible, have plenty of parking space and offer a wide range of quality products. You'll find everything from hot and cold drinks, sandwiches and hot snacks, through to top brand name essentials such as tights, nappies and shampoo – along with regular special offers.

With more than 700 across the UK, open when you need them, Shell Select Shops ensure that your everyday 'top up' shopping trips are made as easy as possible.

(Source: Shell)

Self-Test Questions

1 Why might a wholesaler provide a retailer with a free fascia? Give one example.
2 Give one way in which a retailer may appeal to each of the following senses of the customer: sight, sound, smell, touch.
3 What are 'demand goods'? Why are they also called '80/20 goods'?
4 Give an example of an impulse buy. Where might this type of product be positioned in a shop?
5 Which type of retailer will use the grid-iron store layout? Give one advantage of this kind of layout.
6 Give one way in which a retailer may attempt to prolong the duration of a shopping expedition.
7 What is a 'coordinated display'? Give one example.
8 Give two rules a retailer must remember when lighting a shop.
9 Give three ways in which new stores may be built to be more energy-efficient.
10 Give three uses of a store's 'PA' (public address) system.

evidence indicators

Choose *two* retail outlets to study. They should be different types, for instance a superstore and a boutique, or a convenience store and an antique dealer. You will need to make arrangements to visit the two outlets. Prepare a checklist to remind yourself of the information that you are seeking. This checklist will be based upon the requirements of the report (see below).

Using your findings, produce a report on each retail outlet, giving the following information:

1 the elements used to achieve store design, to include:
   ● the location (high street, parade etc)
   ● the outside appearance – i.e. the fascia, the logo
   ● the inside decor – i.e. walls, floors, ceiling, lighting, atmosphere, fixtures and fittings
   ● the communications methods used by the store
2 the dimension elements used by the store, and the way in which these aim to affect customer behaviour. Include:
   ● sight
   ● sound
   ● smell
   ● touch
3 the type of store layout.
4 the different display techniques used.
5 a conclusion assessing the effectiveness of each store in achieving its objectives.

Examining personal selling

In this chapter, we will:

- examine means of selling different types of consumer good
- look at three different categories of selling
- consider the different stages involved in personal selling
- consider elements of product knowledge
- consider ways of dealing with customer queries

We will cover Element 3.3, Performance Criteria 1, 2, 4, 5, 6.

Selling techniques vary both with the merchandise on offer and with the needs of the customer. Remember that sales personnel cost money and are only employed where shops feel that they cannot sell effectively without them.

WHAT DO SALES STAFF DO?

The customer's decision to make a purchase can be seen as having four stages, often known as AIDA for short – see Figure 9.1. The sales staff themselves tend to be involved in the *desire* and *action* stages. Customers are usually aware and interested already – that's why they have entered the shop in the first place. The seller's task is therefore to focus the customer's interest onto something within the shop which will satisfy his or her needs. As we will see, some products require more selling skills than others, and customers, similarly, vary as to the amount of attention they require.

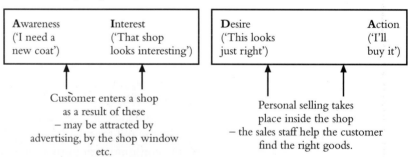

Figure 9.1 The four stages in customer purchase

Ideally, the aim of personal selling is to help customers to find the products they need – and not to sell them something they do not want.

For discussion:

1 For which goods do you feel that you might need help and advice before coming to a buying decision
2 For which goods do you not need help or advice?

(Note: in your answers, try to be fairly precise – to say 'food', for example, is too general.)

3 Can you draw any general conclusions about the type of goods that require personal selling?

TYPES OF GOOD

The goods sold by retailers are called **consumer goods**. These – as we have seen – can be classified as:

- convenience goods
- shopping goods
- speciality goods

Convenience goods – see Figure 9.2 – include:

- **staple goods** – everyday purchases such as frozen food, bread, soap and tea
- **impulse goods** – items we buy on the spur of the moment, such as chocolate or chewing gum

Generally, convenience goods are sold not by the sales assistants but by national advertising, by the layout of the shop and by the way in which the goods are displayed. Most of these goods are prepackaged and standardised and require little product knowledge – we can decide for ourselves whether we need Heinz or Baxters' soup.

Convenience goods tend to be inexpensive, and because we usually need them quite urgently, we enter the shop with the intention of *buying*. Self-service is normal here, and we only need help when we cannot find what we are looking for.

Figure 9.2 Convenience goods

Shopping goods – see Figure 9.3 – include **consumer durables** such as CD players, video recorders, cars and washing machines. They also include clothes and soft furnishings such as curtains and bed linen. Such goods tend to be more expensive than consumer goods, and they are bought less often: the decision to buy here is not urgent and requires more thought.

Customers buying these more expensive goods are more likely to need personal service and advice, so that shops selling shopping goods need an informed sales staff. These stores often stock a variety of competing products to allow the customer choice, and in this case sales staff need to be aware of the differences between brands. Goods such as household furnishings and materials, in which personal taste plays a large part, require particular expertise. Some of the department stores make a feature of expert personal service.

Of course shopping goods can also be obtained from mail-order catalogues, or from the shelves of discount stores like Toys Я Us, where little or no advice is needed. This is a result of growing awareness on the part of consumers and of the availability of advice in specialist magazines.

Speciality goods: a shopping good becomes a speciality good – see Figure 9.4 – when customers ask for it by name: 'We want a Liberty Print, perfume by Paco Raban, Wedgwood pottery or a Ford Fiesta.'

Figure 9.3 Shopping goods

Here, product knowledge is crucial, and sales staff need to be highly skilled at identifying customer needs and then giving appropriate advice.

With some specialised products such as cars, retailers have to gain manufacturer approval before they can become part of the 'dealer network'. This means, among other things, that the sales staff must follow a set of procedures laid down by the manufacturer. (Pages 251 and 252 give some information on Ford dealers.)

Treating goods as convenience goods, shopping goods or speciality goods is a useful way of understanding the selling techniques used by retailers. However, the type of *customer* is also important.

Audi. Vorsprung durch Technik

Figure 9.4 Speciality goods

TYPES OF CUSTOMER

Customers fall into two main categories: those who know exactly what they want, and those who are 'shopping around'. With the former, it is a matter of wrapping the goods and taking the money, whilst with the latter, the customer needs skilful handling if a sale is to be made.

CATEGORIES OF PERSONAL SELLING

We can identify three categories of personal selling:

1 transaction processing
2 routine selling
3 creative selling

1 **Transaction processing.** This is not really selling but merely recording sales details, either in writing, by keying them into a cash register, or, as is increasingly likely, by using a scanner. There may also be a need to wrap the goods and deal with the payment. Little product knowledge is necessary as the customers usually have a clear idea of what they want and frequently serve themselves. Transaction processing is performed by staff at the checkout of the convenience store or supermarket.

The introduction of new technology has gradually reduced the amount of skill and knowledge required. Nevertheless, since sales staff are directly in contact with the public, they must still be efficient, smart, helpful and friendly: the treatment that customers receive may determine whether they return in future or shop elsewhere.

2 **Routine selling.** This is similar to transaction processing, although more product knowledge is required; there is also room for initiative. Sales staff may be asked to: locate the goods, provide some general information about them, and offer some advice.

This type of selling is often associated with non-technical shopping goods such as shoes or clothes in a boutique or cutlery in a department store, though where a customer needs little advice, it may apply also to technical goods such as computers.

Although routine selling normally involves helping the customer to find what they are looking for and perhaps giving advice, it may also be possible to gain extra sales of *related* products by the use of **suggestion selling**. For example, a customer buying shoes may be asked if they need some shoe polish, or a customer buying a computer may be offered a dust cover.

3 **Creative selling.** Creative selling generally involves expensive or technical products where a high degree of specialised knowledge may be necessary. This may apply to both shopping goods and speciality goods; cars, computers and other electrical goods are examples.

A customer who is about to spend a large sum of money will be concerned to make the right purchase, and often needs help and reassurance. Sometimes, a customer has only a very general idea of what he or she needs. For instance, a parent buying a computer as a Christmas present may need a lot of help. It is important that customers do not feel pressurised, and equally important that they have faith in the advice given by the sales staff.

Remember that the categories above overlap, and that the need for creative or routine selling is determined by the type of customer involved as well as by the goods themselves. This is shown in Figure 9.5.

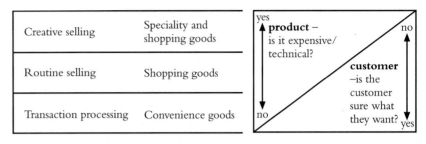

Creative selling	Speciality and shopping goods
Routine selling	Shopping goods
Transaction processing	Convenience goods

Figure 9.5 How the category of personal selling used depends on the type of product on offer

activity

Look at Figure 9.6.

1 What sort of goods will be sold at Peacocks:
- convenience goods
- shopping goods
- speciality goods?
2 What sort of selling will be required?
3 What particular qualities do sales staff need?

NEW STORE OPENING

PEACOCK'S STORES LIMITED, the retail clothing multiple, are opening a new store in CATFORD and require the following personnel:

FULL-TIME, PART-TIME & SATURDAY SALES ASSISTANTS
RETAIL EXPERIENCE PREFERRED

With responsibility for a designated area of the store, your main priority is to provide a courteous and efficient service to customers. General duties will involve the processing of sales transactions using E.P.O.S. tills and maintaining presentation standards within the store.
Applicants should preferably have gained relevant and similar experience with a recognised professional retailer.
In return we offer competitive rates of pay supported by an excellent benefits package including generous holidays, full in-store training and staff discount (after qualifying period).

PLUS MANY OTHER PERMANENT AND TEMPORARY POSITIONS AVAILABLE

Interested applicants should call into:
The Job Centre, 62 - 66 Rushey Green, Catford.

We are an equal opportunity employer.

PEACOCKS
EXCITING OPPORTUNITIES IN RETAILING
STORES NATIONWIDE

Figure 9.6 A staff advertisement from Peacocks

activity

Wheeler Street Motors is a motor dealer which has a parts department open to trade and to retail customers. Details of spare parts are kept in a library of microfiches (small photographs which need to be magnified on a 'reader').

A customer enters, and for once there isn't a queue . . .

Assistant: 'Good morning, sir.'

Customer: 'Morning. Do you have a rear light for a '92 Vauxhall Cavalier, please?'

Assistant:	'I'll need to check. *(Switches on microfiche reader.)* Which side do you need?'
Customer:	'Oh ... er ... *(thinks)* ... off-side.'
Assistant:	'Is it the whole unit or just the glass you need?'
Customer:	'Oh, just the glass, please.'
Assistant:	'Thank you. I won't keep you a moment ... *(looks through the microfiche reader to locate the part)* ... There are several types. Do you have the model number? ... Good. Thank you ... *(continues to look)* ... Right, found it – I'll see if we have one.' ... *(types stock reference number into computer)* ... Yes, we do. Would you like anything else?'
Customer:	'Er ... No, thank you. That's the lot.'
Assistant:	'Right, I won't keep you a moment.' *(Goes to get the part. Returns with the part in a box. Opens the box, and shows the customer.)*
Customer:	'Yes, that's it.'
Assistant:	*(Keys details into the cash register.)* 'How would you like to pay?'
Customer:	'Cash.'
Assistant:	'That will be ... *(Reads price. Customer hands over a £20 note.)* 'Thank you.' *(Puts cash on top of till, counts out change and hands it to the customer with the receipt. Puts £20 note into the till when the customer is satisfied.)*
Customer:	'Thanks very much.'
Assistant:	'Thank you, sir. Goodbye. Who's next, please? Yes madam?'

Now try the following:

1 (a) Does the assistant need expert knowledge?
   (b) Does the customer have a clear idea of what is needed?
   (c) Are the goods of a technical nature?
   (d) Is the customer open to persuasion – i.e. could they also be sold something else?
   (e) Why does the assistant not put the money into the till immediately?
2 What sort selling is going on here, transaction processing, routine selling or creative selling? Your answers from question 1 will help you decide. Look also at Figure 9.5 above.
3 What may be sold by 'suggestion selling' to a customer who has:
   (a) just bought a handbag

(b) just entered a restaurant for a meal?

4 What sort of personal selling (i.e. transaction processing, routine selling or creative selling) would you expect from:

(a) the local Spar convenience store

(b) Marks & Spencer children's clothes section

(c) a double-glazing salesman calling at the door

(d) a high-class jeweller

(e) a record/tape/CD shop such as Virgin/Our Price or Tower Records?

In each case, give reasons for your answers.

STEPS IN PERSONAL SELLING

We have seen that there are different types of personal selling, and that some involve more selling skills than others. The different steps which may be involved are shown in Figure 9.7. Creative selling is likely to involve all of these steps (although sometimes the actual transaction processing itself may be carried out at a separate cash desk). Routine selling will involve some of the steps, whilst transaction processing will normally only involve step number 6. In the rest of this chapter, we will look at what is involved in each of these steps.

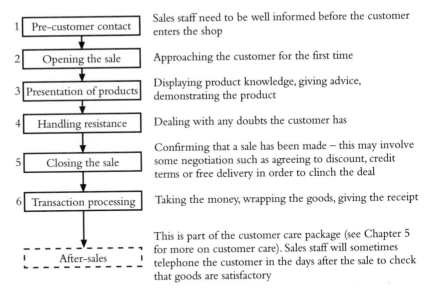

Figure 9.7 Six steps in personal selling

Pre-customer contact

Sales staff need to do their homework if they are to be effective sellers. They need:

- product knowledge, including knowledge of the goods stocked by competitors – this allows an informed discussion of the advantages of the shop's goods as opposed to those of rival shops
- knowledge of stock levels – this avoids selling goods only to find

that the shop is out of stock
- knowledge of delivery schedules – 'You can have it by next Wednesday' – in case the goods need to be ordered
- information on guarantees (sometimes called warranties) and policies about returned goods – 'Take it with you. You can exchange it if you find it's not the right one, as long as the packet isn't opened'

Sales staff must also liaise with the buyers to let them know about customer demands: it is obviously far easier to make sales if the appropriate products are in stock.

Opening the sale Where customers have willingly gone into a shop, it can be assumed that they are at least interested in buying. The salesperson and the customer are complete strangers to each other, and yet it is vital for sales staff to get the first approach right. From the start, sales staff must be courteous. For instance:

- Never keep the customer waiting
- Be aware of the importance of body language: it's not just what you do but how you do it
- Always be tactful
- Remember that you are more likely to sell the merchandise if you sell *yourself* first: the customer must trust you

The salesperson will need to gauge the attitude of mind of the customer. Only then will it be possible to decide on the best way to proceed. The sort of questions that need to be answered are shown in Figure 9.8. Note that not all of these questions would be asked as *direct* questions: it is often possible to pick up useful information from the way in which the customer acts. For instance, some customers appear lost and in need of help, whilst others appear to know what they are looking for and may just need 'Can you find the right size?' or 'Would you like to try it on?'

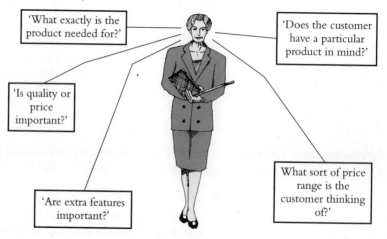

Figure 9.8 Questions for the customer

OPEN AND CLOSED QUESTIONS

In personal selling, a variety of **open** and **closed questions** can be used:

1 Open questions invite the customer to give information, e.g.:
   - Which colour would you like?
   - What exactly do you need it for?
   - Which material were you thinking of?
2 Closed questions are narrower. They ask for a specific response, e.g.:
   - Would you prefer the red or blue?
   - Do you need it for work or home?
   - Do you want pure wool?

It may be best to open with open questions, and then use closed questions to 'home in' on the sale.

Note that the traditional opener, 'Can I help you?', is dangerous: 'No thanks' could be the reply. On the other hand, 'How may I help you?' is far more difficult to turn down.

The presentation of products

This may involve demonstration, explanation and advice. Imagine that a customer coming to a sports shop is interested in a jogging machine. A demonstration here may mean literally showing how the product works by turning it on and explaining the various settings. There may also be an explanation of the various benefits to be gained from this machine.

Upon further questioning, it may be that the customer is concerned to build up physical strength for a particular sport. In this case, advice may be needed as to whether this is in fact the most appropriate machine. Where there are several models, it will be important to explain the difference between them and, perhaps, to explain why the prices vary so much. The skill is to listen to the customer, ask questions to clarify the customer's needs and use product knowledge to suggest the most appropriate solution.

Some general points:

- It is always wise to offer a *choice*. Where the customer is genuinely interested, he or she will feel that it ought to be possible to find something suitable
- The presentation should not be too technical as the customer may feel threatened. On the other hand, where a customer asks technical questions, the salesperson should be able to give relevant advice
- Price and quality are usually related, and this may cause a problem. The customer might ask: 'What's the difference between that model for £79 and that one for £200?' Ideally, the retailer would like to sell the one for £200, but this may be outside the customer's

Figure 9.9 Presenting the product: product knowledge and personal attention at Woolworth

price range. To try to get a sale on the £200 model by suggesting that the one for £79 is really not very good may result in no sale at all.

All suggestions must be positive: 'The £200 one has a more stylish appearance and extra features.' This leaves the cheaper version still perfectly adequate whilst explaining why the other is worth the extra money

The price of a mouse for a computer varies from around £6 to around £40. Assume that a customer needs to replace a mouse that has broken.

1 What would you need to know *before* the customer entered the shop?
2 The customer asks: 'Do you have a mouse for my computer?'
   ● What sort of questions would you ask in order to give the best advice?
   ● What useful things might you be able to guess about the customer just from observation?
3 The customer asks you: 'What do you get for the difference in price?'
   ● What sort of thing would you say?
   ● What would this depend upon?

Handling resistance

Where a customer seems unwilling to go ahead with a purchase, the the sales person must find the *cause* of the objection. Is it a genuine objection, or is the customer just unable to make a decision? Perhaps the customer has decided not to buy, but feels awkward about saying so. The idea here is to reassure the customer, and again, above all, to be positive. Perhaps there is an alternative product, perhaps there has been a misunderstanding about the product, perhaps the cost is more than was at first thought due to hidden extras, or perhaps the customer has not heard of that particular make and needs reassurance. Some of these objections *can* be satisfied.

Resistance to a sale may take many forms:

● 'I'm not really sure. It's a lot of money'
● 'I really wanted a well-known make'
● 'I thought you said VAT was included!'
● 'It's darker than it looked in the window'
● 'I'm not sure now I've got them on'

A customer who is clearly not interested, should be allowed to 'escape' without embarrassment. At least he or she will feel comfortable about returning in future if the shop has been friendly and helpful.

Closing the sale

The rule is 'ABC': 'Always be closing.' The idea is to try to close the sale in a series of steps that make the whole process seem quite logical (and irreversible). Where a choice is to be made it is useful to *summarise* discussions to help the customer decide. Where, for instance, several skirts have been laid on the counter, the ones definitely not needed are removed so that the choice becomes easier.

The ultimate disaster is where the decision is made – 'I've decided to have this one, but in blue' – and the item is out of stock. Here the pre-sales knowledge becomes vital: this possibility should have been foreseen and avoided.

Transaction processing

As we have noted earlier, this involves taking payment, wrapping goods, issuing a receipt and any other associated paper work.

After the sale

The salesperson can now breathe a sigh of relief, but the customer may be wondering: 'Have I done the right thing?' Buying may be a difficult process for many shoppers, not just because they are spending their hard-earned cash but also because they are putting their judgement on the line. This is particularly true in cases where choosing clothes or curtains for the bedroom has taken a lot of time and effort. After the sale, therefore, the customer should be made to feel that the right choice has been made: 'That really does suit you' or 'I'm sure you'll find that very useful' will help a good deal. Reassurance is very important. Research shows that customers read more advertisements about a product *after* buying that product than they do before – possibly because they are trying to confirm that they have made the right choice.

Some shops offer **after-sales service**. This is particularly important with expensive consumer durables which have a fairly long life, such as cars, vacuum cleaners and video recorders. Much after-sales service is dealt with by specialist departments under warranty arrangements and service contracts. However, sales staff may be involved in certain ways:

Case study: sales at Ford Motor Company

The Ford Motor Company sells its vehicles through a network of independent dealers throughout the UK. Research has shown that customer service, and in particular the conduct of and

Figure 9.10 The Ford Motor Company logo

the selling methods used by dealer staff, are vital to Ford sales.

The following guidelines are issued to selling staff:

- Within two minutes of arrival, customers will be courteously acknowledged and advised that a salesperson will be available on request
- The salesperson will demonstrate interest in the customer and establish an advisory relationship by listening to and identifying his or her needs
- All customers will be offered a test drive
- The salesperson and finance and insurance personnel will provide all customers with thorough explanations and a pleasant, non-pressurised purchase experience
- Using a checklist, the salesperson will deliver the vehicle in perfect condition when promised
- The salesperson will introduce the customer to the members of the Service/Parts team to provide reassurance that the customer will be cared for throughout the ownership of the vehicle
- The salesperson will contact all customers 3–5 days after delivery

(Source: information from Ford: 'Ford and its Dealer Network', sheet E70)

- They may contact customers a few days after the purchase to make sure that there are no problems (see the Ford case study above)
- Sales staff will need to be aware of the after-sales package as this is part of the 'product' that they are selling
- Where customers return a product, sales staff need to be aware of company policy. Marks & Spencer, for instance, have for years operated a no-quibble money-back or goods-exchange policy which goes far beyond that required by law

There is more detail on customer service in Chapter 5.

1 Using the Ford information, answer the following:
   - What pre-customer contact do you think that dealers need?
   - How is the sale opened?
   - How is the product demonstrated?
   - How is customer resistance handled? (How is the customer reassured?)
   - What after-sales service is offered?
2 'Hello, this is Nigel speaking. How may I help you?'
   - From a personal viewpoint, does this introduction make the organisation seem more friendly to you?
   - Why do you think that businesses have introduced this kind of routine?
   - Is this an open or a closed question?

activity

Draw labelled diagrams (similar to the one on page 247) showing the practical selling steps required for each of the following customers:

- Customer 1 is very clear about what he or she wants. Here, the best method is to make help available if required and then leave the customer to choose. When the sale is agreed, there may be an opportunity here to make a related sale – a tie to go with the shirt and so on
- Customer 2 has some idea of what is needed – perhaps he or she has seen an advertisement which appeals. However, some more information and advice may be required. Here, the salesperson will *demonstrate* the product, and may, with further questioning, find that a slightly different product is more appropriate – 'Have you considered the Mark II?' Ideally, this second product will be a more expensive one, (this is called 'selling-up')
- Customer 3, like many customers, has only a general idea of what he or she is looking for – a new coat perhaps, or some curtain material. Here, the salesperson needs to go through the whole selling routine. Help and advice are actively sought
- Customer 4 is just looking for ideas, and may not even need to buy on this particular occasion. He or she may be looking for a birthday present or some camping equipment for the summer perhaps. Here, the idea is to give help and advice so that if a sale is not possible at present, the customer is at least encouraged to return later. The salesperson's manner and knowledge plus the ability of the shop to supply the right goods at the right price will be crucial here. Often, a brochure with details and a telephone number is provided for such occasions

PRODUCT KNOWLEDGE

We have mentioned that effective sales staff will have sound product knowledge before the customer enters the store. We will now look at this in a little more detail.

Product knowledge has five aspects. These are demonstrated in the advertisement shown in Figure 9.11.

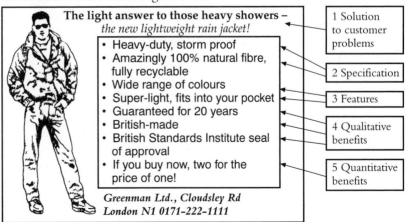

Figure 9.11 An advertisement highlighting the five aspects of product knowledge

1 Look at the Dixons mobile phone advert shown in Figure 9.12. What are the: specifications, features, quantitative benefits, qualitative benefits, solutions to customer problems?

Figure 9.12 A Dixons mobile-phone advertisement

2 Produce an advert for a real, or imagined, product showing the *five* aspects above.

Tangible and intangible qualities

Some of the qualities associated with products are **tangible** and some are **intangible**:

- Tangible qualities are factual ones. For example: 'Made of stainless steel – will not rust', 'an Intel chip inside'
- Intangible qualities are claimed but difficult to prove. For example: 'Made in England', 'Free range eggs', 'Not made with child labour'

Sometimes, firms get into trouble when intangible qualities which are claimed turn out to be untrue.

For each of the three advertisements above – i.e. Greenman, Dixons and your own chosen advert – identify those qualities that are tangible and those that are intangible. You may find it useful to use a table such as the one below:

ADVERTISEMENT	TANGIBLE QUALITIES	INTANGIBLE QUALITIES

The need for broad product knowledge

Case study: Solar Systems – computers for the home and office

Figure 9.13 shows that the core product knowledge is primarily about our own fictional brand of personal computer (PC), but that we also need to know about other brands of PC, other types of computer and other competing products.

A conversation may go like this:

Customer: 'I saw this machine reviewed in *PC User* magazine. Do you have it?' *(Takes out press cutting.)*

Shop assistant: 'Actually, we are a Solar Systems dealer. If you look at the specification, though, you'll see that our brand is practically identical – same memory and cheaper too.'

Customer: 'I don't know a great deal about computers. My friend has a Macintosh that looks really good.'

Shop assistant: 'Very good machine. More expensive than ours, though. The other point is that there are more PCs about. You see, Macintosh computers work on a different operating system. What that means is if you are thinking of taking

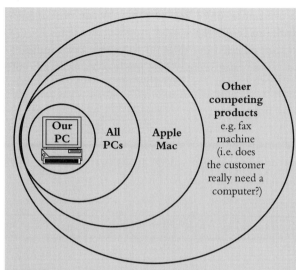

Figure 9.13 A broad product knowledge enables sales staff to satisfy customer needs

discs from one machine to another, a PC is really the best bet. Your disc will work on more machines if it's PC compatible.'

Customer: 'Yours is a PC?'

Shop assistant: 'That's right.'

Customer: 'I see.... I wonder if I really need a computer at all – it seems very complicated. I've seen fax machines for £250.'

Shop assistant: 'Well of course it depends what you need to do. Remember though that with our fax card you can not only use the computer to do the accounts and the word processing but you can also use it as a fax machine. We could do you a special price on the fax card and PC together.'

Customer: 'Really? I didn't realise that computers could send faxes.'

Shop assistant: 'Would you like to have a try? It's all set up and ready to go. Just switch it on.'

Customer: 'Well it seems quite straightforward, and clicking on these pictures makes it easy. What if it goes wrong, though? I wouldn't have a clue!'

Shop assistant: 'They're very reliable but, just in case, all of our machines come with a free, one-year, on-site warranty in other words, we'll send someone round if it goes wrong. You can also phone our hotline to get instant help if you get stuck when you are using it.'

Customer: 'Sounds fair enough. Do you do credit?'

Shop assistant: 'We certainly do – interest-free if you buy before the end of the month.'

How does the assistant here:

- display broad product knowledge
- counter resistance
- close the sale?

WAYS OF DEALING WITH CUSTOMER QUERIES

Checking manual and computer files

Where a potential customer asks for information, it is vital that accurate details be given. This means that stock details, prices and dates for delivery must all be up-to-date. For instance, a customer ringing up about the price of the latest multi-gym must also, if necessary, be told if there are none left. If that person races 10 miles to be there before closing time only to be disappointed, this does nothing for the image of the retailer.

In Chapter 7 we saw that EPOS technology makes it possible for stock details to be updated after each sale. In Argos, the discount store, for example, you can see stock details being checked before your order is processed.

Queries from existing customers often relate to the date and conditions of the original sale. It is vital, therefore, that accurate records be maintained of all sales transactions. If, for instance, a customer calls to ask about a repair to be carried out under warranty, the seller needs to be clear as to whether the warranty terms still apply. Perhaps the expiry date has passed, or perhaps it would normally have expired but special terms were given to this particular customer.

Figure 9.14 A warranty card for an electrical product

In transaction or routine selling, the customer may ask for clarification on 'special offer' or 'sale price' goods. Accurate manual or computer files need to be kept so that there is no confusion and so that clear advice can be given in these situations. We will see the importance of updating recording systems when we look at administration in Chapter 10.

Directing and guiding customers

We have seen that an essential part of the seller's job is to take the trouble to find out a customer's needs so as to give appropriate guidance: a dissatisfied customer is not a good advertisement for a business. We will look at ethics in selling on page 258.

Referring to higher authority

Sometimes, the salesperson does not have the authority to make a decision. It may then be necessary to ask a superior for advice. In transaction processing, this may occur when a checkout cashier asks the supervisor to approve a cheque. In creative selling, this may involve asking a manager for advice on special conditions which may be necessary to clinch a sale:

- 'Can we offer a special discount?'
- 'Is it possible to order one specially for next Thursday?'
- 'Can we arrange a special delivery by noon tomorrow?'

Agreeing to these may clinch a sale, but they may not be usual policy. A supervisor will decide whether they are possible, and if so, whether to give authorisation. As a general rule, managers prefer sales staff to sell by offering extras rather than by offering discounts.

Use of body language

We have seen that the sales staff must read the body language of the customer when first making contact. They must also *send* the right signals. If, for instance, the seller yawns or looks exasperated, anxious or unfriendly, the customer is unlikely to be put at ease. Behaviour that is threatening or rude is simply not good for business.

It is important to be approachable and helpful without being familiar. The salesperson has to be someone the customer can trust.

Use of tone of voice

Tone of voice also conveys signals to the customer. Impatience and frustration have no place in selling. Retailers exist to serve their customers, and they must do what they can to maintain a polite, caring and supportive relationship.

1 When may a supermarket cashier need to refer to higher authority?
2 In what circumstances may a customer ask a cashier to check some information?
3 What sort of direction may a customer in a supermarket seek? Who might provide this help?
4 Where in a supermarket may you get personal service?

PERSONAL SELLING AND ETHICS

The word 'salesman' still often brings to mind an Arthur Daley or Del Boy type of 'conman'. In part, this is due to the experience of customers with door-to-door salesmen and used-car dealers. These retailers may depend upon commission to make a living, and therefore be desperate to make a sale, whether the customer needs the product or not. Traditionally, paying commission was regarded as a way of motivating staff and giving a reward for results. More recently it has been criticised, as it does tend to encourage sales staff to pressurise customers.

activity

SUGAR ATTACKS RETAIL CHAINS

Alan Sugar lashed out yesterday at the trading practices of electrical retail chains, which helped him make his fortune as head of the Amstrad consumer electronics group.

He said he had decided a year ago to sell Amstrad products direct to the consumer because it was no longer profitable to work through retailers which, he claimed, typically added a 30 per cent mark-up to his products and did 'precious little in return'.

He added: 'Sometimes the product becomes quite irrelevant to the retailer and is just something that allows them to get hold of the customer. I, for the life of me, cannot work out why anybody needs to buy an extended warranty worth up to 20 per cent of the product's value – but the salesman will spend far more time selling that, and making a 100 per cent mark-up, than in talking about the product.'

He claimed that in one year his group had taken 20 per cent of the market for direct sales of computers to small companies – equal to IBM's proportion.

(The Guardian, *24 November 1995*)

1 What is Alan Sugar's criticism of 'salesmen' in the electrical retail chains?
2 What is a warranty? What does Sugar say is the real reason why retailers sell warranties?
3 What form of selling does Sugar think is the best for the customer? Do you agree?
4 Daewoo, 'the largest car manufacturer you've never heard of', advertise that in their showrooms their customers will not be approached unless they ask for help. They also advertise that sales staff are *not* paid commission. What do you think are the advantages and disadvantages of commission from the point of view of:
   ● sales staff
   ● the customer
   ● the company?

As we have seen in Chapter 5, customer service is becoming an increasingly important way in which retailers compete. It is important that sales staff do not make misleading claims, for if these prove to be untrue, then a business's reputation may suffer badly. The aim of sales staff should be to 'sell goods that don't come back to customers that do'.

Self-Test Questions:
Chapter 9

1 List the different steps involved in creative selling.
2 Give one example of an 'open' question and one example of a 'closed' question which a salesperson might use.
3 What type of selling may take place in a supermarket: transaction processing, routine selling or creative selling? Explain your answer.
4 From a retailer's point of view, what is the benefit of offering sales staff commission on sales made? What problem may this have from the customer's point of view?
5 A car is advertised as having '16 valve overhead cam, a free car phone' and being 'available on 0% finance'.
Which of the above is a 'specification' and which is a 'feature'?
6 Why is it useful for a salesperson to have knowledge of competitors' products?
7 Which policy is a retailer most likely to approve as a means of closing a sale: reducing the price or providing some 'free extras'?
8 An electric drill provides a solution to a customer need – namely, the need to drill holes. However, the 'potential product' marketed by a retailer provides more than this: it provides other benefits such as a variety of colours and a one-year warranty. What extras might a retailer of home computers provide as part of the 'potential' product?
9 A customer shows resistance to an 'own brand' video recorder. How can the salesperson counter this?
10 A salesperson should know about stock levels and delivery times. Give two examples of when these may be important in making a sale.

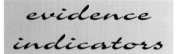

In order to achieve this Element, you will need to take the part of a salesperson in a role-play situation.

TASK 1 *Preparation*

1 Identify *two* selling situations in which you would need to carry out personal selling. Each situation should involve a *different category* of personal selling. If you work in a retail outlet (a part-time job perhaps), then you may use this as one of your categories. In this case, you need to choose only *one* other situation.

Examples you might choose for your role play are:

● checkout operator in a convenience store – using transaction processing; and salesperson in a builder's merchants or a motor-parts shop – using routine selling; or

● sales assistant in a specialist shop such as a shoe shop or a garden centre – using routine selling; and a salesperson in a car showroom – using creative selling

Note: the aim of the role play is to demonstrate personal selling. This may be done more easily through routine selling and through creative selling, since transaction processing is fairly limited.

2 Do some research to gain sufficient product knowledge for your role play. You will need to look only at one particular item, but remember that you need to know about the different models available. One way of doing this is to take a section from a catalogue, perhaps the radio-cassette players from the Dixon's catalogue, or the TVs and video recorders from the Argos catalogue – and preferably something that you are interested in.

3 Your teacher or a friend will be the customer. They must assume a role which will allow you to demonstrate all the steps involved in personal selling. Therefore they should:

- be interested in the type of product you have researched (e.g. they may need a new TV)
- rely on you to find the best one for their needs – they are not really sure about what is available, or about the difference between models
- have a price range in mind and certainly a price limit (though you may need to find out what this is)
- be cautious about buying, but willing to buy the right product ultimately

TASK 2 *Perform the role play*

You are the salesperson. A customer enters your shop. The idea is that you should demonstrate the different steps in personal selling from opening (when the customer enters the shop) to close (when the customer buys). Therefore, you will need to:

- welcome the customer
- discover what her/his needs are by careful questioning
- demonstrate product knowledge when giving advice
- handle resistance
- close a sale
- use appropriate tone of voice and body language

TASK 3 *Compile the evidence*

1 Ideally, the role play will be videoed.
2 You should also write up notes to show that you understand:
   - the different categories of personal selling, and which two you have demonstrated
   - the various steps in the selling process in each case
   - how you demonstrated these steps on each occasion
   - an evaluation of your sales technique

3 *If you actually work in a retail outlet* (as a part-time assistant perhaps), you need only perform one role play. One of your selling categories can be achieved by writing a description of the selling process actually involved in your job. Your work supervisor should sign to confirm that you have demonstrated this type of selling.

MULTIPLE CHOICE TEST: UNIT 3

1 A store with over 50,000 square feet of single-level selling area is called a:
   a discounter
   b superstore
   c hypermarket
   d specialist

2 A shop selling products specifically for left-handed people would be classified as:
   a a specialist retailer
   b a niche retailer
   c a convenience store
   d a general retailer

3 The largest part of the non-store retail market is held by:
   a market traders
   b mail-order houses
   c TV shopping channels
   d on-line shopping via the Internet

The options below are shared by questions 4 and 5.

The following are means by which retailers may compete:
   a provides after-sales service
   b accepts a wide variety of plastic cards
   c accessible to local people
   d sells goods on hire purchase

Which one is most likely to be used by each of the following?

4 a motorway petrol station
5 a small convenience store
6 Which is most likely to be true of a hypermarket?
   a stocks a variety of goods at competitive prices
   b is easily accessible to local people
   c provides a high level of personal service
   d relies upon shop-window displays to attract customers

7 The collapse of the Net Book Agreement is likely to result in:
   a a wider range of books becoming available
   b more small bookshops
   c an increase in the number of books being sold
   d price competition between booksellers

8 The growth in out-of-town shopping during the 1980s led to:
   a more traffic congestion in the high streets
   b more regional shopping malls
   c an end to 'one-stop' shopping
   d a more environmentally friendly form of shopping

9 A local CTN (confectioner, tobacconist, newsagent) is most likely to benefit from:
   a the introduction of the National Lottery
   b the development of out-of-town shopping
   c the legalisation of Sunday trading for all
   d the promise of a minimum wage

10 EPOS and EFTPOS may benefit a retailer in a number of ways. Which of the following is *not* a direct result of this new technology?
   a speeding up the checkout by the use of bar-code readers
   b allowing customers to claim points on their loyalty cards
   c allowing the retailer to give special offers
   d allowing the use of debit cards such as 'Switch'

11 Which of the following is *not* stated in a contract of employment?
   a weekly working hours
   b the rate of pay

c   the amount of annual bonus payable

d   the period of notice required

12   Which of the following trade unions represents shopworkers?

a   USDAW

b   AUEW

c   NATFHE

d   UNISON

13   Which type of store facade allows passers-by to look in the shop window without obstructing the pavement?

a   open

b   recessed

c   straight

d   duplex

14   Which of the following is *not* true?

a   One reason that open store designs are found in indoor shopping centres is that heat loss is not a problem

b   Using double glazing will help cut out traffic noise

c   Having lighted window displays at night presents a security risk

d   Heat from refrigerator motors can be recycled to warm the shop

15   Which sense gives us 80% of the information we receive about our environment?

a   sight

b   sound

c   smell

d   touch

The following options are shared by questions 16 and 17:

a   a baker

b   a convenience store

c   a fashion boutique

d   a builder's merchants

16   Which of the above types of shop would be most likely to rely upon touch to affect buyer behaviour?

17   Which of the above types of shop would be most likely to rely upon smell to affect buyer behaviour?

18   Which of the following is most likely to be an impulse buy?

a   a bottle of wine in an off-licence

b   a bar of chocolate in a convenience store

c   an electric drill in a DIY shop

d   a wheelbarrow in a garden centre

19   Which best describes the boutique style of shop layout?

a   where there are long parallel lines of shop fixtures which channel shoppers from entrance to exit

b   where sections within a single shop are arranged as if they are individual speciality shops

c   where goods of a similar type are arranged so that shoppers may move freely between them

d   where young people shop for fashionable clothes

The following options are shared by questions 20 and 21:

a   theme

b   lifestyle

c   coordinated

d   classification dominance

20   Which of the above describes a display of gifts for Mother's Day?

21   Which of the above describes a display in which shop models are shown wearing an outfit made of matching items?

22   Which *two* of the following apply to 'transaction processing'?

i   Staff have to be smart, efficient, friendly and helpful

ii   This involves selling complex or expensive goods

iii   Staff need to be able to locate and describe goods, and they may also suggest extra (add-on) purchases to go with items already chosen

iv   It is the sort of work carried out at a supermarket checkout

a   i and ii

b   ii and iii

c   iii and iv
d   i and iv

23 Which *two* of the following are examples of
    open questions?
    i   'May I help you?'
    ii   'How may I help you?'
    iii 'Which colour would you like?'
    iv   'Would you prefer the grey or the blue?'
    a   i and ii
    b   ii and iii
    c   iii and iv
    d   i and iv

24 Which of the following is likely to be the last
    step in the selling sequence?
    a   demonstrating product knowledge
    b   using questions to find out customer needs
    c   summarising the advantages of the product
    d   countering customer resistance by allowing
         the customer to use the product

25 Which *two* of the following may give rise to
    customer resistance to buying?
    i   The customer realises that there is a one-
         year warranty included in the price
    ii   It appears that the price quoted does not
         include VAT
    iii The product will need to be ordered from
         the manufacturer
    iv   Delivery to the customer's premises can be
         arranged
    a   i and ii
    b   ii and iii
    c   iii and iv
    d   i and iv

26 A customer says that a product is beyond her
    price range. Which of the following responses
    is most likely to meet this objection?
    a   agreeing that the product is expensive
    b   ignoring the objection
    c   explaining that the product is very high
         quality and therefore excellent value for
         money
    d   suggesting a less expensive alternative

27 Which is the most appropriate response to
    customer resistance?
    a   Ask questions to find out why the
         customer is unsure
    b   Ignore the resistance
    c   Use technical language to show the
         customer that you are knowledgeable
    d   Recommend another local retailer

28 Which of the following is a sign of customer
    resistance?
    a   asking for a demonstration of the product
    b   asking whether credit terms are available
    c   pointing out that a competitor's product
         has a higher specification for a similar price
    d   reminding the shop that they have offered
         free after-sales service to all customers

29 You work for a computer retailer where there
    is a telephone 'hotline' to answer customer
    queries. You ask each caller for their invoice
    number before proceeding with their query.
    The *immediate* reason for this is:
    a   the problem may need specialist advice
    b   you wish to check that they actually are
         one of your customers
    c   from this you can find the type of machine
         they have
    d   you need to check that you have the
         correct manual available

30 A customer asks you about a word-processing
    package. You do not have enough product
    knowledge to answer. Which of the following
    is the *best* response?
    a   Admit that you don't know and apologise
    b   Suggest that the customer look through the
         manual
    c   Find a colleague who can answer the query
    d   Suggest that the customer write to the
         manufacturer

Administration and finance

C H A P T E R   1 0

Investigating administrative processes for selling

In this chapter, we will:

- look at how administrative processes coordinate the work of different departments in a retail organisation
- consider those administrative processes involved in selling
- work through an example showing the documents used in credit sales

We will cover Element 4.1, Performance Criteria 1, 2, 3, 4, 5, 6.

WHAT ARE THE AIMS OF RETAILERS?

Look at these mission statements:

W H SMITH

Why we are in business:

We are in business to delight our customers by offering them:

- memorable products
- good value for money
- legendary service

We want:

- our shareholders to get a competitive return on their investment
- our suppliers to profit from our success
- the communities in which we work to be proud of our presence

As we achieve all of this our future will be secure and profitable.

(Source: W H Smith 1995 Annual Report)

TESCO

Corporate objectives

Tesco is committed to:

- offering customers the best value for money and the most competitive prices
- meeting the needs of customers by constantly seeking, and acting on, their opinions

regarding innovation, product quality, choice, store facilities and service

- providing shareholders with progressive returns on their investment
- improving profitability through investment in efficient stores and distribution depots, in productivity improvements and in new technology

- developing the talents of its people through sound management and training practices, while rewarding them fairly with equal opportunities for all
- working closely with suppliers to build long-term business relationships based on strict quality and price criteria
- participating in the formulation of national food industry policies on key issues such as health, nutrition, hygiene, safety and animal welfare
- supporting the well-being of the community and the protection of the environment

(Source: Tesco 1995 Annual Report)

The two businesses are not competitors, but they say similar things:

- They both need to make a profit for their owners (the shareholders)
- They will achieve this by providing the right products at the right price and by creating a good public image

The mission statements above were taken from the (1995) annual reports of the two companies (available in reference libraries or directly from the companies). Look at the aims of other large retailers. Are these similar to those above? Are there any differences?

Retailers usually face a great deal of competition. They make profits by providing those goods that the customer wants and supplying these goods in the most effective and efficient manner possible. There are three main stages here, each of which may involve a number of different processes:

1 *Obtain goods.* This may involve:
    - identifying customer needs
    - identifying suppliers
    - negotiating terms
    - ordering
    - transporting goods
    - making payments
2 *Store and display goods.* This may involve:
    - stock (or inventory) control
    - advertising
    - window dressing
    - displaying goods
    - setting an appropriate price
    - making sure that the shop is open at appropriate times, is clean, is secure and is warm
3 *Sell goods.* This may involve:
    - contacting customers
    - serving customers

- giving advice
- tailoring goods to customers' requirements

There may also be a need to:

- deliver goods
- offer credit
- send invoices and statements
- collect payment, chase debtors
- provide after-sales service
- get feedback from customers

All of this takes a lot of organisation.

THE NEED FOR ADMINISTRATION

Figure 10.1 Elements of administration

Administration is about setting up routines, systems and procedures so that a business can work efficiently from day to day. It concerns the way in which a business is organised to achieve its aims and objectives (see Figure 10.1). If a business is disorganised, it will lose out even if the products are good. For example:

1 Customers may be lost through:
- being kept waiting
- goods being out of stock
- staff being impolite or badly informed
- incorrect information being given
2 Stock may be lost or damaged by:
- poor storage systems leading to breakages or other damage
- poor stock control resulting in perishables passing their sell-by

date or seasonable/fashionable goods remaining unsold
- poor security, resulting in 'shrinkage' (the polite word for stealing)

3 Money may be lost through:
- customers being given credit without their credit limits being checked
- customers not being chased for their debts
- invoices being incorrectly filled in
- forms being mislaid

If proper procedures are in place, these problems should not occur. In practice this usually means that there will need to be a set of rules that everyone understands and a set of standard documents or forms allowing all relevant information to be recorded on each occasion. We will look at documents used in buying and selling later in this chapter and in Chapters 11 and 12.

Administration must not become an end in itself so that 'red tape' hinders the operation and slows down decision-making – 'bureaucracy gone mad'. Nevertheless, it is important for a business to have efficient systems: many smaller business owners are surprised to find out just how much paper work there is to be done in the evenings.

DEPARTMENTS WITHIN A RETAILING OUTLET

In a small organisation – the local corner shop for example – there might be one person responsible for absolutely everything. Once a year, the owner will perhaps employ an accountant to see that the books are in order for the Inland Revenue for tax purposes, and for the Customs and Excise for VAT.

A slightly larger organisation might have a small number of sales staff in the shop and a single office where the owners carry out administrative duties. They may share these duties, or perhaps one may be responsible for the wages and accounts, one for buying and so on.

Organisations which are larger still will have whole specialist departments, each employing a number of people to perform particular functions. For example, the structure might be as shown in Figure 10.2.

How departments work together

The different departments will need to work together to serve the overall needs of the organisation – see Figure 10.3, for instance. The flow of accurate information between the various departments is crucial to the smooth running of the business.

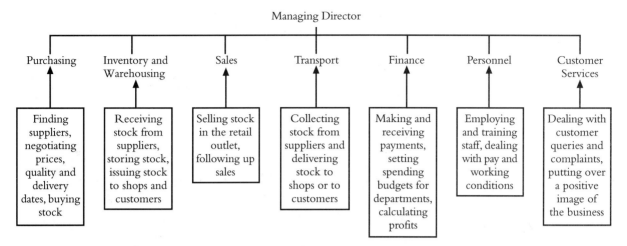

Figure 10.2 Typical specialist departments in a large retailing organisation

Buyers in the purchasing department order goods. The sales department tells them what customers want, and the inventory section lets them know which lines are running low in the warehouse.

These goods are stored in the warehouse by the inventory section. They tell buyers which stocks are running low, and send goods to replace stocks on the shop shelves.

The goods are transported to the shop where they are displayed on the shelves. As the goods are sold, replacement stock is ordered from the warehouse.

The goods are sold by the sales staff in the shop. Sales staff need product knowledge, and this may come from the purchasing section which bought the goods in.

The accounts section calculates the business profits (value of sales – cost of purchases – running costs = profit). These figures come from across the different departments.

Figure 10.3 How different departments work together in the organisation

1 The sales staff talk to customers. How can this help the purchasing section?
2 What information does the transport section need from the sales department before it can deliver goods to the customer?
3 Why does the warehouse need to know how much stock the sales staff have sold?
4 What information does the accounts section need in order to calculate the business profits? Which departments does it get this information from?

AN EXAMPLE OF HOW DEPARTMENTS WORK TOGETHER

Imagine that you buy a new CD player from a discount warehouse such as Argos or Comet. What stages are involved in this transaction?

1 You notice an advertisement in your local paper for a discount warehouse which has a good selection of CD players. The prices appeal to you as there is a special offer 'while stocks last'. You also notice that you will be able to pay using your credit card.

   So far, two departments have been involved in getting you interested. The advertisement has been placed by the company's **sales department**; and the **finance department** will have been involved in decisions about prices and discounts, and also in deciding whether to allow credit, and whether to accept plastic cards as a means of payment – some stores, for instance, will not accept credit cards.

2 You arrive at the store. It is clean, warm and tidy: the firm subcontracts its maintenance, cleaning and repairs to an **outside contractor** which offers 'total building care'.

   You choose a CD player from the glossy catalogue (designed by **sales**) and write down the details on the standard form provided. The sales assistant keys the reference number into the **stock** database. This is maintained on a *real-time* basis so that it is updated every time a sale is made. If the stock report shows that the item is available, the sale can go ahead; if not, they have lost a customer. You are in luck. The sales receipt is printed up showing the details of the sale - see Figure 10.4. You pay by credit card.

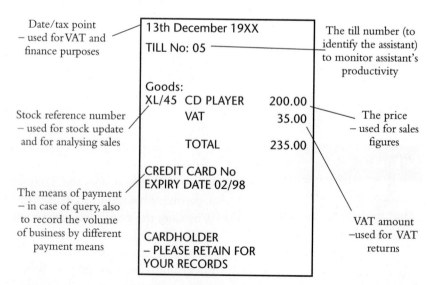

Figure 10.4 The information found on a typical sales receipt

The EPOS (electronic point of sale) machine records the sale and updates the stock records. Ultimately, the sales figures will be processed by the **finance section**.

3 You are given a reference number and asked to wait a few moments whilst the **stores section** locates the item and sends it to the desk for you to collect.

If necessary, the retailer will arrange for delivery by the **transport section**. Some firms prefer to subcontract the delivery to an **independent carrier**.

Should you have any queries, you can contact the **customer services** section.

Finally, across the organisation, the various members of staff will have been recruited and trained by the **personnel** section.

1 Which departments use the various items of information on the customer receipt?
2 Identify the departments involved when you buy a pair of shoes.
3 It is becoming increasingly common for retailers to subcontract some functions to outside companies rather than to set up their own department. What are the advantages, for a retailer, in 'outsourcing' its building maintenance, its computer-systems maintenance and its delivery service?

Remember that the exact way in which a retail outlet will operate is determined by factors such as its size and the nature of the products it sells. The example below shows how stock control at Sainsbury's involves sending information collected by sales assistants, via head office, to the various storage depots around the country.

Case study: stock control at Sainsbury's

The major supermarkets aim to maintain a full range of stocks without the need to **stockpile**, and this means that they need to reorder on a daily basis. The requirements of each particular branch come from information collected at the checkouts via the EPOS (electronic point of sale) system. The computer is able to analyse exactly what has been sold and therefore what needs to be reordered. There are two types of good:

1 **shelf-lines** are only held on the store's shelves. These are goods which have a limited shelf-life, such as meat and dairy products. Fast-moving shelf-lines will be

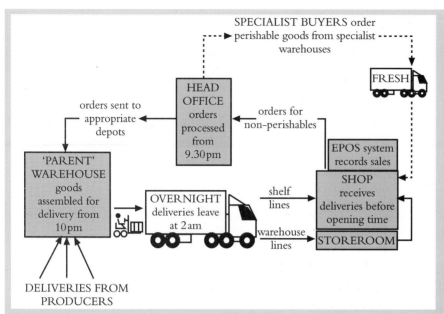

Figure 10.5 The stock-control process

reordered on a 24-hour cycle (order today for delivery tomorrow), whilst slower-moving shelf-lines will be reordered less often – perhaps three times a week.

2 warehouse lines have back-up stocks in the store's warehouse so that the shelves can be refilled as necessary during the day. These are non-perishables such as canned goods and dry goods like rice and sugar. Typically, these stocks will be assessed and replaced on a weekly basis.

The use of new technology – especially EPOS – has speeded up the supply chain. The instant updating of stock information has made the link between selling and reordering automatic.

The stock control process is illustrated in Figure 10.5.

(Source: J Sainsbury PLC)

activity

1 Which departments do you think are involved in the distribution process above? Briefly explain how they work together to achieve the smooth running of the operation.
2 Stocks are sold on a FIFO (first in first out) basis. Why is this?
3 Give the advantages of delivering overnight for each of the following: the customer, the driver, the shop.
4 Large retailers operate a 'de-stocking programme' – i.e. not holding more goods at a branch than is necessary to meet customer demand. How could 'stockpiling' prove to be expensive?
5 The manager at each branch decides which goods will be shelf-lines and which will be warehouse lines. Which of the following is most likely to fall into which category:
   ● cream
   ● bread

- baked beans
- spaghetti
- tomatoes
- fish fingers
- fresh fish?

ADMINISTRATIVE PROCESSES USED FOR SELLING

In the rest of this chapter, we will look at the various administrative processes involved in selling. In Chapter 11, we will look at the administrative processes used in buying.

Sources and uses of sales information

A retailer must have access to good-quality sales information. A good administrative system will enable the relevant information to be collected and made available as and when it is needed.

Retailers need to be able to answer the following questions:

- Are sales increasing or decreasing?
- Which goods are in demand?
- How many of these goods are we selling? Do we need to restock? Is there any wastage? (Perhaps goods are damaged in storage, or stolen, or perhaps they are passing their sell-by date and being thrown away)
- Which are our most profitable lines?
- What do our customers think about our products?
- Are we doing as well as our competitors? Do we need to market ourselves better – advertise perhaps or maybe give special offers?
- Which goods are selling locally? Should we stock these?
- Which goods are selling nationally? Should we stock these?

Sales information can come from within the organisation – perhaps captured on forms or input into the computer by staff in the course of their day-to-day activities – and it can also come from outside sources – Table 10.1 gives a summary.

CUSTOMERS

Feedback from customers can be gained when sales staff attempt to sell products, or when customers come back with queries and comments. Some retailers provide questionnaires – see Figure 10.6 – with tick-boxes for customers to complete. These ask about the nature of customer satisfaction, and usually leave a space for suggestions.

Shops selling durables will have a better chance of collecting customer information. This is because: customers generally need more advice during the selling process with this kind of good than they do with convenience goods; there is often after-sales service; and there

Table 10.1   Sales information

SOURCE OF INFORMATION	HOW IT IS COLLECTED	TYPE OF INFORMATION
Internal information:		
Customers	Questionnaires, after-sales contact, feedback to sales staff	Information about the demand for goods Details of customer satisfaction
Enquiries from potential customers	Records of enquiries (usually input into computer database)	Interest in products Effectiveness of promotion
Response to publicity		
Sales staff questionnaires	Customer feedback	Advantages and disadvantages of the retailer's products as opposed to those of competitors
Sales records	EPOS, EFTPOS, till roll, sales documents (see page 204)	
Stock-control figures	EPOS system Manual or computer-generated stock records Stock taking	Quantities sold of various lines
External information:		
Trade magazines (both local and national)	Subscribe to magazines	New product information/trends
Official statistics	Local reference library On-line service providers	Local and national sales data

may be hire purchase or credit arrangements which also provide opportunities for collecting information.

High-turnover shops which do not offer credit terms (e.g. grocers, petrol stations, DIY superstores) find it more difficult to monitor customers. Recently, loyalty cards have enabled them to find out more about their customers through the application form for these cards.

ENQUIRIES

These may be logged to provide information about the effectiveness of advertising and the nature of customer interest, and to provide potential targets for future publicity.

Suppose, for example, that you telephone a computer supplier after reading about a special offer in *PC User* magazine. It is likely that your details and the nature of your call will be noted, and you may be asked:

- 'Have you dealt with us before?'
- 'If so, what is your post code?' (Postcodes cover a few addresses only, and can be used to locate you in the customer database)
- 'If you have not dealt with our company before, may we have your

COOPERS

HELP US TO BE BETTER

Please take a moment to let us know your views

Date .... Time ....
Location ....

HOW OFTEN DO YOU VISIT COOPERS ?

First Visit ☐   Once a week to
More than once a week ☐   once a fortnight ☐
                        Less often ☐

PLEASE LIST THE PRODUCTS YOU HAVE JUST BROUGHT

....
....

PLEASE GIVE YOUR VIEWS ON THE FOLLOWING :

	Excellent	Good	Fair	Poor
Quality of Drink	☐	☐	☐	☐
Choice of Drink	☐	☐	☐	☐
Quality of Food	☐	☐	☐	☐
Choice of Food	☐	☐	☐	☐
Speed of Service	☐	☐	☐	☐
Staff Friendliness	☐	☐	☐	☐
Quality of Environment	☐	☐	☐	☐
Value for Money	☐	☐	☐	☐
Overall Impression of Unit	☐	☐	☐	☐

ARE YOU ..... MALE ☐ FEMALE ☐
WE WOULD APPRECIATE YOUR COMMENTS :

Figure 10.6 A Coopers questionnaire designed by Traveller's Fare Ltd who run food and drink outlets at railway stations

name, address and telephone number?' (These can then be added to the database)

- 'Do you represent another organisation?'
- 'How did you hear of our company?'
- 'How can we help you?'

All of this helps an organisation to build up a picture of their customers, their area of interest, where they live and the effectiveness of their promotion.

RESPONSE TO PUBLICITY

A retailer will attempt to measure the level of increased interest resulting from publicity or advertising. For example:

- A car dealer needs to know whether offering interest-free credit is likely to attract customers
- The major supermarkets need to know how much interest there is in loyalty cards

Some retailers invite customers to send back tear-off slips from newspaper advertisements, possibly to request further information. Here, a reference number will identify the newspaper or magazine where the advertisement was placed. In this way, a retailer can see the effectiveness of particular forms of publicity.

MERCHANDISE REPORT

DEPT.	FL	UNITS	NET VALUE	%	LF	%LF	£LF
05	1	1	19.99	3	80	10	0
06	1	1	79.99	10	36	5	2
09	1	0	0.00	0	40	5	0
12	1	4	103.96	13	48	6	2
13	1	0	0.00	0	8	1	0
19	1	6	65.94	8	48	6	1
22	1	7	120.93	15	76	10	2
24	1	1	3.99	1	12	2	0
25	1	4	15.96	2	16	2	1
27	1	5	102.95	13	42	5	2
29	1	4	20.96	3	126	16	0
34	1	2	6.98	1	14	2	0
35	1	2	9.98	1	24	3	0
79	1	0	0.00	0	48	6	0
Sub Total		37	551.63	70	618	81	1

Figure 10.7 An EPOS till printout

SALES STAFF

Sales staff are in direct contact with the customer and are in a unique position to gauge customer response to their organisation. They will quickly be aware of any advantages and disadvantages their products have when compared to those of their competitors.

STOCK-CONTROL FIGURES AND SALES FIGURES

The till print-out shown in Figure 10.7 was created using an EPOS (electronic point of sale) system. Remember that details of all sales recorded by an EPOS system will be stored in the firm's computer, and can be used to provide reports about total sales and goods in stock. Sales figures can be broken down to show: sales of different lines of stock; sales by department; busy and slack times; the most common methods of payment by customers; and the efficiency of sales staff.

LOCAL AND NATIONAL TRADE MAGAZINES

Trade magazines provide specialist information for retailers in different categories. The magazines with the largest circulation are shown in

Table 10.2. Some of these are provided through the trade and are not otherwise available, whilst others are available on subscription or through newsagents. In practice, the magazines make their money through advertisements, and to ensure a wide enough circulation to attract advertisers, they may circulate free copies on a controlled basis.

Table 10.2 Trade magazines with a large circulation

CATEGORY	MAGAZINE	CIRCULATION (DECEMBER 1995)
Food and drink – groceries	*The Grocer*	51,559 weekly
	Asian Business	48,486 fortnightly
	Convenience Store	46,396 fortnightly
Food and drink – licensed sales	*Publican*	31,831 weekly
	Off Licence News	25,195 weekly
Food and drink – fish selling	*Fish Trader*	2,454 monthly
Forecourt	*Service Station*	16,370 monthly
Newsagents	*CTN (Confectioner Tobacconist, Newsagent)*	17,536 weekly
Greetings cards	*Greetings & Gift Stationer*	6,976 alternate months
Booksellers	*The Bookseller*	13,172 weekly
Electrical goods	*Electrical & Radio Trading*	8,046 weekly
Garden centres and equipment	*Garden Trade News*	6,077 10 issues per year
Hardware and DIY	*DIY Week*	16,443 fortnightly
Motor trade	*Glass's Guide Car Values*	41,878 monthly
	Glass's Guide Commercial Vehicle Values	12,169 monthly
	Autotrade	30,900 monthly
	Tyres & Accessories	6,536 monthly
Pharmacies	*The Pharmaceutical Journal*	44,363 weekly
Perfumery and cosmetics	*Beauty Counter*	13,664 monthly
Duty free trade	*Frontier*	4,998 15 issues per year

What do trade magazines contain, and who reads them?

Case study: *Convenience Store* magazine

Trade magazines are targeted at buyers in a particular trade. Here are details for the magazine *Convenience Store*:

- Editorial policy: six-page news section covering all aspects of the industry. Regular drinks news and features, new products and promotions, marketing advice, and business articles covering areas such as stock-taking and theft
- Price: £2 per copy, or £45 per year (26 copies)
- Fortnightly circulation 1995: 46,396 (UK: 46,361; overseas and Eire: 35)
- Target readership: independent retailers, retailers stocking groceries, CTNs (confectioner, tobacconist, newsagent), petrol forecourts, cash-and-carries

In 1995, ESA Market Research Ltd concluded that *Convenience Store* was received by more neighbourhood grocers than any other trade title.

Features and advertisements, in addition, give advice and sales information.

Figure 10.8 A cover of *Convenience Store* magazine

(Source: BRAD December 1995)

activity

1 Ask your local convenience stores which trade magazines they receive. It is almost certain that they will receive some. Do they pay? Ask if you can have a copy which they have finished with – most will be quite happy to help you.
2 The advertisement in Figure 10.9 appeared in *Convenience Store*.

- What information does it give that would be useful to a retailer?
- In what ways is the advertisement different from ones aimed at the consumer?

Figure 10.9 An advertisement from *Convenience Store* magazine

Manufacturers' news sheets

Manufacturers also produce their own news sheets, often showing recommended retail prices. An example is shown in Figure 10.10.

OFFICIAL STATISTICS

The Central Statistical Office (CSO) produces figures which may be of

Product	Price per case or price to the retailer (the trade price)	Price to the consumer (the retail price)**
Medium Curry Paste 290g × 12 12 jars of 290 grams in each case)	£13.49	£1.35 per jar
Hot Curry Paste 290g × 12	£13.49	£1.35
Tandoori Curry Paste 300g × 12★	£13.49	£1.35
Creamed Coconut 2 × 50g sachets × 12 (2 'convenient recipe-sized sachets' in a box)	£5.49	55p per box
Korma (Cooking Sauce in a can) 360g × 12	£8.50	85p per can
Rogan Josh (Cooking Sauce in a can) 370g × 12★	£8.50	85p
Tikka Masala (Cooking Sauce in a can) 365g × 12	£8.50	85p
Kashmir Malai (Cooking Sauce in a glass jar) 420g × 12	£12.90	£1.29 per jar
Goan Masala (Cooking Sauce in a glass jar) 450g × 12★	£12.90	£1.29
Bombay Rezala (Cooking Sauce in a glass jar) 440g × 12	£12.90	£1.29

Note ★Are these products the best value? (Some shops show the price per gram)
Note ★★Retailers can use these prices as a guideline
Why do you think retailers charge the same prices for sauces in jars even though the weights are different? Have you ever bought any?

Figure 10.10 Do you like curries? Recommended retail prices (Adapted from a price list in *The Grocer*, 5 October 1996)

use to national retailers who are interested in general trends. These may be purchased from HMSO (Her Majesty's Stationery Office), but they are also available in the reference sections of public libraries. Appendix I shows information from Business Monitor SDA 25.

Look at Appendix I on retail businesses in 1993.

1 Which goods have the highest profit margin, and which have the lowest?
2 In which trade are there the most businesses? And the most shops?
3 Draw one chart based upon the figures. Explain what it shows.

HOW DOES A RETAILER USE SALES INFORMATION?

An independent convenience store might use sales information as follows:

Comparisons with other businesses

Businesses find it useful to compare their own sales and profits with those of their competitors. One business will not divulge management information to a rival, but general comparisons can be made from a number of sources:

- **Company accounts.** The 1985 Companies Act requires all companies to send summaries of their yearly accounts to Companies House where they are made available to the general public on request. The larger companies will publish an annual report, usually in the form of a glossy booklet

  The accounts show figures such as those for sales, costs and profits, as well as a summary of the general company policy and its success over the year. One business may look at the sales and profits of its competitors.

  Sole traders and partnerships do not need to publish their figures in this way, however:
- Smaller businesses will be able to get advice on the sort of profits their business should be expecting from their bank's small-business advisor, the local Chamber of Commerce, the local trade association or their accountant
- Organisations such as Verdict Research publish figures for different types of retailer. (We quote them a number of times in this book)

Restocking

The aim here is to hold the right amount – neither too much nor too little – of the right kind of stock.

- Too little stock results in customers being turned away. The retail trade is highly competitive, and customers will quickly take their custom elsewhere
- Too much stock may result in:
  - unsold goods perishing or being sold off cheaply
  - money being tied up unnecessarily
- Where a retailer has an EPOS system, detailed stock and sales information will be available immediately. For the small retailer, (without EPOS) it will be necessary to review stock records periodically and to reorder when stock reaches the minimum level

activity

Item: Starter motor SM/15   Location: Bay 11   Reorder level: 5
Card no: 5

DATE	IN FROM/OUT TO	STOCK IN (UNITS)	STOCK OUT (UNITS)	BALANCE (UNITS)	REORDER DATE	UNITS ORDERED	SUPPLIER/ORDER NO
1 May	Balance B/f			9			
5 May	SI 2003		4	5	5 May	15	Motec Ltd Order 346
8 May	SI 2025		1	?			
10 May	PI 4500	15		?			
15 May	SI 2054		2	?			
25 May	SI 2086		1	?			

Note:
SI = sales invoice (used where goods
are sold to customers)
PI = purchase invoice (used where
goods are received from the supplier)

1 Draw up a table like the one shown and complete the balance column by replacing the question marks with the goods remaining in stock on each date.
2 Which documents provide the information for 'stock in' and 'stock out'?
3 What do you think determines the minimum stock allowed before stock is reordered? Try to give two different factors. (Hint: remember that a business does not want to run out of stock.)
4 Businesses do not want to hold too much stock – why do you think this is? What could happen to a greengrocer, a sports shop stocking seasonal goods such as tennis rackets, a computer shop and a music shop selling CDs if too much stock were held by these outlets?

Identifying market needs

Businesses continually canvass the views of customers to find out the needs of the market. Tesco, the most successful supermarket chain by early 1996, receives 35,000 comments a year at its head-office customer service department. Under its 'Customer First' policy, the company has introduced:

● *Customer panels*. Groups of customers are invited to tell the store manager and head-office colleagues what they think of their local store. Where appropriate, these points are followed up and improvements are made
● *a one-in-front policy*. This is a way of cutting checkout queues, introduced after listening to customers. Where there are more than two people at the checkout, another till will be opened. This carries on until all checkouts are staffed
● *first-class service*. Staff, whatever their job, are encouraged to use their initiative to help customers. This may involve helping people when their car won't start or perhaps calling up a friend when a customer

is not feeling well. This all helps to improve the image of the company.

(Source: Tesco Annual Report and Accounts 1995)

Identifying market trends

Trade magazines will carry articles on market trends. Issues may include 'Is the customer influenced by the green/environmentally friendly image?', 'Is Britpop really dead?', 'Is there a resurgence in the market for real ales?', 'Is the threat of BSE really hitting sales of English beef?' For example, the *Asian Trader* magazine carried the following information on trends in sales of bread:

MARKET SURVEY
BREAD

One of the biggest growth areas in the total bread market is the rolls and morning goods sector, which is currently showing a nine per cent year on year growth. This growth looks set to continue – good news for the independent retailer because of the high prices the items command. Products from this sector tend to be impulse purchases, so there is great potential for the retailer to carve out additional profit opportunities.

(Source: Asian Trader, 5 January 1996)

How could a small retailer use this information?

Retail Newsagent magazine produced the figures in Table 10.3 in January 1996.

Table 10.3 National newspapers circulation and market share

TITLE	AVERAGE DAILY CIRCULATION JAN–DEC 1995	CHANGE ON JAN–DEC 1994	MARKET SHARE 1995
Dailies			
Daily Mirror	2,525,310	+1.3%	31.3%
Daily Record	747,688	−0.5%	9.3%
Daily Star	744,024	no change	9.2%
The Sun	4,053,257	−0.6%	50.2%
	8,070,280	+0.1%	100.0%
Daily Express	1,270,642	−5.1%	34.6%
Daily Mail	1,832,441	+3.3%	49.9%
Today	570,899	−4.4%	15.5%
	3,673,981	−1.0%	100.0%
Daily Telegraph	1,049,399	+0.9%	39.0%
Financial Times	294,977	+1.0%	11.0%
Guardian	397,364	−0.9%	14.6%
Independent	293,566	+4.5%	10.9%

TITLE	AVERAGE DAILY CIRCULATION JAN–DEC 1995	CHANGE ON JAN–DEC 1994	MARKET SHARE 1995
Times	657,857	+21.4%	24.4%
	2,693,162	+5.35%	100.0%★
Sundays			
News Of The World	4,717,656	−1.5%	48.9%
Sunday Mirror	2,547,392	−0.6%	26.4%
Sunday Sport	301,729	+4.1%	3.1%
The People	2,079,218	+2.4%	21.6%
	9,645,995	−0.3%	100.0%
Mail On Sunday	1,998,887	+2.0%	59.1%
Sunday Express	1,382,686	−8.5%	40.9%
	3,381,573	−2.6%	100.0%
Independent On Sunday	327,014	+1.2%	12.0%
Observer	463,413	−6.0%	17.0%
Sunday Telegraph	683,065	+5.1%	25.1%
Sunday Times	1,252,880	+1.3%	46.0%
	2,726,372	+0.9%	100.0%★

Source: ABC

★ May not add up to precisely 100% due to rounding up or down of figures

These articles may use official government statistics or those from private research organisations. The figures in Table 10.3 were compiled by the Audit Bureau of Circulations (ABC).

1 In 1995, one 'quality' newspaper cut its prices to win extra sales. Which paper do you think this was?
2 Use a spreadsheet package to illustrate the figures shown in Table 10.3 in the form of a chart.
3 Do you think a small newsagent would find these figures useful?

Identifying profitable lines
Internal sales information will enable retailers to identify their most profitable lines. A computerised accounting package can produce rapid reports from sales data over a particular month or year.

The report shown in the table gives an example of the sort of sales analysis that is possible.

CANDID CAMERAS LTD			STOCK PROFIT REPORTS – MONTH TO DATE			
STOCK CODE	DESCRIPTION	QUANTITY SOLD	SALES VALUE (£)	COST OF SALES (£)	PROFIT (£)	PROFIT MARGIN (%)
DX300/1	DX-300 ZOOM MK1	60	4,800	3,600	1,200	25
DX300/SZ	DX-300 SUPERZOOM	20	3,400	2,600	800	24
XL22/AM	XL-22 AUTOMATIC	35	2,170	1,400	770	35
RM2/MF	RM2-MINIFOCUS	70	3,850	2,800	1,050	27
FL/95	FLASH-95	25	750	775	(25)	(3)

1 Which line has the highest percentage profit margin?
2 Which line gives the highest profits?
3 Which line should be discontinued? Why?

Identifying wastage

Stock reports such as that above can also identify wastage. For instance, why is the FLASH-95 actually making a loss? Perhaps the item is being sold below cost because it is not a popular line, or perhaps some of these items have been thrown away as they are either damaged or simply obsolete. The report shown does at least highlight that this particular line is unprofitable.

Where goods have a limited shelf-life, wastage can be minimised by ensuring that the first stock in is sold first – i.e. first in first out (FIFO). Shelves in supermarkets are arranged so that the stock nearest to its sell-by date is at the front.

Business documents used in buying and selling

When goods are bought and sold, the transaction may be either cash or credit:

- *Cash purchases and sales.* Literally, 'cash' means notes and coins. In practice, a 'cash sale' is one in which immediate payment is made – perhaps in cash, perhaps by cheque, perhaps by plastic card. Cash sales are normal when consumers visit retailers for their daily shopping. Some smaller retailers purchase their stock for cash at the 'cash and carry'
- *Credit purchases and sales.* Here, the buyer has an account with the supplier, and is allowed to settle this at some future date. Credit sales are usual in business, when, for instance, a retailer purchases stock from a wholesaler, or a wholesaler from a manufacturer. More expensive consumer goods such as cars, cookers, freezers and washing machines are also available on credit terms. Generally, the consumer will pay in a number of instalments over a period of time

Here we will look at the documents used when sales and purchases are on credit – see Figure 10.11. (We will look at methods of payment and cash transactions in Chapter 12.)

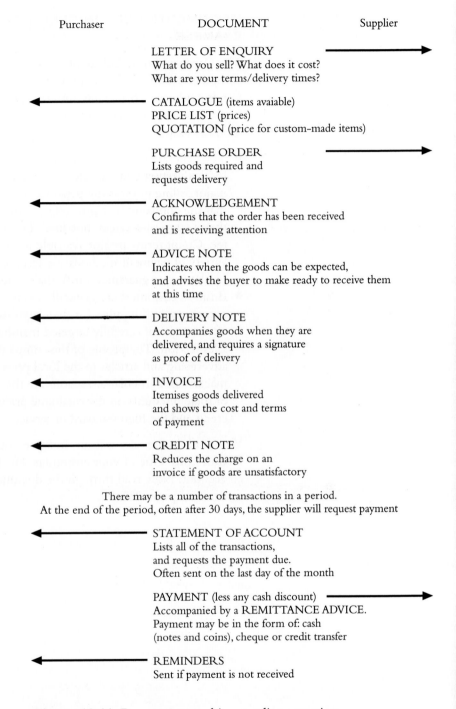

Figure 10.11 Documents used in a credit transaction

DOCUMENTS USED IN CREDIT SALES – A WORKED EXAMPLE

The Hardwarehouse Ltd supplies a comprehensive selection of computer products from its premises in an industrial estate in North London. Customers include both the general public and local businesses. Most of the latter have accounts which they settle on a monthly basis.

- The general public, who visit the retail counter, are attracted by local advertisements, articles in PC magazines and word of mouth. A major selling point is the personal attention and after-sales services that the company is able to offer, both on the premises and through their technical-services 'hot-line'. Local delivery is provided for a fee. Credit terms are not available to non-trade customers, though a variety of payment methods are accepted, including: cash, cheque (with cheque guarantee card), major credit cards and debit cards
- Business customers are generally organisations wanting the equipment and supplies for their own use. Many became customers after a series of carefully targeted mailshots by The Hardwarehouse's sales section. The profile of the company was also raised by advertising and articles in the local press and features in specialist magazines. Particular attractions are the competitive prices, the offer of trade discounts on the catalogue prices, the availability of 30-day credit and the high standard of service

You work in the sales section. Imagine you are the sales supervisor, Dennis Lotis. One of your customers, Hi-Tec Ltd, has recently opened an account. Now read through the documents used in opening the account on pages 287–96.

1 Enquiry. You receive the following enquiry (Figure 10.12):

HI-TEC LTD

43 Chip Lane
Romford
Essex RM5 3MB

Tel: 01708 665 777   Fax: 01708 665 778   VAT Reg No 454 5432

1 October 19-6

Account no: HTL/95
The Managing Director
The Hardwarehouse Ltd
20 Park Drive
London N5 3MW

Dear Madam/Sir

As you will know we have been a regular customer for nearly two years. During that time you have supplied us with software and consumables on credit terms with settlement made on receipt of your monthly statement.

We are currently expanding our business and would be pleased to receive from you a.s.a.p.:

  Details and prices of stand-alone computer systems
  Details of charges for carriage
  Terms and conditions on which these goods are supplied

Yours faithfully

Helen Shapiro

H Shapiro (Ms)
Purchasing

Figure 10.12 A letter of enquiry

2 Catalogue and price list. You reply by return of post, enclosing a catalogue and price list (Figure 10.13):

THE HARDWAREHOUSE LTD

20 Park Drive   Tel: 0171-224-6600
London N5 3MW   Fax: 0171-224-6611

2 October 19-6   VAT Reg No: 233 6123 15

Account no: HTL/95

Ms H Shapiro
Purchasing Department
Hi-Tec Ltd
43 Chip Lane
Romford
Essex RM5 3MB

Dear Ms Shapiro

Thank you for your enquiry of 1 October.

I am sending you our current catalogue and price list for stand-alone systems as requested. I also enclose latest details of software and stationery.

We are able to offer the following terms:

Monthly credit terms as at present. Settlement, strictly net, within 5 days of statement
20% trade discount on all orders
Carriage free on all orders over £1,000, otherwise £15 + VAT
Delivery within 5 working days

I will look forward to receiving your order.

Yours sincerely

Dennis Lotis

D Lotis
Sales

Enc

CATALOGUE and PRICE LIST

THE HARDWAREHOUSE LTD

20 Park Drive
London N5 3MW

Tel: 0171-224-6600
Fax: 0171-224-6611

VAT Reg No: 233 6123 15

PENTIUM SYSTEMS	Hard disc size	
PS/1000	210Mb	£1,475
PS/1001	270Mb	£1,490
PS/1002	340Mb	£1,505
PS/1003	430Mb	£1,515
PS/1004	540Mb	£1,565

Pentium system includes: 8Mb RAM, 1.44 Mb 3.5" floppy disc drive, 14" low radiation monitor, keyboard, mouse, mini tower or desktop case, 12-month on-site warranty, MS-DOS and Windows (latest updates)

PRINTERS

24 Pin

PRD/500	Ariel 380 80 column	£179
PRD/501	Ariel 390 80 column	£259
PRD/502	Ariel 390 Flatbed	£329

Laser		**Pages/minute**	
PRL/200	Maxprint 60	4	£449
PRL/201	Maxprint 80	8	£845
PRL/202	Maxprint 90	8	£1,209

SOFTWARE

Business accounting
A/10	Sage Accountant+	£194
A/11	Sage Book-keeper	£95
A/12	Sage Financial Controller	£320
A/13	Folio Payroll	£80

Spreadsheets
S/50	Supercalc	£69
S/51	Lotus 1-2-3	£225
S/52	MS Excel	£225

Personal Finance
PF/10	Quicken	£29
PF/20	MS Money	£25
PF/30	Sage Moneywise	£35

Databases
D/20	Boorland Dbase	£235
D/21	DataEase	£375
D/22	MS Access	£222
D/23	Paradox	£249

Wordprocessing
W/60	Lotus Ami Pro	£135
W/61	MS Word	£223
W/62	Wordperfect	£205

Games on CD
G/01	RAM Raider	£21
G/02	Hard Driver	£25
G/03	Magic Max	£25
G/04	Storm Force	£19
G/05	Return of Quark	£23

CONSUMABLES

Printer paper
Print-Bond, A4 white per pack (500 sheets)   £2.50
Print-Bond, A4 white per pack (2,500 sheets) £12.00

Printer Cartridges
TO/700 Maxprint toner £50

Figure 10.13 A catalogue and price list

3 Purchase order. You receive the following order (Figure 10.14):

HI-TEC LTD

43 Chip Lane
Romford
Essex RM5 3MB

Tel: 01708 665 777 Fax: 01708 665 778 VAT Reg No 454 5432 89

ORDER

Date: 5 October 19-6

To: Sales Department The Hardwarehouse Ltd 20 Park Drive London N5 3MW	Delivery details: Please deliver to the address above Times: 9am – 5pm

ORDER NO 5004	ACCOUNT REF HTL/95	REQUESTED BY a.s.a.p.	TERMS Net monthly

Quantity	Product code	Description	Unit price
1	PS/1003	Pentium system with 430Mb hard disc	1,515.00
2	PRL/202	Maxprint 90 laser printer	1,209.00
5	S/52	Microsoft Excel	225.00

Authorised by: *H Shapiro*	Position: *Purchasing Manager*	Date: 5/10/-6

Figure 10.14 A purchase order

4 Acknowledgement. After checking stock levels, you acknowledge the receipt of the order (Figure 10.15) and confirm that the goods will be supplied as agreed:

ACKNOWLEDGEMENT

THE HARDWAREHOUSE LTD

20 Park Drive
London N5 3MW

Tel: 0171-224-6600
Fax: 0171-224-6611

6 October 19-6

VAT Reg No: 233 6123 15

Your order no: 5004
Your account no: HTL/95

Ms H Shapiro
Purchasing Department
Hi-Tec Ltd
43 Chip Lane
Romford
Essex RM5 3MB

Dear Ms Shapiro

Thank you for your order of 5 October for the following:

      1 PS/1003 Pentium system with 430Mb hard
         disc @ £1,515.00
      2 PRL/202 Maxprint 90 laser printer @
         £1,209.00
      5 S/52 MS Excel @ £225.00

The matter is receiving our attention and we confirm that delivery will be to your business address within 5 days on the terms agreed.

Yours sincerely

Dennis Lotis

D Lotis
Sales

Figure 10.15 A letter of acknowledgement

5 **Advice note.** You have arranged for delivery with the carrier that you use. You now send an advice note (Figure 10.16) to ask the customer to be ready to receive the goods on this date:

ADVICE NOTE

THE HARDWAREHOUSE LTD

20 Park Drive
London N5 3MW

Tel: 0171-224-6600
Fax: 0171-224-6611

8 October 19-6

VAT Reg No: 233 6123 15

To:
Purchasing Department
Hi-Tec Ltd
43 Chip Lane
Romford
Essex RM5 3MB

ADVICE NOTE NO	1413
YOUR ORDER NO	5004
YOUR ACCOUNT NO	HTL/95

The items listed below will be delivered on:	10th October 19-6

Quantity	Product code	Description	Unit price
1	PS/1003	Pentium system 430Mb hard disc	1,515.00
2	PRL/202	Maxprint 90 laser printer	1,209.00
5	S/52	MS Excel	225.00

Delivery by: own van   Delivery address: as above
Number of items   8

D Lotis

D Lotis
Sales Manager

Figure 10.16 An advice note

6 **Delivery note.** All of the goods ordered have been packed for delivery. The driver is given a delivery note (Figure 10.17) made out in triplicate. The customer will keep one copy, and the carrier will keep the second copy and return the third copy to you the supplier. The driver will not leave the goods until there is a signature confirming delivery. If it is found that some items are missing or that there is obvious damage, then the delivery note will be amended to show this before it is signed. Some buyers have their own goods-received note.

DELIVERY NOTE

THE HARDWAREHOUSE LTD

20 Park Drive
London N5 3MW

Tel: 0171-224-6600
Fax: 0171-224-6611

10 October 19-6

VAT Reg No: 233 6123 15

To:
Purchasing Department
Hi-Tec Ltd
43 Chip Lane
Romford
Essex RM5 3MB

DELIVERY NOTE NO	1413
YOUR ORDER NO	5004
YOUR ACCOUNT NO	HTL/95

Quantity	Product code	Description
1	PS/1003	Pentium system 430Mb hard disc
2	PRL/202	Maxprint 90 laser printer
5	S/52	MS Excel

Delivery by: own van   Delivery address: as above

Number of items   8

Goods received as detailed above:

signature: *Edmundo Ross*

PRINT name: *EDMUNDO ROSS*

D Lotis

D Lotis
Sales Manager

Figure 10.17 A delivery note

7 Invoice. Now that the goods have been delivered, you are able to prepare and send an invoice (Figure 10.18) to show the charge for these items. You will retain two copies, one for the sales department records and one for the accounts section.

The invoice has the same stock details as the acknowledgement, the advice note and the delivery note, and normally it is only necessary to key this information in once to prepare all four documents. ('E & OE' stands for 'errors and omissions excepted'.)

INVOICE

THE HARDWAREHOUSE LTD
20 Park Drive
London N5 3MW

Tel: 0171-224-6600
Fax: 0171-224-6611

12 October 19-6

VAT Reg No: 233 6123 15

To:
Purchasing Department
Hi-Tec Ltd
43 Chip Lane
Romford
Essex RM5 3MB

INVOICE NO	8835
YOUR ORDER NO	5004
YOUR ACCOUNT NO	HTL/95
TAX POINT	as date

Quantity	Product code	Description	Unit Price £	Total price £	Trade discount @ 20%	Net £
1	PS/1003	Pentium system 430Mb hard disc	1,515.00	1,515.00	303.00	1,212.00
2	PRL/202	Maxprint 90 laser printer	1,209.00	2,418.00	483.60	1,934.40
5	S/52	MS Excel	225.00	1,125.00	225.00	900.00

Terms:

E & O E

add carriage	0.00
Sub-total (excl VAT)	4,046.40
add VAT @ 17.5%	708.12
TOTAL DUE	4,754.52

Figure 10.18 An invoice

8 **Credit note.** Some days later, Hi-Tec inform you that one of the printers is faulty. They return this printer to you as agreed, and you accept responsibility. As you are unable to replace the item immediately, you prepare a credit note (Figure 10.19) to reduce the amount that the customer will be charged. Again, there will be one copy for the sales section and one for the accounts section.

CREDIT NOTE

THE HARDWAREHOUSE LTD

20 Park Drive
London N5 3MW

Tel: 0171-224-6600
Fax: 0171-224-6611

20 October 19-6

VAT Reg No: 233 6123 15

To:
Purchasing Department
Hi-Tec Ltd
43 Chip Lane
Romford
Essex RM5 3MB

CREDIT NOTE NO	562
REF INVOICE NO	8835
YOUR ACCOUNT NO	HTL/95
TAX POINT	as date

Quantity	Product code	Description	Unit price £	Total price £	Trade discount @ 20%	Net
1	PRL/202	Maxprint 90 laser printer	1,209.00	1,209.00	241.80	967.20

Reason for credit:
Printer returned as faulty

add carriage	0.00
Sub-total (excl VAT)	967.20
add VAT @ 17.5%	169.26
TOTAL DUE	1,136.46

Figure 10.19 A credit note

9 **Statement of account.** At the end of the month, the accounts section sends a statement of account (Figure 10.20) to the customer. This lists the transactions made over the month, shows the amount now due and asks for payment. A **remittance advice** is attached so that the payment can be identified.

The statement shows the following:

- the position at the start of the month. The customer owed £600 brought forward from September
- that the customer paid this amount by cheque on 4 October
- that the invoice was sent on 12 October for the goods delivered
- that the credit note was sent on 20 October

Notice that the balance due is calculated at each stage. The invoice and credit note numbers are also shown so that the statement can be checked.

STATEMENT OF ACCOUNT

THE HARDWAREHOUSE LTD

20 Park Drive
London N5 3MW

Tel: 0171-224-6600
Fax: 0171-224-6611

31 October 19-6

VAT Reg No: 233 6123 15

To:
Purchasing Department
Hi-Tec Ltd
43 Chip Lane
Romford
Essex RM5 3MB

YOUR ACCOUNT NO	HTL/95

Date	Details	Debit	Credit	Balance
1 Oct	Balance brought forward			600.00
4 Oct	Cheque		600.00	0.00
12 Oct	Invoice 8835	4,754.52		4,754.52
20 Oct	Credit note 562		1,136.46	3,618.06
	Balance now due			£3,618.06

Terms: payment within 5 days of this statement
strictly net

- -

REMITTANCE ADVICE

THE HARDWAREHOUSE LTD

20 Park Drive
London N5 3M1

Tel: 0171-224-6600
Fax: 0171-224-6611

ACCOUNT	HI-TEC LTD	ACCOUNT NO	HTL/95
DATE	31 October 19-6	AMOUNT	£3,618.06

Figure 10.20 A statement of account

For this activity, use the price list on page 289.

1 You work for The Hardwarehouse Ltd. Using today's date, produce sales invoice number 9925 for the following transaction:
- a customer, Ginola Ltd buys:
  - one PS/1001 Pentium system
  - one PRL/200 laser printer
  - one W/60 Lotus Ami Pro
- Terms are:
  - no delivery required
  - 20% trade discount
  - VAT at the current rate
- Other details:
  - order number 324
  - account reference GIN/96

2 Produce a statement of account dated 31 January 19-7 for L J Silver. Show the balance due at each stage. Details are:
- 1 January, balance brought forward £500 (owing from December)
- 4 January, purchased goods for £780 (invoice number 4334)
- 7 January, sent a cheque to pay off the opening balance
- 18 January, bought more goods for £1,650 (invoice number 4390)
- 21 January, received a credit note (number 412) for £45 – after returning damaged goods

The dispatch and delivery of goods

Where a retailer transports goods, it is important that:

- the goods be sent to the correct destination. The goods may travel from a storage depot to one of the stores, or from a store to a customer
- the goods be transported safely. This may mean careful handling, careful packing or maintaining correct temperatures. The tilapia case study on page 313, for example, shows that it can be vital to keep the 'cold chain' below 3 °C

Transport may be by the firm's own vehicles or by independent carriers such as Parcel Force, Securicor Omega, ITN or DHL.

1 When you are out and about, notice the names on delivery vehicles – some will be shop names, some will be manufacturers, others will be specialist carriers.
2 Which shops run their own vehicle fleets? What do they sell?
3 Which manufacturers deliver? Why do you think this is so?

4 Computer firms (such as The Hardwarehouse Ltd in the worked-through example above) frequently use independent carriers. Why is this so? (Think of the way the goods are packed.)

WHY AN ACCURATE AND SAFE DISPATCH OF GOODS IS IMPORTANT

- *Customer satisfaction.* Clearly, it may cause great inconvenience to a customer if goods are either damaged in transit or sent to the wrong place. The careful handling and careful labelling of boxes will help to prevent damage. The forms that we have used are designed to ensure that delivery dates and addresses are recorded accurately. Notice that the delivery may not be to the customer's address: the documents have a space to indicate exactly where the delivery is to be taken. The advice note is designed to ensure that the customer will be available to receive the goods
- *Avoiding breakage.* Breakages and damage will cost the retailer money. Notice that the credit note is used when goods are faulty – this may be a result of damage in transit. Where goods require special handling, retailers may prefer to undertake their own delivery.
- *Business performance.* We have seen that, increasingly, retailers are attempting to reduce the time between ordering and delivery: they now order more frequently and expect rapid delivery. The idea is to reduce the size of stocks, with the following advantages for business efficiency:
  - Money is not 'tied up' in stocks
  - Expensive selling space is not used for warehousing
  - There is less chance of breakages or theft, or of stocks deteriorating

  However, this Just-in-Time system does rely upon the accurate delivery of goods in perfect condition
- *Monitoring stock.* The accurate dispatch of goods enables a business to effectively monitor stock levels – which is vital for reordering purposes. Although the retailer will need to physically stock-take (i.e. to actually count the goods) at intervals, it should be possible for them to calculate how much stock is in hand by comparing the figures for stock received with details from invoices showing stock sold. Of course, this is only possible if the forms are accurately completed and the correct goods have been dispatched.

Self-test questions:
Chapter 10

1 Give three possible problems which may result from carelessness when dispatching goods to customers.
2 Give an example of how the purchasing and sales departments of a superstore may work together.

3 What is the function of the inventory department?

4 A business will record sales made at the till. Give three uses a business may have for this sales information.

5 What is the purpose of an advice note?

6 What is the purpose of the delivery note? Why are there a number of copies of this document?

7 Give five items of information shown on an invoice. What is the purpose of this document?

8 Which items on a statement of account *increase* the amount due, and which *reduce* it?

9 What is meant by the term 'cold chain'? What happens to goods if the cold chain is broken?

10 Give two sources of national sales data available to a retailer in the grocery trade.

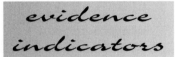

evidence indicators

PART 1

Scenario

You are a trainee working in the sales section at The Hardwarehouse Ltd where your duties include completing sales documentation. You have just opened an account (SOL/96) for a new customer, Solar Systems Ltd of 21 Spa Road, Liverpool.

Transactions

On 15 January 19–7, you receive an enquiry from Solar Systems asking you to quote for the supply and delivery of:

- one Pentium system with at least 500Mb of hard disc
- one laser printer capable of 4 pages per minute
- one copy of Sage Financial Controller accounting software

Your manager suggests that you quote:

- the catalogue price less 20% trade discount
- delivery on the usual terms
- VAT at the current rate
- payment to be upon receipt of the monthly statement

Your tasks:

1 Prepare a quotation to be sent to the customer. (You also send the new catalogue for information.)

2 You receive order no. 3344, dated 20 January, requesting delivery on the terms quoted. Prepare:
   - an acknowledgement of the order, dated 21 January
   - an advice note (no. 2005) dated 23 January (stating that delivery will be on the 25th)
   - a delivery note (no. 2005) dated 25 January

- an invoice (no. 9021), dated 27 January
- a statement of account for the month, dated 31 January

PART 2

An existing customer, Discount Disks of 45 Hove Road, Brighton, Sussex (account no.: DIS/95), requests a quotation for a 66Mhz Pentium system with between 300Mb and 400Mb of hard disc.

1 Prepare a quotation for this dated 8 February 19-7. (Use the same terms and conditions as those offered in Part 1 above.)
2 The quotation is accepted and the goods are ordered (order no. 4050) on 14 February. Prepare:
   - an acknowledgement of the order, dated 15 February
   - an advice note (no. 2045), dated 17 February (stating that delivery will be on the 19th)
   - a delivery note (no. 2045), dated 19 February
   - an invoice (no. 9233), dated 21 February
   - a statement of account for the month, dated 28 February

PART 3

Write notes to explain the purpose of each of the selling documents that you have completed.

PART 4

1 Select two retailer outlets for study. Name the retailers and the trade(s) in which they operate.
2 For each:
   - identify the sources of sales information that they may use
   - give the type of information that each of these sources may provide
   - give details of how each retailer uses this information
3 Draw an organisation chart for each of the outlets to show the main departments.
4 Give an example for each outlet to show how different departments work together to achieve the smooth running of the organisation.
5 Explain the reasons for the importance of the accurate and safe dispatch of goods. Give examples of how one of your organisations achieves this.

Investigating administrative processes for buying and receiving goods

In this chapter, we will:

- consider the role of the buyer in small and large retailers
- examine the buying process
- look at how buyers locate and choose their suppliers, and at negotiations, orders and deliveries

We will cover Element 4.2, Performance Criteria 1, 2, 3, 4, 5.

THE BUYER

Most retailers work in a very competitive market, and customers who cannot find what they want will quickly go elsewhere. Effective selling will only take place if the right products are on the shelves at the right price. The buyer is responsible for ensuring that this is the case.

The buyer's job is to:

- plan the type and variety of goods to be stocked
- locate suppliers
- choose actual goods to be stocked – e.g. particular brands
- negotiate with suppliers so as to buy as cheaply as possible
- ensure that goods are of the right quality
- ensure that the supplier is reliable and will deliver on time

There is a difference between the way in which small and large retailers buy:

- The smaller retailers will select their stocks from what is on offer at the wholesaler – or, if they are buying direct, at the manufacturer
- The larger retailers carry a vast range of stock and frequently employ specialist buyers who are experts in their own particular area. Larger retailers can use their buying power to drive hard bargains. A supplier not wishing to miss out on a large order may be willing to enter into a contract involving: changing the production method, adapting their products, or developing new products to the buyer's own particular specifications. For instance, Asda may want a particular taste of wine, a particular production method (e.g. organically grown food), apples with no blemishes or fish of a certain size.

The buyer must:

- know the market – e.g. what is in fashion? What are the trends? Who are our customers?
- be able to drive hard bargains: what price? Do we get discounts? How quickly can you deliver? Can we have credit?

- understand their own business and its policies – e.g. what is our image? What is our product mix? Are we aiming for a particular style?
- understand what will work most effectively in a particular store – e.g. how quickly do goods 'turn over'? What is their shelf-life? Can we store these products? Is there room to display them properly?

THE BUYING PROCESS

The process for buying products is shown in Figure 11.1. The documents associated with each stage will be familiar from the earlier section on buying and selling documents (see Chapter 10, pages 285–296).

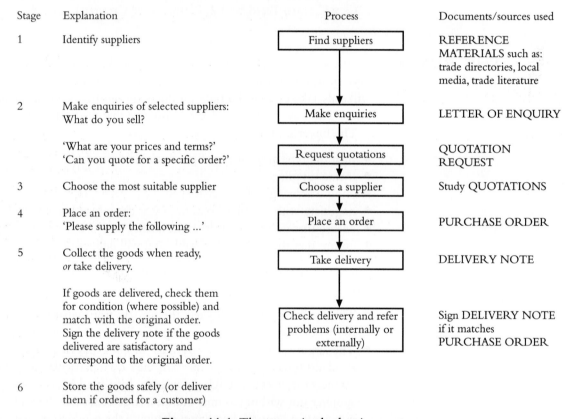

Stage	Explanation	Process	Documents/sources used
1	Identify suppliers	Find suppliers	REFERENCE MATERIALS such as: trade directories, local media, trade literature
2	Make enquiries of selected suppliers: What do you sell?	Make enquiries	LETTER OF ENQUIRY
	'What are your prices and terms?' 'Can you quote for a specific order?'	Request quotations	QUOTATION REQUEST
3	Choose the most suitable supplier	Choose a supplier	Study QUOTATIONS
4	Place an order: 'Please supply the following ...'	Place an order	PURCHASE ORDER
5	Collect the goods when ready, *or* take delivery.	Take delivery	DELIVERY NOTE
	If goods are delivered, check them for condition (where possible) and match with the original order. Sign the delivery note if the goods delivered are satisfactory and correspond to the original order.	Check delivery and refer problems (internally or externally)	Sign DELIVERY NOTE if it matches PURCHASE ORDER
6	Store the goods safely (or deliver them if ordered for a customer)		

Figure 11.1 The stages in the buying process

If any problems occur, these need to be referred to the appropriate section:

1 *Internal problems* may include:
   - inappropriate goods ordered
   - goods ordered that are not yet required causing unnecessary stockpiling

These matters should be referred to the purchasing section.

2 *External problems* may include:
   - the late delivery of goods

- goods delivered that were not ordered
- goods that were ordered not delivered
- goods damaged in transit

Some problems may be avoided by carefully checking deliveries. However, although it will be possible to check that the correct number of packages have been received, it is not usually possible to check that the goods are in working order. As a result, the goods may be signed in only for a problem to be discovered at some later stage. In this case, it will be necessary to request a **credit note** from the supplier.

Please reread the section on business documents in Chapter 10 (pages 285–296), but this time, imagine that you are working for Hi-Tec Ltd, the buyer.

The section on *buying documents* in the *Evidence Indicator* may be attempted now.

Sources of information on suppliers

Some businesses such as franchises and voluntary retail cooperatives (e.g. Spar) have permanent arrangements with suppliers. However, for some businesses, finding suppliers who offer suitable terms may be a problem. Rather like the consumer, the retailer has to shop around.

There are a number of sources of information on suppliers, ranging from the business's own records to freely available local information, or to specialised publications. Much of the information will be available at the local reference library, and some of it will also be distributed through the trade.

Possible sources of information include the following:

- *Internal records*. A business will often keep its own record of suppliers in the same way that it will keep a database of customers. The information will usually be compiled from past dealings with suppliers, but there may also be details of potential suppliers built up from publicity materials, on new products, which have been filed for future use
- *Trade registers and directories*. These give lists of businesses involved in particular trades. An example is:
  - *Kelly's Directory of Manufacturers and Merchants*
- *Trade magazines*. There are a large number of trade magazines specialising in different types of retailing – a list of those with the largest circulation is shown on page 276 in Chapter 10. Manufacturers and wholesalers are able to target retailers by advertising in these magazines, many of which are circulated free by post. Retailers are also able to keep up with new developments and gain tips for increasing profits
  - *BRAD* (British Rate and Data Guide) – provides a full list of trade publications

Figure 11.2 An advertisement for Country Choice plus other sources of supply

Wholesalers and manufacturers are keen to sell, and so will advertise in the appropriate publications.

What does Country Choice (see Figure 11.2) deliver? (See the 'One Stop' case study on page 172 in Chapter 7.)

- *Trade associations.* Many trades have their own trade associations which are able to help members with specialised information. Examples of trade associations include: the British Educational Suppliers Association, the British Fur Trade Association, the Greeting Cards Association, The Hardware Federation and the Association of Convenience stores (ACS)
- *Classified directories.* The Yellow Pages – 'Let your fingers do the walking' – is a classified directory published by the Yellow Pages division of British Telecommunications plc (see Figure 11.3). It lists the telephone numbers and addresses of businesses organised under headings such as 'Builders' merchants', 'Mobile telephones' and 'Wholesale stationers'. The directory is distributed free to users of BT telephone services.

  The Thomson's Directory (see Figure 11.3) is a local directory of businesses and services distributed free to households and businesses. Businesses are classified under general headings according to their trade. Thomson's suggests that businesses should 'Give buyers the information they need to ensure they call you', and that the way to do this is to place an advert with the directory

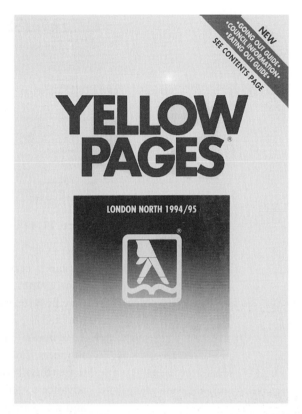

Figure 11.3 Classified business directories

- *Exhibitions, conferences and trade fairs.* These are organised around a particular theme, and usually represent a particular trade. The idea is to give businesses a showcase to display their products. (See Figure 11.4.) Information, free samples, brochures, advice and contact numbers are all available. Latest developments and new ideas are also on display. Entry is normally restricted to those from the trade. Although there may be an entry fee, complimentary tickets may also be circulated to a targeted number of retailers or distributed with trade journals

1 Look up wholesalers of clothing, newspapers, nuts and bolts.
2 Why do you think so many trade exhibitions are held in Birmingham?

- *Catalogues.* As we saw in the section on selling, suppliers will produce their own catalogues and price lists. These will normally be sent out in response to a customer enquiry. The catalogue may

DIARY DATES

Euroshop '96
The world's largest trade fair, Euroshop '96, will feature shopfitting, display and merchandising.
Messe Düsseldorf
February 24-28
49 0211 4560 991

ICB '96
The International Confectionery, Biscuit and Ice Cream exhibition claims to be the only dedicated confectionery exhibition in the UK.
NEC, Birmingham
March 3-5
0171-610 3001

Taste of the West
Minister of Agriculture Douglas Hogg will open this third Festival

of West Country Food and Drink.
Matford Centre, Exeter
March 20-21
01392 445675

Retail Security '96
The first security exhibition specifically for CTNs and c-stores features everything from shutters to CCTVs.
Lord's Banqueting Suite
March 24 (one day only)
0181-944 0955

Foodex Meatex
Four daily workshops, dealing with different aspects of food hygiene, will take place at the food and meat industries' exhibition. Subjects covered include food safety and handling, workwear, maintenance of flooring areas, hygiene

training and cleaning systems.
NEC, Birmingham
March 24-27
0121-622 6860

Association of Convenience Stores
Annual conference of the Farnborough-based trade association.
The Palace Hotel, Torquay
April 28-30
01252 515001

Food & Drink Expo '96
Around 550 exhibitors are expected to take stands at the fair. The show, which is organised by Blenheim, will also feature catering, fresh produce and ingredients fairs.
NEC, Birmingham
April 28-May 1
0181-742 2828

CIBUS '96
The eighth International Food Exhibition CIBUS will take place in Parma, Italy. This year there is a separate exhibition dedicated to confectionery, as well as greater coverage of fish products and health foods.
Parma, Italy
May 9-13
0171-435 9632

Forecourt Shop & Convenience Retailing '96
A highlight of the show will be the New Product Awards, which are the only product awards for the convenience industry. Entries are limited to exhibitors only.
NEC, Birmingham
June 4-6
0181-742 2828

Figure 11.4 Trade fairs and exhibitions for suppliers

contain a certain amount of detail and perhaps illustrations or photographs, and may be costly to produce. For this reason, there may be a separate price list which can be rapidly (and cheaply) updated if prices change

- *Local media.* The local press or radio may give information about suppliers. For example, where there is to be a feature on a particular trade, then businesses connected with this will be informed in advance to see whether they wish to take advantage of the publicity and place an advertisement.

There is often a local free press which survives entirely on revenue from classified advertisements. Suppliers may be found in this, although the general nature of the readership means that it is more likely to contain information about local retailers than about wholesalers

- *Word of mouth.* Personal recommendation is a reliable way of choosing suppliers. Retailers may be prepared to help one another with advice. They may be friends or relations or they may meet as members of a particular retailing organisation such as the Society of Independent Retailers or the Association of Convenience Stores. Remember that many retailers have a lot in common and may not necessarily be in direct competition with one another.

1 In recent years, Yellow Pages has put some well-known advertisements in the media: remember J R Hartley looking for his book on fly-fishing, and more recently taking up golf? The line 'Let your fingers do the walking' is also still used.
    Since Yellow Pages is free, why is it advertised on TV?
2 Look up 'Trade associations' in your local Yellow Pages, and note which ones are mentioned. Telephone or write to one of these. Find out what services it provides for its members.

activity

Assume that you wish to set up a business printing your own designs of T-shirts.

1 Use local sources of information to:
- identify two suppliers of plain T-shirts
- obtain details of terms and conditions offered, including: minimum quantities supplied, price, delivery times, mode of delivery, terms of payment, methods of payment accepted

2 Interview the manager of your school/college canteen. Where do supplies come from? What are the terms and conditions? Is one or a number of suppliers used?

The following case studies use fictional names but are based upon interviews with two actual businesses.

Case study: MX Ironmongers

MX is a general DIY store based in North London. The business has two shops a few hundred yards apart in a local shopping area so that some custom comes from those visiting the other shops nearby. There are no employees, and the two owners look after one shop each. The main selling point is that the owners understand the stock that they sell and, despite the small premises, are likely to have what you are looking for; in fact, they seem to have everything.

The general appearance is that of organised chaos. From floor to ceiling, there are: trays of nuts and bolts, light fittings, reels of cable, tins of paint, batteries, buckets, locks and so on. There is also a key-cutting service. Although the average purchase comes to a few pounds, some more specialised items are also stocked – e.g. gate hinges at £28 each.

Modernising the shop would take time, cost money and probably do little to improve business. As it is, however, the shop provides a genuine service to local people, and although there is a sizeable local population, it is not likely that a larger DIY chain will set up in the immediate area.

Interview with the proprietors
How do you find out about suppliers?
We look in Yellow Pages and specialised trade papers such as *The Trader* which comes out every month.

We also belong to the Hardware Federation which is based in Birmingham. The Federation sends us trade information and also provides *The Grey Book* each year. This gives recommended retail prices of items.

Where do you buy your stocks?
90% of the time, we use wholesalers. They open on Sunday mornings, so we usually collect the goods ourselves to save on delivery costs.

For some goods, we get delivery from manufacturers. Sometimes, we get the manufacturer's details from the label on the goods. We may contact them to see if they will supply us direct.

How do you pay?
We often pay cash. Sometimes when goods are delivered we have one month to pay. We had to provide references from our bank before we were allowed credit, and similarly before we were allowed to pay by cheque. If suppliers are to deliver £500 worth of goods, they need to be sure that we will pay them.

What payment do you accept?
Cash, or for a large payment, a cheque with a banker's card. Nothing else, no credit.

A last word?
No-one can teach you this business, you learn from experience. Sometimes, we will get something especially for a customer, but we have to be careful. If we buy too much, it may take a year or more to sell it.

Case study: Crescent Mini Market

Crescent Mini Market is a small neighbourhood convenience store in a residential area in North London. The shop, which measures approximately 3 metres by 7 metres, has one unit for frozen food, one for ice cream and two cool units for dairy products and prepacked meat. There is also a cool-drinks cabinet, a central shelf unit, some wall shelving and a counter. Goods stocked include: tinned food, prepacked frozen food such as fish fingers and pizzas, prepacked meats and dairy products, bread, canned and bottled drinks, newspapers and magazines. The owner, Mr Patel, has two ways of stocking his shop:

1 Most of the food and drink is collected from a cash-and-carry in his own van.
2 Other items, such as cigarettes, newspapers and magazines, and bread, are delivered by the suppliers' own vehicles. As the order for bread was low, the existing bread supplier stopped delivering: he wanted a £100 minimum order. A new supplier was found by word of mouth. He will deliver because he also has to visit another small customer nearby.

With the cash-and-carry, administrative procedures are kept to a minimum. There is no need to order goods, but instead merely to drive to the warehouse, select the goods, pay for them and drive them back to the shop. The trip is similar to a visit to a supermarket.

For goods that are delivered, the following procedure is usual:

- A 'rep' visits the shop to take the order. A copy of the order is retained for reference
- The delivery is made by van, the goods are checked against the order and the delivery note is signed
- An invoice is sent and, depending upon the arrangement, this is either paid immediately or logged on the account which is in turn paid when a statement is received at the end of the month

Copies of magazines such as *Convenience Store* are delivered free. Sometimes, *The Grocer* is purchased.

1 Where do small retailers find out about suppliers?
2 Why do small retailers tend to use a cash-and-carry? What is the particular advantage?
3 Retailers such as MX and Crescent Mini Market rarely buy on credit. Why not?
4 Why may some suppliers be reluctant to deliver to small shops?

Choosing a supplier

Having located suitable suppliers, a retailer will need to select the ones that offer the best terms. Considerations might be:

- convenient location
- low prices
- discounts for bulk buys
- a willingness to accept small orders
- variety and quality
- credit facilities
- free delivery

When choosing suppliers, a retailer may send a **letter of enquiry** to gain general details, or request a **quotation** for particular goods.

- A letter of enquiry may be used to obtain general details of the type of goods available. Where the goods are standard (probably with a brand label), a catalogue and price list will show the various stock lines, the prices and the general terms and conditions upon which these may be supplied. Most standardised goods are priced in this way – e.g. groceries, electrical goods and office supplies
- A quotation is required for non-standard goods. These may be special orders made to the retailer's particular requirements, such as specially printed T-shirts or a particular pattern of dress

Remember that wholesalers and manufacturers do not sit back and wait for orders but promote themselves through the pages of trade publications. The Londis advertisement quoted in the extract below was taken from *Asian Trader*. It shows that wholesalers are keen to 'sign up' small retailers for regular supplies. The idea of a 'partnership' between suppliers and retailers appears in the mission statements of many businesses. The idea is that both parties can benefit if each has a clear understanding of the other's needs: the supplier gets a regular outlet, while the retailer gets the goods the customers want.

1 Read the article on the next page. What advantages does the Londis arrangement offer:
   - to the retailer
   - to the wholesaler?
2 What is a symbol independent? (See page 175.)

Why the Londis Health Check is important

If your store has a minimum £5,000 turnover – or the potential to reach that figure – and is in the Londis distribution area, you owe it to yourself to take the Londis Wholesaler Health Check. It is carried out free of charge . . . [and] . . . will show you if you're buying at the most competitive prices.

. . . Actual invoices from your . . . wholesaler . . . are compared . . . with the Londis standard. . . . Also taken into account are costs of membership, technology, fascia rental, etc. This . . . enables Londis to calculate the annual saving you could make . . . if you decided to join our group. This usually averages between 2 and 5 per cent . . .

(Source: Asian Trader, *5–18 January 1996)*

The buying power of large retailers

Large retailers have the power to drive hard bargains with suppliers, and they will only make agreements with those who are prepared to meet their demands. It is not only price, quality and reliability that determines what they buy: they are also interested in production methods. The Body Shop, for instance, has built its success on obtaining supplies which are produced without harming animals and with a concern for the environment. The John Lewis Partnership will not sell imported rugs made by young children. Sainsbury's agrees with farmers that production methods should be 'friendly' to the land. These companies are aware that a 'green' image sells goods.

Case study: B&Q

B&Q, the DIY chain, will only deal with suppliers who are committed to protecting the environment:

All our suppliers must get involved

For the past three years it's been company policy that *all* our suppliers have their own environmental policy and action plan. This means they must know what damage their products are doing and have a meaningful action plan to reduce that impact.

Each supplier has been given a

personalised report outlining what their environmental strengths and weaknesses are with an appropriate grading from A to F. All suppliers who were an F grade had to be at least a C before 30th June. We achieved the target. By 30th November all suppliers which are E or D should be at least C grade. Suppliers not committed to our policies will be delisted.

(Source: The Guardian, *24 October 1994)*

Case study: fair play for toy workers

If you went down to the shops yesterday you might have been surprised – teddy bears were picketing, not picnicking, at a leading London toy store to publicise the plight of their makers in Asian factories ...

Supported by the World Development Movement, the teddies and giant soft toys were outside Hamley's, Regent Street.

WDM head of campaigns Harriet Lamb said that at least 250 Asian toy workers have been killed and hundreds more injured in industrial accidents and factory fires since 1993. She said some employees were paid 42p an hour for a 10-hour day and worked a six or seven-day week.

The WDM has joined forces with the TUC and the Catholic Institute for International Relations to negotiate a safety code with the industry to ensure toy companies check out their suppliers.

(Source: The Guardian)

Case study: W H Smith: buying power

Following the breakdown of the Net Book Agreement (which had prevented price-cutting by booksellers), W H Smith, the UK's biggest bookseller, announced that it was imposing far tougher terms on its suppliers. The company has asked for a 48% discount on books supplied, a 60-day credit period and books to be on **sale or return** (SOR).

Although the collapse of the Net Book Agreement reduced prices, it did not lead to extra growth in book sales, and it is feared that many small publishers may close down.

1 Why are suppliers prepared to change their production methods to suit large retailers?

2 Which two documents may a buyer send to find out the price of a supplier's goods?

3 Sometimes a supplier will send a standard catalogue and price list to a retailer. However, for some goods a quotation is sent. Name goods which are priced in each of these two ways, and explain why there is a difference.

4 Why is W H Smith able to dictate such hard terms to publishers?

5 What was the Net Book Agreement? What has happened since it collapsed in late 1995?

Placing an order When the retailer has agreed terms and conditions with the supplier, goods will be requested by means of a purchase order. There is an example of such an order (sent by Hi-Tec Ltd) on page 290. Notice that this specifies the items required, the quantity, the delivery date, the delivery address and the terms and conditions agreed.

With advances in new technology, paper-based documents are being replaced by **electronic data interchange** (EDI) whereby 'electronic documents' may be sent directly from the retailer's computer to the computer of the supplier. EDI speeds up the whole process of ordering. Now that suppliers are able to respond more quickly to orders, the retailer is able to hold less stock. The furniture retailer MFI, for instance, has found that this has a number of advantages, including:

● less need for expensive warehousing at branches

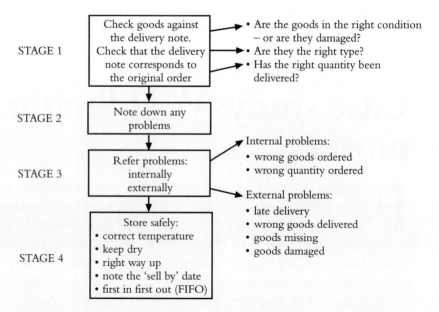

Figure 11.5 The stages in taking delivery of goods

- less money 'tied up' in stock
- less likelihood of damage or loss of stock
- branch warehouses can be used to increase the selling space of the store

EPOS systems (see page 204) also help with ordering. Records of sales and stock levels are instantly updated so that managers have the information needed to reorder the correct items without delay.

Taking delivery of goods   It is important to have standard procedures for taking delivery of stock. These help to avoid errors such as paying for stock not received and accepting damaged or incorrect stock. The usual stages are as shown in Figure 11.5 (left).

Case study: Sainsbury's – specialised buying/special delivery

Whilst small retailers search for suppliers in trade magazines, the large retailers employ specialist buyers who are able to travel the world in search of new products. Often, these retailers have such buying power that they can dictate the way in which the supplier operates.

Mike Wildman, deputy manager of Sainsbury's Technical and Development Department, has the job of sourcing new products. In 1992 he received a sample of red tilapia, a farmed fish, from Jamaican Broilers, one of his existing suppliers. The taste was right, and because customers were now showing an interest in new exotic fish, so was the timing. However, before a deal could be made, some product development was needed.

Tilapia is a farmed fish, so its size can be controlled – this is vital as the European market requires fish to be 10–12 inches (around 27 cm) long and ¾–1 lb (around 400 grammes) in weight. Experiments with feed

and different types of water were made, and tasting panels were set up. Eventually, convinced that the fish might be viable, Wildman flew to the Caribbean to visit the Barton Isle fish farm. He needed to make sure that the company could meet the strict code that Sainsbury's demands of all its suppliers. After some adjustments to the plant's hygiene and refrigeration, the factory was given the seal of approval and a contract was signed.

There is just a 48-hour difference between the time the fish is caught and the time it appears on the slab in the supermarket. 10,000 fish a week are supplied in this way.

Day 1
1 Fish are caught at 4 pm.
2 Processing takes 30 minutes. Here, the fish are graded, weighed, washed, gilled, gutted, scaled and placed in 30 lb bags (14 kg). They are then packed in ice in insulated cartons, and from now on the temperature must

remain below 3 °C: the 'cold chain' must be maintained as the fish pass from one form of transport to another.

3 The fish are transported by lorry from the farm to Kingston Airport (Norman Manley International). This takes 3 hours.

4 The scheduled British Airways flight to the UK takes off at 9.45 pm and lasts 9 hours.

Day 2

5 At 11.40 am, at Gatwick Airport, the Ministry of Agriculture, Fisheries and Food inspects the export documents and checks the cargo: damaged packing could mean that the goods are condemned as unfit.

6 The goods are loaded onto lorries and transported to Bluecrest at Grimsby. This takes 4.5 hours.

7 The goods are designated an 'overnight commodity', meaning that they must get to stores very quickly. Quality control is carried out to see that the fish are in good condition. They are then 'gas packed' in carbon dioxide and nitrogen, and sealed in packs for further transport.

8 Delivery is carried out by road throughout the UK.

Day 3

9 A final check is carried out at the store: is the temperature still below 3 °C? The fish is then displayed in ice on the slab ready for when the store opens.

(Source: adapted from Sainsbury's 125 years Celebration Supplement)

1 Why is a supplier such as Jamaican Broilers prepared to adapt its products to suit a customer such as Sainsbury's?

2 How do large companies like Sainsbury's find their suppliers?

3 How did Sainsbury's know that Jamaican Broilers produced a fish called tilapia?

4 What problems could occur in the transport of the product?

5 At what stages are the goods checked by Sainsbury's?

6 Explain the terms: gas packing, overnight goods, quality control, cold chain?

7 Why do you think EDI (electronic data interchange) is necessary for documentation in cases like this?

Self-test questions:
Chapter 11

1 Give five sources from which a small DIY shop may find out about suppliers.

2 Put the following processes into the correct sequence: make enquiries, find suppliers, take delivery, choose a supplier, place an order.

3 Some goods need to be transported in special conditions. What is meant by the term 'cold chain'? To which sort of goods does it apply?

4 The Yellow Pages is a 'classified' directory. What does this mean?
5 A retailer of furniture has approached a number of suppliers with a view to making an order. The retailer is interested in price. Give *two* other factors which are important when choosing a supplier.
6 An order form is always numbered. Why is this?
7 When goods are delivered by a wholesaler:
   ● which document must the retailer sign as proof of receipt of goods?
   ● Which *other* document should the retailer check the goods delivered against?
8 What is the purpose of a trade association? Name *two* associations.
9 Why might a retailer visit a trade exhibition?
10 Many larger retailers are trying to speed up the supply chain. Cutting the time between order and delivery means that they do not need to hold so much stock. Give *two* advantages of this to the retailer.

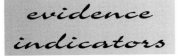

evidence indicators

1 Identify an area of the retail trade which interests you – e.g. DIY, groceries, records/tapes/CDs, clothes. Assume that you are a retailer in your chosen line of business, and give your business a name, an address, a telephone number and a fax number.
   Design a letterhead and an order form (use the documents on pages 287 and 296 as examples, or alternatively look at the designs used by businesses that you know).
2 Use information sources to identify *two* possible suppliers to your trade. Carefully note the information sources that you have used and the details of the suppliers that you have identified. Explain what has attracted you to these suppliers.
3 Complete buying documents using your headed paper (these documents will not actually be sent). You will need:
   ● two letters of enquiry – one to each of your potential suppliers, requesting a catalogue/price list
   ● two letters requesting a quotation for a particular order – one letter to each supplier
   ● two order forms – one to each supplier
   NB: you will need to supply unit prices and catalogue numbers. You can either:
   ● obtain a price list from a supplier, or, if you do not have access to the supplier's prices:
   ● work backwards from retail prices in shops to calculate what a realistic buying-in price would be.★
4 Investigate the purchasing and delivery processes for two different products in two different outlets. You should:

- Draw labelled diagrams to illustrate the stages involved in the purchasing process for each product. Identify the documents used at each stage
- Explain the procedures used by each outlet when taking delivery of these products

★ To calculate the purchase price:

(a) Find out the normal gross margin for the products you wish to buy — a number of these are shown in Appendix I on page 345.

(b)   £ sales price × margin % = gross profit in £s
             sales price − profit = purchase price
       For example, for a product selling at £2 with a 25% gross margin:
             £2 × 25% = £0.50 gross profit
             £2 − £0.50 = £1.50 purchase price

Investigating documentation required for financial transactions

In this chapter, we will:

- look at how and why financial records are kept
- examine different methods of payment

We will cover Element 4.3, Performance Criteria 1, 2, 3, 4, 5.

WHY DO WE NEED TO KEEP FINANCIAL RECORDS?

Even in a small business, it is not possible to remember all of the daily financial transactions that occur. Written records are therefore essential: without them, no-one knows what is going on and it is impossible to check anything.

In order to work efficiently, a business needs an organised system of record-keeping. We need a set of standard documents and a standard set of procedures. If responsible staff leave, go on holiday or are ill, then it should still be possible to find the information we need.

Business financial records are produced for the benefit of two main groups of people:

1 **Managers.** Financial records provide internal information which enables managers to run their business more effectively.
2 **Stakeholders.** Financial records provide information required by **stakeholders** – i.e. all of those who have a right to know about the business. Some of this information, such as the annual accounts, is required by law.
   Stakeholders may include:
   - owners (sole traders, partners, company shareholders)
   - management
   - customers
   - suppliers
   - employees
   - subcontractors (such as the independent carrier used for deliveries)
   - the bank manager
   - the government (especially the Customs and Excise for VAT, and the Inland Revenue for tax)

We shall examine the use of financial records by these two groups in more detail a little later on.

WHAT DO WE RECORD?

Input

The system of financial recording is illustrated in Figure 12.1.

There is an original document for all financial transactions. The details from these documents are recorded in the business accounts.

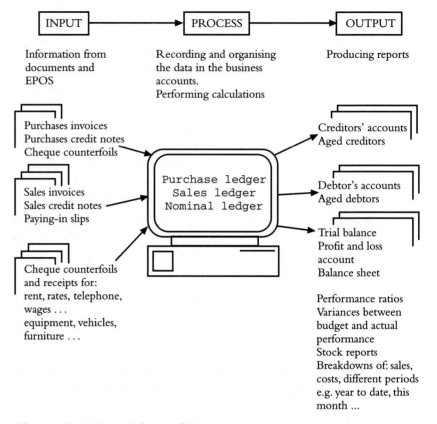

Figure 12.1 Financial recording

The documents include:

- **invoices** which show charges for goods bought or sold
- **credit notes.** These reduce the charge on an invoice (where, for example, the goods are returned as faulty)
- **cheques**, **credit cards** and **debit cards counterfoils** and **credit transfer details (giro)**
- There are also **bills** (**invoices**) and **receipts** for running costs (**overheads**) and for the purchase or sale of assets such as cars, furniture and equipment

Output   The accounting system can provide a number of standard reports for day-to-day use. These include:

1 In the sales ledger:
    - **Debtors' accounts** – showing what each customer owes. It also shows: how much business has been done with each customer, what the credit limit is, and whether this has been exceeded
    - the **aged debtors' report** which shows how long outstanding amounts have been owed. This should be regularly checked, and overdue bills chased

2 In the purchases ledger:
   ● **creditors' accounts** showing what we owe to each supplier
   ● the **aged creditors' report**. This report shows for how long we have owed money to our suppliers. As with aged debtors, the time periods shown are: 30 days, 60 days, 90 days and more than 90 days

3 In the nominal ledger:
   ● details of accounts for: **assets** (things we own), **liabilities** (what we owe), **incomes** such as sales, and the numerous **expenses** such as rates, rent, light and heat, and so on
   ● the **bank account** – showing money received and paid. The current balance is particularly important
   ● the **trial balance** which summarises the balances on the various accounts

THE PURPOSES OF FINANCIAL RECORDS

Monitoring business performance

From day to day, managers need to know how the business is progressing. They need answers to questions concerning such matters as:

● Cash flow: what is the bank balance? Can we pay the wages this month?
● Creditors (the suppliers): how much do we owe? Who do we owe it to? When is it due?
● Debtors (the customers): who owes us money? How much do they owe? Is it due yet?
● Performance: did the sales staff meet their targets? Are expenses being kept within the budgets?

At various stages during the year, managers also need **progress reports**. These include:

● an analysis of sales – e.g. what is selling, and what is not?
● an analysis of departmental performance, e.g. which department is doing well, and which is not?
● monitoring against pre-set budgets – e.g. are we keeping down costs? Are sales up to target?
● profit and loss for the month and the year to date
● stock reports – e.g. which stock lines need reordering?
● aged debtors report. Managers use this to analyse trends in payment by customers – e.g. is it taking longer than previously for customers to settle their bills? It also helps to highlight bad debts (debts that cannot be collected).

S.W.I.T.S.	(Store Weekly Information Tracking Sheet)	STORE	Moviedrome

STORE MANAGER	Jane Willis	WEEK ENDING	11-May

REVENUE		A	B	C	D	E
DAY	DATE	Sales revenue – budget	Sales revenue – actual	Variance (+ or – budget)	Sales revenue last week	Variance (+ or – last week)
				B – A = C		B – D = E
Mon	5-May	700	750	50	710	40
Tue	6-May	800	760	(40)	820	(60)
Wed	7-May	800	830	30	790	40
Thu	8-May	800	620	(180)	580	40
Fri	9-May	800	810	10	740	70
Sat	10-May	1,500	1,200	(300)	1,650	(450)
Sun	11-May	600	550	(50)	350	200
Totals		6,000	5,520	(480)	5,640	(120)

Sales last year	Percentage up or down against:	Budget	(8.00%)
		Last week	(2.13%)
5,000		Last year	10.40%

SALES ANALYSIS							
DAY	DATE	Movies	Confectionery	Games	Blank tapes	Head cleaners	Other
Mon	5-May	390	70	175	85	20	10
Tue	6-May	455	75	130	65	15	20
Wed	7-May	440	62	158	120	20	30
Thu	8-May	330	55	130	90	10	5
Fri	9-May	450	83	127	110	24	16
Sat	10-May	524	186	320	120	35	15
Sun	11-May	328	56	100	45	7	14
TOTALS		2917	587	1140	635	131	110

Weather

Temperature	17°C
Conditions	
Grey but fine, except: Thursday, heavy rain	

New releases

1) Grey Rain 2
2) The Brother
3) For Ever Amen
4) Long Way Home
5) Chain Saws and Roses
6) Rough Diamond

Promotions/TV/sporting events/local and world events/school and Bank Holidays

May Day Bank Holiday on Monday 5th
FA Cup Final Saturday afternoon (10th May)

Store Manager signature:	*Jane Willis*	Date	*11-May*

(Source: based on a SWITS sheet used by Blockbuster Video)

Study the SWITS sheet for Moviedrome.

1 Explain the following terms: budget, actual and variance.
2 Why do management need a SWITS sheet like the one shown?
3 On which days did the shop:
   - do better than the budget set for the week
   - do worse than last week?
4 Are sales up or down compared to the same period last year?
5 By what percentage are sales below budget?
6 From the information available, can you suggest why this is?
7 Which of the stock lines brings in the most money?
8 Which of the stock lines would you describe as an 'impulse' buy?

Producing annual accounts

By law, all businesses must produce annual accounts at the end of each financial year. These will include:

- a **profit and loss account** – to show profit (or losses) over the financial year
- a **balance sheet** to show what the business is worth at the year end

All businesses must make these accounts available to the Inland Revenue. In addition, all companies are required by the Companies Act 1985 to *publish* their accounts within a time limit. This means that they must send a copy to Companies House where, for a fee, they can be inspected by anyone who is interested. They must also send a copy to all of their shareholders, each of whom is invited to the **annual general meeting** (AGM) where the directors report on the year's progress.

Annual accounts are used by the stakeholders for a variety of purposes:

- The Inland Revenue calculates **tax** on the basis of business profits. Sole traders and partners are charged **income tax**, whilst companies pay **corporation tax**
- HM Customs and Excise collects **value–added tax** (VAT). All businesses with turnover over a certain level (as decided in the government's annual budget) must register for VAT, and this means that they must first collect VAT on their sales and then, after claiming back any VAT paid on their purchases, send the difference to the Customs and Excise. Generally, VAT returns are made each **quarter**
- The bank and other lenders are interested in the business's accounts since these show whether the business is able to repay its loans. Where a business wishes to borrow money, it will normally need to provide some evidence of how it has performed over the past three

years – usually, the bank asks for copies of the annual accounts which were given to the Inland Revenue

- Shareholders have invested money in company **shares**, and they are interested to see how the directors have used these funds. If the company is profitable, then the value of the shares may increase. Shareholders will normally receive part of the profit in the form of a **dividend payment**.

Retailers aim to make a profit by providing a service for which their customers are willing to pay.

- The gross profit is made by selling stocks for more than they cost to buy
- The net profit (operating profit) is the final profit after business running costs have been paid

Net profit is used as follows:

- Part is paid as corporation tax
- Part is paid to the owners (the shareholders)
- The rest is 'ploughed back' into the business

Case study: J Sainsbury PLC – Annual Accounts 1995

PROFIT AND LOSS ACCOUNT OF J SAINSBURY PLC FOR 52 WEEKS TO 11 MARCH

		1995 £m	1994 £m	notes:
	Sales	11,357	10,583	value of sales made in Sainsbury stores
less	Cost of sales	10,241	9,574	cost of buying in the stock and selling it
	Gross profit	1,116	1,009	Profit on sales
less	Operating costs:			
	Administrative expenses	217	213	costs of running the operation
	Other costs	54	418	e.g. salaries, advertising etc.
	Interest charges	36	9	interest on loans
	Operating Profit (before tax)	809	369	Net profit after all costs are accounted for
less	Tax on profit	273	227	Corporation tax based on profits
	Profit after tax	536	142	Profit available to Sainsburys after tax of which:
less	Dividends	212	190	(i) paid to shareholders
	Retained profit	324	(48)	(ii) 'ploughed back' into the company for future developments such as building new stores etc.

BALANCE SHEETS AS AT 11 MARCH

		1995 £m	1994 £m		
	Fixed Assets	4,950	4,869	(a)	land, buildings, equipment etc. – long lasting assets
	Current Assets				
	Stocks	509	303		
	Debtors	172	160		
	Cash at bank	201	89		
		882	552	(b)	cash or 'near cash'
less	**Creditors due within one year**	1,836	1,607	(c)	to be paid within the year
	Net current liabilities	(954)	(1,055)	(d)	(b) – (c)
	Total assets less current liabilities	3,996	3,814	(e)	(a) + (d)
less	**Creditors due after one year**	707	673	(f)	loans, mortgages etc.
		3,289	3,141		value of the business
	Share capital	452	452		invested by shareholders
	Reserves (retained profits)	2,837	2,689		retained profits
	Shareholders' funds	3,289	3,141		value of the business

STATEMENT OF DIRECTORS' RESPONSIBILITIES

The directors are responsible for keeping proper accounting records which disclose with reasonable accuracy at any time the financial position of the Company and to enable them to ensure that the accounts comply with the Companies Act 1985. They are also responsible for taking reasonable steps for the prevention of fraud and other irregularities.

REPORT OF THE AUDITORS TO THE SHAREHOLDERS OF J SAINSBURY PLC

In our opinion the accounts give a true and fair view of the affairs of the Company at 11 March 1995 and of the profit . . . for the 52 weeks then ended and have been properly prepared in accordance with the Companies Act 1985.

Coopers & Lybrand
Chartered Accountants
and Registered Auditors
London
9 May 1995

1 How much profit did Sainsbury's make (before tax) in 1994 and in 1995?
2 Calculate the % profit margin for each year:
   % profit margin = operating profit (before tax)/sales × 100
   This shows how many pence Sainsbury's make for each £1 you spend.
3 In Europe and the USA, the profit margin for supermarkets is 3%. How does Sainsbury's compare?
4 Make a list of Sainsbury's stakeholders. Why will each be interested in the accounts?
5 Sainsbury's has issued 1,800,000,000 shares. How much dividend did each share earn in 1994, in 1995?
6 What is the share price today? (Use today's newspaper.)
7 According to the balance sheet, how much is the company worth?
8 What was the value of stocks held by Sainsbury's in March 1995?

AUDITING THE ACCOUNTS

The role of the auditors is to check the accounts. There are:

- **internal auditors** who are employed by the retailer to check that the financial records are accurate. They are also interested in whether the accounting system is working efficiently, whether it is secure and whether it is producing the right information
- **external auditors** who are employed by company shareholders to check that the directors have produced accounts which give a 'true and fair view' – in other words, that the accounts are not misleading

Notice the auditors' report on the accounts of J Sainsbury as shown in the case study. Coopers & Lybrand are external auditors. They are a firm of accountants appointed by the shareholders to check that the annual accounts can be trusted.

1 Why do the shareholders appoint independent auditors such as Coopers & Lybrand?
2 Were the auditors satisfied with the accounts of J Sainsbury PLC? What again are the *four* important words here?

ENSURING SECURITY

Financial records must be *secure*: that is, they must be accurate, they must be honestly prepared and there must be checks to avoid **fraud** (the falsifying of records) and theft. Security is maintained by carrying out routine checks on the business books, and the internal audit is part of this process. Notice also that the Sainsbury's directors' duties include the prevention of fraud.

One rule is that no single individual should be in sole charge of the finances. One of the largest frauds of recent times, the Nick Leeson affair in Singapore, occurred because the company, Barings Bank, did not have anyone else to check what was going on.

1 What are the two types of auditor? What is their purpose?
2 How does a retailer achieve a gross profit? What is net profit?
3 Name two security threats to a business's finances. What may be done about each?
4 What is a business 'stakeholder'? Give five examples of stakeholders, and say exactly what interest each may have in the business.
5 Give three different pieces of information that managers may get from financial records.
6 Why does a supermarket *not* need to keep customer accounts? What sort of business *would* need to keep them?
7 What is a 'bad debt'?

METHODS OF PAYMENT

The exact financial records that a retailer will keep depend upon the methods of payment that are accepted and used by the business. Some small retailers may rely mainly upon cash, whilst the larger stores and mail-order houses will use a variety of methods. The possibilities are:

- cash
- cheque
- credit card
- debit card
- vouchers
- credit agreements
- direct debit
- standing order
- electronic funds transfer

Cash: notes and coins

Consumers are the main users of cash, and in many cases, it is the only means of payment accepted by retailers such as small shops and public houses and vending machines. Cash is less frequently used as a means of settlement in credit transactions, and it is rarely used in transactions between businesses.

The main advantages with cash are that payment is immediate and there is little paper work – perhaps just a written receipt or a print-out from the till.

The major problem is security. Cash needs to be stored safely, for it can be lost or stolen, and may therefore provide dangers for the responsible staff. It is also inconvenient and time-consuming in that it has to be counted and then transported to the bank.

Note that the term 'cash' may be used in a wider sense simply to mean immediate payment as opposed to a credit sale where payment is at some future date. For example, **cash-on-delivery** (COD) or **cash** with order (CWO) agreements may accept payment by a number of means such as cheque, debit or credit card.

Cheque

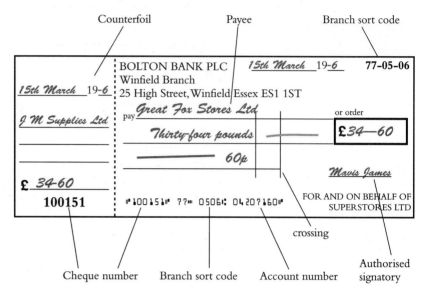

Figure 12.2 A cheque

The cheque shown in Figure 12.2 is an instruction from the drawer, Mavis James, to the company's bank. It asks for £34.60 to be transferred from her account to the payee, J M Supplies Ltd. Notice that:

- the cheque is written so that it would be difficult for the payee to alter the amount by adding more numbers – changing it to £134.60 would not be easy
- the **counterfoil** is completed so that this can later be checked against the bank statement

A cheque is normally **crossed** – see Figure 12.3 – when two parallel lines are drawn across the face of the cheque. This makes the cheque more secure because a crossed cheque cannot be cashed over the bank counter – it must be paid into a bank account. (An uncrossed or 'open' cheque *can* be cashed.) Additional instructions, known as either **'general crossings'** or **'special crossings'** may be written within the crossing lines:

1 General crossings:
   - 'and co': this simply draws attention to the crossing
   - 'a/c payee only': the cheque can only be paid into the account of the named payee. Without this the cheque may be **endorsed** (signed on the back) to instruct payment to a different payee
   - 'under sixty pounds': this prevents the cheque being altered fraudulently

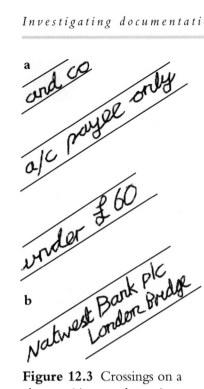

Figure 12.3 Crossings on a cheque: (a) general crossings, (b) a special crossing

2 Special crossings:
- 'Natwest Bank PLC – London Bridge': the cheque must be paid into a particular bank – even a particular branch

CHEQUE GUARANTEE CARDS

Where a cheque is for a substantial sum, a trader will normally wait for it to be **cleared** before supplying the goods. (Of course, an exception may be made where the payee is known and trusted.) Clearing takes three or four working days.

Alternatively, a **cheque guarantee card** – see Figure 12.4 – may be used. If the card number is written on the back of the cheque, if the cheque is signed in the trader's presence and if the sum is below the limit shown on the card – normally £50 or £100 – and the cheque card has not expired, then the cheque is guaranteed. This does restrict the size of cheque that can be used, but the goods are now available *immediately*.

Cheque cards often double as either credit cards or debit cards (see below).

Banks only issue cheque cards to approved customers, and the amount guaranteed depends upon the customer's financial standing.

PROBLEMS WITH CHEQUES

Cheques and cheque cards must be examined carefully before they are accepted. (Notice the procedure at a supermarket till when the supervisor is called over to authorise cheques.)

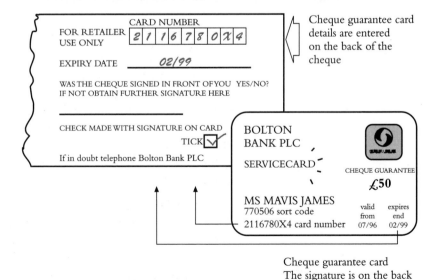

Figure 12.4 A cheque guarantee card

'Bouncing' or dishonoured cheques

Cheques which are not cleared are sent back to the drawer marked 'R/D' (return to drawer). Reasons may be:

- incorrect completion, including: inappropriate date, alterations not initialled, no signature or a signature which does not match the bank specimen, or money in the box which does not match the amount in words
- insufficient funds in the account and no cheque card (or an out-of-date cheque card)

'Stale' cheques

Where a cheque is six years old, the bank will not honour it. In practice, a bank will normally consult the drawer once a cheque is six months old.

Lost or stolen cheques

The drawer can stop a cheque where it has been lost or stolen, or where there is some suspicion about the payee. However, this is not possible where it is guaranteed by a cheque card.

BANKER'S DRAFT

This is a guaranteed cheque which can be used for large amounts. Payment is guaranteed as it is written by the bank itself rather than by the customer. Building societies write similar cheques for savers whose accounts do not provide cheque books. Some banks charge a fee of around £5 for this service.

Plastic money   **Credit cards** and **debit cards** involve the use of:

- manual machines which make out a receipt in triplicate with copies for the customer, the trader and the card company. Details are printed by pressing the receipt against the embossed card. A phone call may be necessary to establish the creditworthiness of the customer.
    The till receipt for the goods may be stapled to the card receipt
- electronic machines through which the card is 'swiped'. The magnetic strip on the back of the card links with a central computer which checks the card's details. A receipt is printed in duplicate, and the issuer's computer is updated automatically. The system is known as EFTPOS (electronic funds transfer at the point of sale)

In either case, the trader claims immediate payment, (less a commission for the service) either from:

- the credit card company or
- the debit card holder's bank

CREDIT CARDS

There are various types (see Figure 12.5):

- cards issued by the banks often in conjunction with card companies. These include Access, Barclaycard, the Co-operative Bank
- cards issued by specialist card firms including American Express and Diners Club
- store cards such as those issued by Debenhams and John Lewis

Figure 12.5 Examples of credit cards

This is a popular form of payment, and there is a trend for other organisations to enter the field – credit cards are now issued by Vauxhall Motors, Oxfam, even the Labour Party!

A credit-card holder is sent a monthly statement by the card company which may be paid either in full or by instalment. This is a convenient and popular method of buying, but interest rates can be high – perhaps 2% or 3% per month.

Recently, most card companies have started to charge an annual fee to renew their card (around £10 at the time of writing). This is because a significant number of customers use the card as a convenient method of payment but avoid the interest charges by paying their statements in full each month.

Read the following extract:

CARDS REMAIN FLEXIBLE FRIENDS DESPITE HIGH INTEREST RATES

Britons like plastic. There are now nearly 53 million credit and debit cards in circulation, according to The International Card Game – a report just published by the Credit Card Research Group.

Consumers spent an average of nearly £1,400 in 1994 on each of their credit cards. The typical purchase was £36.

The average outstanding balance per card is about £420. This suggests that the typical

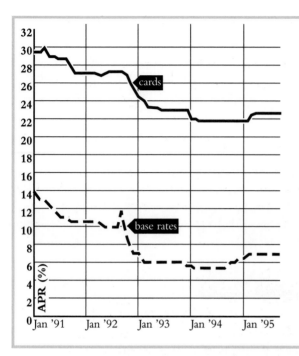

cardholder spends more than £93 a year servicing the debt.

The UK is expected to follow in the footsteps of the US credit card market over the next few years. In the US there are two cards for each head of the population – twice the UK level.

[Figure 12.6] shows the gap between base rates and the average APR (annual percentage rate) charged by the five largest credit card issuers.

Figure 12.6 The gap between base rates and the average annualised percentage rate (APR) charged by the five largest credit card users

1 Look up credit card rates – a selection can be found in Sunday newspapers. Which gives best value?
2 Choose a card and work out the interest charge for a year if your average outstanding balance is £200 per month.

DEBIT CARDS

The operation here is similar to that of a credit card: the difference is that here the trader is paid straight from the customer's bank account. In a sense, it is a guaranteed cheque without a chequebook. The service is free to the customer (who is not borrowing money), but, as with a credit card, the trader is charged a percentage on each sale.

Switch is the major brand of debit card.

PLASTIC CARDS AND SECURITY

Plastic cards pose a security risk: they are easily lost and can be used by anyone able to forge the signature. A credit card can be used over the phone simply by quoting the card number. Where the card being used has been reported as lost, the electronic card machine will warn the retailer.

EFTPOS (ELECTRONIC FUNDS TRANSFER AT THE POINT OF SALE)

This is the system mentioned above where debit or credit cards are processed through a computerised link from the cash register to the bank or card company. EFTPOS is discussed in more detail on page 204.

Vouchers   There are a variety of vouchers available:

- Gift vouchers such as record tokens and book tokens have been traditional presents from stores such as Boots and W H Smith. More recently, other stores have joined the act – even the supermarkets. It is now possible to give a friend from £1 to £50 worth of groceries for their birthday! (See Figure 12.7.)

Figure 12.7 Gift vouchers from Waitrose

- Some products have vouchers printed on the packet – e.g. 20p off the next packet of washing powder. In addition, the supermarkets produce magazines which encourage loyalty by offering vouchers for money off future purchases at the store
- **Loyalty cards** – e.g. see Figure 12.8 – are a new version of an old idea. On the basis that it is more difficult to attract new customers

than it is to keep existing ones, retailers are now offering plastic cards which ring up points in line with the value of purchases made (previously they offered stamps). These cards can be exchanged at some future date for vouchers which can be spent in the store. The Tesco Clubcard is regarded as a major reason why Tesco was able to become the leading supermarket in early 1996 (see pages 186 and 189)

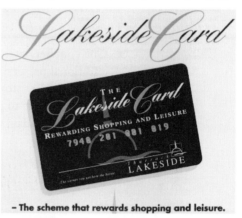

Figure 12.8 The Lakeside loyalty card

Case study: Loyalty vouchers

ASDA OFFERS TO ACCEPT ALL DISCOUNT VOUCHERS

Asda announced yesterday that its stores will accept promotional vouchers from any supermarket chain.

Tesco, whose Clubcard loyalty vouchers are the main target, last night branded the ploy an 'empty gesture', but it will keep Asda's name in the headlines.

Archie Norman, Asda's chief executive said the move was 'a bit of fun really'. He launched the idea in seven stores last weekend, 'People got upset so we thought we would do it in all our stores' Mr Norman said.

Asda is experimenting with its own loyalty scheme but had yet to decide whether to proceed nationally. 'Our customers want lower prices now,' he said. 'Vouchers are manipulative. We are saying to people: You don't need to feel captured.'

Mr Norman promises real service, 'not something you suddenly produce with a national advertising campaign'.'

(Source: adapted from The Guardian, *15 December 1995)*

1 How does the retailer record the points you earn on a loyalty card?
2 Tesco's student clubcard requires only 30 points per quarter to qualify. Why do you think that supermarkets (along with banks) aim special promotions at students? (Remember, it's a loyalty card.)
3 The evidence is that the Tesco card has been very successful. Who else offers loyalty cards, and what is the thinking behind them?

Credit agreements

The success of some retailers depends upon their making credit sales – mail-order houses are a good example. Consumers may find some goods – especially consumer durables – too expensive to buy outright.

With a credit sale, the consumer takes possession of the goods immediately but pays for them in instalments over the following months. Often, a percentage of the total price is required as an initial deposit, and normally interest is charged. The exact terms will be set out in a **credit agreement** which is a legal contract signed by the consumer. Often, the credit agreement is not between the consumer and the retailer but between the consumer and a finance company which pays the retailer immediately. The consumer then repays the instalments (and the interest) to the finance company.

Direct debits and standing orders

Direct debits and standing orders both allow the holder of a bank account to set up a series of automatic payments through the banking system. Both services allow funds to be transferred directly from one bank account to another.

DIRECT DEBITS

Under this arrangement, the holder of a bank account completes a **direct debit mandate** giving the bank permission to pay a named creditor on demand. This system is useful where the amounts vary and time periods are irregular. Services such as gas and electricity can be paid in this way, as can invoices from suppliers.

STANDING ORDERS

Here, the account holder completes a **standing order mandate** – see Figure 12.9 – instructing the bank to make equal payments at regular intervals to a named payee – e.g. £200 per month, payable to J P Estates until further notice. Standing orders are used where there are regular payments of fixed amounts – thus insurance premiums, rent and hire purchase instalments may be paid in this way.

Creditors favour direct debit, even where a standing order would be appropriate: direct debit puts them in control and saves them time and money – they request payment when they want it, there is no problem of late payment, and there is no expense of processing cheques and sending reminders.

As a precaution, it is wise for the payer to state an upper limit on the direct debit mandate; if bills exceed this sum, the bank will seek confirmation before paying.

Although the payments are made automatically, the payee will send regular statements to confirm the amounts paid. As with cheques, payment will only be made where there are sufficient funds or overdraft facilities available.

STANDING ORDER MANDATE

To ___BOLTON BANK PLC___

Address ___25 High Street Winfield Essex ES1 1ST___

	Bank	Branch Title (not address)	Code Number
Please Pay	MIDLAND	GILLESPIE ROAD	66-02-07
	Beneficiary		Account Number
for the credit of	FASTFIT LTD		0 5 3 7 2 1 6 2
	Amount in figures		Amount in words
†the sum of	£30		THIRTY POUNDS

	Date and amount of 1st payment		Date and frequency
commencing	5/4/-7 *now	£60	and thereafter every 5th of month
	Date and amount of last payment		
*until	5/2/-8	£20	
quoting the reference	MJS	2053	and debit my/our account accordingly

* This instruction cancels any previous order in favour of the beneficiary named above, under this reference
† If the amount of the periodic payments vary they should be incorporated in a schedule overleaf

Special instructions

Signature(s)___Morris James___ Date ____

Title and number of account to be debited ___SUPERSTORES LTD___ 0 4 2 0 7 1 6 0

*Delete if not applicable

Note: The Bank will not undertake to
(i) make any reference to Value Added Tax or pay a stated sum "plus VAT"
(ii) advise payer's address to beneficiary
(iii) advise beneficiary of inability to pay
(iv) request beneficiary's banker to advise beneficiary of receipt.

Figure 12.9 A standing order mandate

Electronic funds transfer

Various electronic means of funds transfer are now available via EDI (electronic data interchange). An example is BACS (Bankers Automated Clearing Services) by which a business will prepare a computer disc or tape with details of payments to be made. The BACS computer will process these payments so that funds are taken from the business's bank account and transferred directly to the accounts of the various payees. This system of 'credit transfer' is useful where a large number of payments need to be made. Examples include wage and salary payments to employees, payments of dividends to shareholders and payment of suppliers' accounts.

1 Perhaps you have seen the following notices. What is the point of each of them?
- 'Please use correct money – driver carries no cash'
- 'This safe has a time delay'
- 'These machines use tokens only'
- 'No cheques for goods below the value of £10'

2 Which is the most convenient means of paying for each of the following? Which means of payment do you think the business would prefer? Briefly give your reasons.
- Paying the milkman £6 for the week's milk
- Paying the electricity bill of £100 for the quarter
- A retailer settles up with the cash-and-carry for £350
- A haulier pays the monthly diesel account at a petrol station – £400

RECEIPTS DOCUMENTS

The methods of payment available to customers, as described above, are also the methods by which suppliers receive payment. Documents specifically associated with records of payments are:

- receipts
- cheque counterfoils
- paying-in slips
- counterfoils for debit and credit cards
- bank statements

Receipts

Receipts – see Figure 12.10 – act as proof of purchase and proof of payment. They are particularly important in transactions involving cash payment where no other evidence exists. For payment of accounts, where credit has been allowed, receipts will often be issued only on request. This saves the payee time and money, and such payments are also thought unnecessary as they are usually by cheque or credit transfer and can be verified via the bank. For example, if Hi-Tec Ltd settles the account shown on page 295 by cheque, there will not be a receipt unless it is requested; however, it will still be possible to verify that payment has occurred by looking at the bank statement.

A receipt will:

- describe the goods that have been purchased and itemise the cost
- indicate that payment has been made
- indicate the means of payment used
- show when the purchase was made

Cheque counterfoils

Where a payment has been made by cheque, the **cheque counterfoil** will be retained. Technically, this is not a receipt, neither is it proof of payment, but assuming that it has been accurately completed, it does act as a record of payment. The bank statement will confirm that payment has actually taken place.

Paying-in slips

Cash and cheques are paid into the bank by means of a **paying-in slip** (also called a **credit slip**) (see Figure 12.11). The counterfoil will be stamped by the cashier at the bank as proof of receipt.

(a)

```
        THANK YOU FOR CHOOSING

     TESCO

------------------------------------
                        £
   PEANUTS          #    0.92
   WEBSTERS         #    2.49
   ENTRE 2 MERS     #    2.99
   F/HSE CHEESE          1.30
   RIO RIVA         #    0.37
   DR PEPPER        #    0.35
   IRN BRU          #    0.35
   7 UP CAN         #    0.35
   T/TSSE X4GREEN   #    1.62
   HOOCH LEMONADE   #    0.99
   HOOCH LEMONADE   #    0.99
   HOEGAARDEN 33C   #    0.99
   HOEGAARDEN 33C   #    0.99
   PREMIUM ALE      #    1.19
   PREMIUM ALE      #    1.19
   COOKING OIL           0.49

   TOTAL                17.57
   CHEQUE               17.57
   CHANGE DUE            0.00
------------------------------------
   CARD NO 63400400017384857
   POINTS THIS VISIT        3
   BALANCE NOT AVAILABLE
------------------------------------

           THANK YOU
     FOR SHOPPING AT TESCO
        SOUTHWARK BRANCH
   TELEPHONE NO 0171 237 1866

     VAT NUMBER 220430231
   THIS IS NOT A VAT RECEIPT

   12/07/96 17:31 022 2423 3235
              3189
```

```
      IN DE VREDE
     DONKERSTRAAT 13
     8640 WESTVLETEREN
     TEL. 057-40.03.77

     HA  18 DEC 95 13:48

   2 6 FLESSEN EXTRA      624.00
   2 LEEGGOED +            36.00
   1 KRUYDEKOECKE         110.00
   3 CONFISERIE           105.00
   1 KAAS                 119.00
   ==============================
   TOTAAL               994.00

   FF                    177.50


      VRIJDAG  GESLOTEN

   Tick   9      Kelner x  0 x
```

(b)

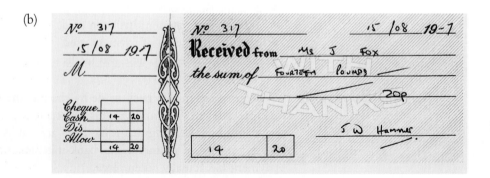

Figure 12.10 Examples of receipts: (a) till receipts for cheque and cash payments, (b) a handwritten receipt as used by small retailers

(a)

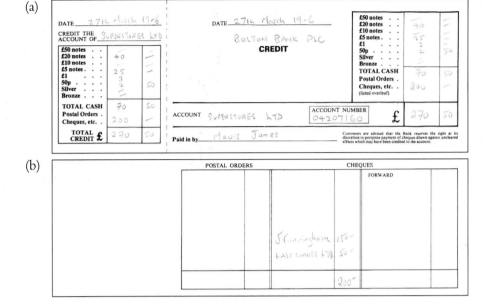

(b)

Figure 12.11 A paying-in slip: (a) front and (b) back

Counterfoils for debit and credit cards

The counterfoils produced by EPTPOS systems for debit and credit cards – see Figure 12.12 – also act as receipts documents.

Bank statements

Ultimately, most receipts and payments will pass through the business's bank account. Most businesses will keep a cash book to record receipts and payments into and out of their bank account. The bank will also keep a record of the bank account and will send the customer regular copies in the form of a **bank statement**.

THE NEED FOR ACCURACY OF DOCUMENTS

Documents are used to provide a clear, permanent record of business transactions, and issues that might arise here are:

- *accuracy*. Inaccurate documents lead to misunderstanding and confusion. For instance, where a payment of £30 from a customer is recorded inaccurately as £20, then the customer may be invoiced for £10 that has in fact been paid. Such mistakes are bad for customer relationships
- *security*. Where financial information is inaccurate, then security becomes an issue. The business must ensure that transactions are being carried out accurately and honestly. It is good practice to put checks into the system to ensure that financial transactions are approved by a senior officer and that any errors in financial recording are discovered at an early stage

(a)

(b)

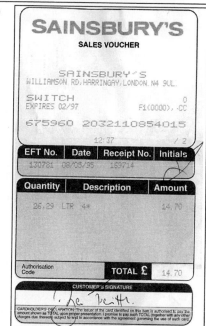

Figure 12.12 Examples of (a) a credit-card counterfoil,
(b) a debit-card counterfoil

- *reliability of data.* We have seen that financial records are used both by management and by outside agencies such as the Inland Revenue and HM Customs and Excise. Errors in these records may have serious consequences:
  - Declaring profits or sales incorrectly may lead to charges of fraud if it is thought that the business is trying to evade tax or VAT payments
  - If managers work from incorrect figures, then the decisions that they take may not be appropriate
  - If external auditors discover that the business accounts are misleading and do not present a 'true and fair view', then this will be shown in the annual report. As a result, investors may be unsure about putting money into the business

Customer satisfaction   An inefficient business will not provide customer satisfaction. If, for instance, invoices are incorrect, if cheques to suppliers bounce, or if direct debits continue to be withdrawn after bills have been settled, then customers will lose confidence in the business. Customers are not just buying products, they are also buying service and image, and they will be put off where this fails to match up to expectations.

activity

1 Produce a handwritten receipt for the cheque shown on page 326.
2 Write the cheque in payment for the Tesco bill shown on page 336. What steps would the retailer take to ensure that the cheque is valid?
3 Calculate the value in £ sterling of the purchases in Belgian Francs shown on page 336. Which credit cards does Sally Line accept? (See page 338.)
4 What advantage is there for Sally Line in accepting such a wide range of credit cards?
5 Credit cards can be expensive. Why are they so popular? What are the problems for the retailer?
6 Explain the difference between:
   ● a credit card and a debit card
   ● a standing order and a direct debit

It is clear from Table 12.1 that cash receipts and payments need to be checked immediately, since it will be impossible to prove what was paid at some later date. For payments by other means, such as cheques, there is documentary proof of the payment through the banking system.

Notice that bar-code readers, 'swipe card' machines and cheque-printing machines remove much human error from the financial recording process.

Security checks for financial documents

It is necessary to have a system of security checks to ensure that financial transactions are carried out correctly, accurately and honestly. Procedures might include:

● the authorisation of orders: it should not be possible for junior staff to finalise decisions about orders. A system should be in place by which a senior member of staff should authorise any order by **countersigning**. This will prevent:
  – the ordering of unwanted or inappropriate goods
  – the ordering of goods on unfavourable terms
  – the ordering of goods without sufficient funds to pay for them
● checking goods received upon delivery. Delivery notes should bear the signature and the printed name of the recipient; this will certify that the goods listed have indeed been received, and will also certify when they were received and who received them. The original signed note will be returned to the supplier, and duplicates will be retained by the customer and the carrier

Table 12.1   Possible problems created by incorrect financial records

DOCUMENT	POSSIBLE ERROR	IMMEDIATE EFFECT	POSSIBLE LONG-TERM EFFECT
Cheque	A customer cheque is not signed or dated, or the amount in the box does not match the amount in numbers	The cheque bounces	The loss of the supplier if there are continual errors – alternatively, the supplier will not provide credit but insist on cash on delivery
	The cheque is made out for an incorrect amount	A dispute with the supplier	The cheque is corrected
Credit card receipt or debit card receipt	An incorrect amount is charged by the supplier on the EFTPOS machine	The supplier will either gain or lose on the deal. Either the supplier or the customer will be unhappy	Disputes with customers or suppliers are bad for business. However errors such as this are usually isolated
Standing order mandate	Incorrect amounts are paid The payment period may be incorrect	The payee will dispute underpayments	If corrected quickly, there should be no further problems
Direct debit mandate	Incorrect charges are made, or charges continue after the debt is paid	A dispute with the payee	Details should be amended quickly – thereafter, there should be no further problems. However, the bank account should be checked regularly to see that no unauthorised payments are being taken
Receipt	An incorrect amount, or incorrect items, shown	The customer has no proof of purchase	This should be checked at the time – if cash is paid, it will be difficult to rectify later
Paying-in slip	An inaccurate record of deposits into the bank account	The cashier should notice this, otherwise there will be too little or too much in the bank account	It will not be possible to trace incorrect cash amounts – cheques, however can be traced

- checking invoices against goods-received notes: the goods charged on the invoice should correspond to those signed for on the goods-received note.
- checking invoices against orders: each invoice should bear the reference number of the order upon which it is based. Before an invoice is paid, a check should be made against the original order, and goods which were not ordered should not be paid for. If such goods have been delivered, they should be returned and a credit note requested
- authorised cheque signatories: business cheques will usually bear the name of the business rather than the name of the signatory. The bank will have specimens of the signatures of all authorised signatories, and a cheque will only be honoured where the signatures match. Often, a business cheque will need at least two signatures: where a single officer is in charge of the cheque book, there is always the chance of misuse of funds or of undetected errors

- ensuring that plastic debit and credit cards are valid by checking:
  - the date that the card expires
  - the signature on the card against the signature of the card holder
  - that the card is valid for the sum being paid – a card will have a limit
  - that the card is not on a list of stolen or lost cards – if a card has been reported missing, then EPTPOS machines will display a warning message and stop the transaction
  - that, where a cheque card is used, the correct number is written on the cheque, the card is still valid, the signature matches and the cheque does not exceed the limit that is guaranteed. These will all be checked by the retailer

  As debit and credit cards become more common, so does card fraud
- comparing till figures with cash received: till operators are responsible for taking over a cashfloat when they come on duty. When they leave the till, the till's contents should equal the contents of the original float *plus* cash received for sales *less* cash taken to the bank. Where this is not so, then either an incorrect figure has been keyed into the till or the wrong cash has been received or given in change.

  Where EPOS systems with bar-code scanners are used, then the price of the goods *will* be accurate as it is read automatically. Any discrepancies here will occur either in receiving the incorrect payment or in giving the incorrect change.

Self-test questions:
Chapter 12

1 What is meant by gross profit? What is meant by net profit? In which of the year-end accounts can these items be found?
2 What is the job of the auditors? Why are they needed?
3 Retailers who offer a variety of payment methods are likely to make more sales. In this case, why do small retailers often insist on 'cash only'?
4 What is a 'loyalty card', and what is its purpose? Give *two* examples.
5 What is the difference between a 'credit card' and a 'debit card'?
6 How may a business check the honesty of its checkout operators?
7 What does EFTPOS stand for? Give *two* examples of how this may help a retailer.
8 How may a business guard against a partner using business cheques for his personal expenses?
9 Give *two* likely effects of a business sending out an incorrect invoice.
10 Give *two* reasons why a business will require orders for new stock to be authorised by a senior member of staff.

Mabern Supplies is a retail outlet selling groceries and general household items. There is also an off-licence section.

Although most of the customers pay by cash, in order to maximise their income, the owners, Mable and Ernie Moss, have decided to accept payment by a number of other means, including: cheque (with a valid guarantee card), credit card and debit card.

Mabern prices goods according to the wholesaler's (Buy-line Ltd's) — list of recommended retail prices (see the table). Below are details of some of the financial transactions for today:

1 The goods sold over the counter include:
   - Customer 1, payment by cash:
     - 1 loaf of Nutraslice white bread
     - 1 tin of baked beans
     - 1 packet of oven chips
     - 1 box of 12 fish fingers
     - 1 tub of Dayglo ice cream
   - Customer 2, payment by cheque:
     - 2 tins of lemonice cola
     - 4 tins of Frolic
     - 1 bottle of Royal Flush (kingsize)
     - 2 packets of Lincolnshire sausages (8 pack)
     - 2 loaves of Nutraslice white bread
     - 1 packet of Park Lane tipped (10 pack)
     - 2 litres of skimmed milk
   - Customer 3, payment by Switch card:
     - 1 bottle of Graham's Gin (75 cl)
     - 4 bottles of tonic water (50 cl bottles)
     - 8 cans of Mad Monk Ale
   - Customer 4, payment by credit card:
     - 10 National Lottery tickets (at £1 each)
     - 4 jars of Brazilia coffee

2 During the afternoon, the following is deposited at the bank:
   - 5 × £20 notes
   - 17 × £10 notes
   - 24 × £5 notes
   - 46 × £1 coins
   - 62 × 50p pieces
   - 37 × 10p pieces
   - £4.50 in copper

BUY-LINE (Cash and Carry) LTD
Unit 6 West Road Grantham Lincolnshire
tel: 01476 12345 fax: 01476 67890
Recommended retail price list

Item	Unit	RRP (£)
Bread		
Nutraslice white bread	loaf	0.38
granary	loaf	0.62
Tins		
baked beans	tin	0.28
garden peas	tin	0.22
Frozen		
oven chips	packet	0.85
fish fingers	box of 12	1.55
fish fingers	box of 6	0.80
Dayglo ice cream	tub	0.93
Flans/pizzas		
Ovenready flans	each	1.70
Italiano	each	1.55
Meat		
Lincolnshire sausages	pack (8)	1.55
bacon	pack (8)	1.95
Soft drinks/mixers		
lemonice cola	can	0.30
orangeice cola	can	0.30
tonic water	bottle (50 cl)	0.65
Aquasprings mineral water	bottle (75 cl)	0.60
Pet food		
Frolic	tin	0.48
Cleaner		
Royal Flush (kingsize)	bottle	0.85
Royal Flush (economy)	bottle	0.55
Cigarettes		
Park Lane tipped	pack (10)	1.20
Park Lane tipped	pack (20)	2.39
Coffee		
Brazilia	jar	1.85
Milk		
Skimmed	1 litre	0.45
full cream	1 litre	0.45
Spirits		
Graham's Gin	bottle (75 cl)	8.90
Sporan single malt	bottle (75 cl)	13.50
Beer		
Mad Monk Ale	can (440 ml)	1.20
Derby Old Brown	can (440 ml)	1.25

TASK 1

Using today's date and the price list shown above, carry out the following:

1 Calculate the bill for each customer.
2 Assuming that each pays as indicated, produce:
   - the relevant receipt document for each customer
   - the cheque and the counterfoil for customer number 2
   - the paying-in slip for the money deposited at the bank

TASK 2

Investigate *two* different distribution outlets. From your studies, produce a report to describe and explain:

- six different payment methods used by the outlets – give the advantages and disadvantages of each method
- potential security problems with these methods of payment – explain the security checks which are used

TASK 3

Write explanations of the following:

- why retailers need to keep financial records
- why it is essential to complete financial documents accurately. Illustrate your answer by explaining what may happen if documents are incorrectly completed

Answers to Unit tests

UNIT 1					
1 = d	6 = c	11 = d	16 = d	21 = d	26 = d
2 = b	7 = d	12 = c	17 = b	22 = b	27 = b
3 = c	8 = b	13 = d	18 = c	23 = d	28 = a
4 = b	9 = d	14 = b	19 = c	24 = d	29 = c
5 = c	10 = b	15 = c	20 = c	25 = c	30 = b

UNIT 2					
1 = c	6 = d	11 = b	16 = a	21 = c	26 = d
2 = c	7 = a	12 = d	17 = a	22 = d	27 = b
3 = a	8 = c	13 = b	18 = c	23 = c	28 = d
4 = c	9 = b	14 = b	19 = c	24 = b	
5 = b	10 = d	15 = c	20 = d	25 = d	

UNIT 3					
1 = c	7 = d	13 = b	19 = b	25 = b
2 = b	8 = b	14 = c	20 = a	26 = d
3 = b	9 = a	15 = a	21 = c	27 = a
4 = b	10 = c	16 = c	22 = d	28 = c
5 = c	11 = c	17 = a	23 = b	29 = b
6 = a	12 = a	18 = b	24 = c	30 = c

Appendix I

Table I.1 Retail business statistics for 1993

	BUSINESSES	OUTLETS	PERSONS ENGAGED (000s)	RETAIL TURNOVER (£ MILLION)	GROSS MARGIN (%)
Total retail businesses	201,841	305,827	2,337	141,887	30.3
All food, drinks, tobacco	68,505	95,352	970	62,672	23.4
NON-SPECIALISED STORES					
Non-specialised stores	23,700	38,175	858	59,471	25.4
Mainly food, drink or tobacco	21,407	32,169	689	49,785	23.1
Other	2,293	6,006	169	9,686	37.3
SPECIALISED STORES					
Specialised food, drink or tobacco	47,098	63,183	281	12,887	24.2
Fruit and vegetables	6,979	8,746	34	1,144	30.5
Meat	10,179	13,172	53	2,409	29.4
Fish	999	1,218	3	149	30.4
Bread, cakes, confectionery	5,986	8,500	51	1,133	47.6
Alcoholic and other drinks	9,066	14,085	58	3,894	17.0
Tobacco products	11,888	14,718	69	3,651	16.5
Other	2,000	2,744	13	506	29.3
Pharmaceutical, medical and cosmetic	7,063	12,333	86	5,494	26.1
Dispensing chemists	6,058	10,244	66	4,398	23.9
Medical and orthopaedic	223	370	2	76	37.1
Cosmetic and toilet articles	782	1,718	19	1,020	35.3
Other new goods in specialised stores	86,611	143,673	948	53,109	36.0
Textiles	2,971	3,940	13	508	40.4
Clothing	13,583	29,893	276	17,305	38.1
Footwear and leather goods	3,209	10,517	66	2,703	43.9
Furniture, lighting, household	7,998	12,870	72	5,121	38.5
Electrical household goods, radio, TV	5,767	10,801	67	6,181	28.9
Hardware, paints and glass	6,219	8,252	78	5,179	40.6
Books, newspapers, stationery	14,929	22,870	166	5,323	26.8
Floor coverings	3,805	5,177	19	1,603	37.5
Photographic, optical, office supplies	996	1,459	7	556	31.0
Other	27,134	37,894	185	8,632	36.9
Second-hand goods	5,013	5,917	15	985	38.7
Retail sales not in stores	31,683	41,762	147	9,860	40.5
Mail order	2,316	2,650	53	5,755	45.5
Stalls and markets	11,281	18,921	39	1,685	35.2
Other	18,086	20,190	54	2,420	34.5
Repair of personal and household goods	672	785	3	81	51.8

Source: *Business Monitor*

Index